TOWARDS THE 1994 SYNOD OF BISHOPS

AUSTIN FLANNERY, OP
EDITOR

DOMINICAN PUBLICATIONS

First published (1993) by
Dominican Publications
42 Parnell Square
Dublin 1
ISBN 1 871552 41 9 ✓

Cover design
David Cooke

Origination
Dominican Publications

Printed in Ireland by
The Leinster Leader Ltd
Naas, Co Kildare

About *Religious Life Review*: It is published six times a year by Dominican Publications, edited by Austin Flannery, OP.

Annual subscription rates: Republic of Ireland: IR£12.81; Northern Ireland: Stg£10.92; Great Britain: Stg£11.28.

Plans for 1994: A series of articles on 'The Place and Role of Religious in the Church'. Contributors include Seán O'Riordan, CSsR., Helena O'Donoghue, RSM, Damian Byrne, OP, Luciana Mendez Almeida, SJ, President Episcopal Conference of Brazil, Michael Amaldaloss, SJ.

Plus a series on Ministry on the Margins: AIDS, Prisons, Working for Justice, etc.

CONTENTS

SECTION THREE: GROUP RESPONSES

SECTION FOUR: SURVEY AND VIEWS

ABBREVIATIONS

AA   *Apostolicam actuositatem*, Decree on the Apostolate of Lay People
AG   *Ad gentes*, Decree on the Church's Missionary Activity
CCEE   Council of Episcopal Conferences of Europe
CCEO   *The Code of Canon Law for the Oriental Churches*
CIC   *The Code of Canon Law*
CLAR   Conference of Latin American Religious
CMIS   World Conference of Secular Institutes
CMRS   Conference of Major Religious Superiors (Of Irish and of English and
        Welsh religious — up to recently.)
COR   Conference of Religious (new name for CMRS of England and Wales)
CROI   Conference of Religious of Ireland (new name for Irish CMRS)
EN   *Evangelii nuntiandi*, Evangelization in the Modern World, Paul VI
F1   *Vatican II: Conciliar & Postconciliar Documents*, ed. A Flannery OP
F2   *Vatican II: More Postconciliar Documents*, ed. A Flannery OP
LCWR   Leadership Conference of Women Religious (US)
LG   *Lumen Gentium*, Dogmatic Constitution on the Church
MR   *Mutuae Relationes*, Directives for Mutual Relations between Bishops
        and Religious in the Church
PC   *Perfectae Caritatis*, Decree on Up-to-date Renewal of Religious Life.
PO   *Presbyterorum ordinis*, Decree on the Ministry and Life of Priests
UCESM, Union of Conferences of Major Superiors of Europe
UISG   International Union of Superiors General (Of women religious).
UMSM   Union of Major Superiors of Men (United States)
USG   Union of Superiors General (International, men religious)

Foreword

MARIAN O'SULLIVAN, OP
President, Conference of Religious of Ireland

The publication of this collection of writings on the forthcoming synod on consecrated life is timely. Since the publication of the *Lineamenta* in 1992, the religious of the world, with their customary diligence, have been reflecting, questioning, responding to questionnaires, dialoguing among themselves and with their bishops on that ancient and mysterious phenomenon in the Church which we call religious life.

The calling of a person or group of persons to devote themselves totally to the search for the divine has been known for thousands of years, notably in Hinduism and Buddhism. In the Christian tradition religious life came into being as a counter cultural way of living the Gospel at a time when the Church had become over-identified with the Roman Empire. Religious orders and congregations have come and gone ever since, according as the Spirit called them in response to changing needs.

To-day religious life appears to be in decline, at least in the countries of the West. Is this because there is no more need for community witness to the divine presence and action in the world? Or is it because yesterday's answers are no longer adequate for todays questions?

The Synod to be held in November 1994 has already prompted in-depth reflection on the meaning and purpose of religious life. This may well be the occasion for a new outpouring of the Spirit in a deep renewal and re-orientation of ministries necessary for our times or in a flowering of new charisms.

This volume is welcome as a contribution to the ongoing reflection and an invitation to broaden and deepen the discussion, thus liberating the spirit of truth, freedom, worship and service among us.

Introduction, and a Word about Contributors
AUSTIN FLANNERY, OP

All of the contributors wrote on religious life today and the 1994 Synod for *Religious Life Review*, their articles appearing between January and September, 1993. They were very well received. This we know because people wrote and told us that they liked them, but also — a more reliable thermometer — because the circulation of the periodical increased.

So it seemed a good idea to collect the articles into a book, adding the *Lineamenta*, or draft disucssion document, and a number of statements on religious life — in the context of the coming Synod — by various groups and of surveys, most of which had not appeared in *Religious Life Review*. About our contributors, all of whom will be familiar to readers of *Religious Life Review*: Desmond O'Donnell, OMI, now works in Australia, having been for several years a Rome-based member of the General Curia of his order, a job which brought him into contact with religious in many parts of the world; Seán Fagan, SM, is Secretary General of his order, has written extensively on religious life and has facilitated many general and provincial chapters for other orders; Fintan Sheeran, SS CC, another well-known facilitator, is in charge of formation for his order in the US; Flannan Markham, SS CC teaches the history of religious life at Maynooth College; Jan Kerkhofs, SJ, is professor of theology at Louvain University and, as chairman of the steering committee of the European Value Systems Study Group, has come to know more than most about Europe's and indeed the western world's rapidly changing beliefs and values; Joan D Chittister, OSB, American Benedictine, is one of the most highly regarded writers and lecturers on the religious life: she enthusese audiences in Ireland and Britain as well as in the US; Seán O'Riordan, CSsR, long-time professor of moral theology at the Alfonsianum, Rome, is a highly regarded writer and lecturer on religious life; Helena O'Donoghue, RSM, was President of the Irish CMRS (before it changed its name) and is General of the Killaloe Mercy Sisters. Peter Hebblethwaite, author of well received lives of John XXIII and Paul VI is also a highly-regarded jouralist.

It was Jan Kerkhofs who drew the statement by the German Superiors to my attention and it was Joe Dargan, SJ, who secured copies of both German statements for me. It was Seán O'Riordan who drew my attention to Luigi Cuccini's article on the canvassing of the views of superior generals and who got me a copy of it. Grateful thanks to them both.

ONE
Clerical Religious: Taking Stock for the Synod

DESMOND O'DONNELL, OMI

An event like the 1994 Synod cannot but influence the understanding and direction of religious life in the future, so that our response to the consultation is important. The men's Union of Superiors General (hereafter USG.) began their preparation in May, 1992, by holding a meeting addressed by Frs. Jesus Alvarez, C.M.F., Bruno Secondin, O.Carm. and John Fullenbach S.V.D. They held a second meetings in November, 1992 and another in May, 1993.

Similar meetings have taken place in each country and congregation. In its June 1992 letter the USG insisted: 'It will be urgent to analyse and reflect and ensure the communication of ideas from everyone.'

This chapter develops my replies to the USG questionnaire which was sent in Autumn 1992 to Generalates in Rome. I should note that I have mainly active clerical Congregations in mind, even if some of what I say applies to other religious as well.

To blame ourselves for our present problems, or to seek solutions from within alone, would be tantamount to blaming Noah's ark for the flood or patching the ark without some knowledge of floods. Few observant people would deny that we are at a unique time in history. Because we seem to be approaching near total discontinuity, some speak of 'the end of history'. The modernity-postmodernity debate continues and the word 'secularization' is common coinage among concerned religious people.

Because the present psycho-historical dislocation is gradually causing the disappearance of traditional sources of identity-strength for individuals and institutions, religious life is being affected deeply. No synod can change this. Technology favours discontinuity, moving us willy nilly from history' s slow development of cultures and institutions to a situation of rapid cultural and institutional upheaval. With different degrees of awareness, all people are undergoing some stress and disorientation; we religious are no exception. Predictably, some deny this, some 'dig in', others offer a diffused response and still others lower their private lifeboats. But many are working hard in their search for solutions or, better still, for a constant Gospel-based solution-finding process.

Can we ask the Synod to realistically recognize that change is not what it used to be? While we can and must define some evangelical and ecclesial non-negotiables, we must also recognize that detailed directions can quickly become irrelevant today. Universal blueprints can paralyse essential local life-giving experiments and adaptations. History shows that Congregations came into being as practical responses to changed situations that were unnoticed by the Church in general. Then, Church law helped their development in most cases but, in others, real development was hijacked and stultified by legalism from within and without.

Clerical religious have an advantage and a disadvantage in their priestly status. Because priesthood in the Church is part of a system whose function is largely guaranteed at present, its immediate future seems clear and safe enough. Despite the fact that priesthood has never been univocally defined in church history, it has survived even when the performance of its members was very low.

A PRIEST COULD STILL FIND A JOB

As distinct from most lay religious, a priest who does not pray, preaches carelessly, visits his people rarely, performs the liturgy routinely and perhaps does not effectively believe in God, could probably still find a job. This makes survival easier and renewal less urgent. Perhaps it is for this reason too that 'clerical congregations committed to ministry forget more easily the prophetic and charismatic dimensions of religious life.'[1] Depending on one's point of view, all this can favour or disfavour the continuance of clerical religious life without renewal of its 'religious-ness'.

However, most Superiors General and a good number of priest religious are now aware that renewal of their congregations is intimately dependent on their understanding of how the ministry of priest religious will be exercised in the Church of the future. At the end of a scholarly article on this subject, we read: 'In the vast majority of orders and congregations founded since the 13th century, ministry has been at the centre of their self-understanding. Definitions and descriptions of religious life that fail to take full account of this indisputable fact are, no matter what their other merits, misleading and harmful.' [2]

I do not think that the Synod can honestly disregard the real problems arising from the clerical dimension of most men's congregations. Unless we name this problem, our growth or decline as clerical congregations might have much to do with our clerical status and depend very little on our being religious.

NECESSARY DISTINCTIONS

To cover over important distinctions by using umbrella words is never helpful for very long. This is why the Synod should recognize the very real distinction between contemplative, active lay and active clerical congregations. Much smothered ambiguity and many useless exhortations have come from official failure to write about these real differences. For instance, to speak about 'community' as a univocal experience for the three groups leads many priest religious to disregard entirely other excellent aspects of Roman exhortations. It is also very difficult to see what contemplatives, groups of lay religious and most missionary priest religious have in common even when we speak of prayer together.

When a religious becomes a priest and is engaged in ministry today, new modalities are added to his being a religious even regarding the vows, as I will show. The secularity which priestly ministry brings to religious life must influence anything said about clerical religious today.

When crisis and confusion are accompanied by awareness, creativity usually emerges. This fact underpins the good news about most religious congregations today; the people in the curias of religious orders are mostly conscious and as clear as the situation allows about the challenges facing us. Chapter agendas continue to show this. There is a healthy discontent as older definitions, symbols and meanings are no longer found helpful. We have all moved comfortably away from phrases like "state of perfection', 'separation from the world', 'seeking God alone' or thinking that we have 'chosen a higher way of life' than our lay brothers and sisters — even if deeper meanings in these phrases might be emerging. Nor do we expect the Synod to supply simplistic answers to the complexities which must be lived.

Most of us are still unclear even about some phrases used in Vatican II about religious life: 'bind themselves to the Lord in a special way', 'follow Christ with greater liberty' (PC, 1.) 'by a narrower way' (LG, 1 3 .), 'to derive more abundant fruit from the grace of our baptism' (LG, 44.) and 'consecrate himself more fully to God in a new and special way'.(LG, 44). Just how we are 'consecrated' more than our baptised and confirmed married brothers and sisters is not clear to everyone either. These core obscurities can be fruitful launching points for discussion prior to and during the Synod, since identity is crucial to fruitful survival for all groups today.

In his talk referred to earlier, Bruno Secondin put it this way: 'But almost thirty years after Vatican Council II, there is a feeling that it is still difficult to consolidate its doctrine around key principles. The key words have increased but their meaning is still under discussion. The lexicon has certainly been enriched. Such words as consecration, following, charism, ecclesiality, sign and witness, prophecy, insertion, inculturation, evangelical counsels, fraternal life etc., are not interpreted in the same way by theologians. All claim to be faithful to the impetus of the Council.'

No one can expect the Synod Fathers to clear up all the older questions and much less so the emerging ones; may we ask them not to try, but rather to join us in the journey while we live and minister with the problems? May we also ask them not to try to reach agreement through ambiguity? Even religious obfuscation remains obfuscation and then undermines the many helpful things coming in official documents. How much better to say that certain things are not clear and, having listened well — especially to the ten Major Superiors officially present at their gathering — to offer tentative guidelines which will help us to continue living and ministering fruitfully for God's Kingdom. Karl Rahner called it *docta ignorantia futuri* — perhaps a difficult stance for those of us from whom people expect transparent clarity and final answers.

UNLOVING CRITICS

If the Synod Fathers take this more humble, less legalistic and non directive approach, it would help undermine the position of those who have ceased to listen with open minds to Roman documents. It is sadly a fact that in some countries many religious have become unloving critics of the Church, partly, I suspect, in response to the uncritical lovers who sometimes author official documents.

Most of us have lived to see changing emphases in the theology and practice of religious life. We remember when, like all other people, institutions supported us well, until something changed when personalism and the human potential movement arrived, to stress the importance of individual growth in the 1960s. Then community with a fairly inward direction was seen to be important, until we more recently rediscovered that all of our congregations were founded for mission, which community is meant to express and facilitate. I sense that many clerical religious have hardly noticed these changes or have not reflected on them. Can the Synod say something about the usefulness of the learning which accompanied this journey and encourage a critically reflective but open stance before the inevitable changes ahead? May we ask if the apparent recent calls from above to move backwards are meant to counter extreme individualism or to be a statement against an unwelcome prophetic stance? Any attempt to freeze the theology of religious life or to domesticate the Spirit will not be helpful.

'Since the final norm of religious life is the following of Christ as it is put before us in the Gospels, this must be taken by all institutions as the supreme rule' (PC, 2). Our new Constitutions and much recent writing show that we are growing in our awareness of this need for radical Christian living. Perhaps rather than an isolated stress on Christ as liberator, man of prayer or man for others — each of which phrases could be used to defend an ideology — we need to emphasise Christ as the loving, faithful Son of the Father and to express this in our prayer-life and vowed living first of all. Let the Synod remind us once again of the message in these words: 'But news of him kept spreading, and large crowds would gather to hear him and to have their sickness cured, but he would always go off to some place where he could be alone and pray' (Lk. 5:15,16). Encourage us to hear again: 'Without me you can do nothing' (Jn.15:5) lest we over-rely on surveys, task forces and process. At the same time, may we ask the Synod Fathers to hesitate well before even hinting at a return to a quasi monastic spirituality.

For clerical religious especially, the vow of poverty— however we name it — is not easy to live meaningfully; ministry and money can become very mixed. This is another example of where the Synod will have to speak to us priests directly, rather than include us in their exhortation to contemplatives and active lay religious. Clerical credit cards have come to stay; many priests and Sisters in institutions handle bigger sums of money than the Province of which they are members and they have little choice but to dress, drive and dine differently from other members of their congregations. So too have useful but costly seminars and sabbaticals become part of ongoing education everywhere. Just how I witness to poverty to my hardworking married brothers and sisters today is unclear to me — as I am sure it is to them. I doubt if the Synod can give us answers here; this is just an appeal for words that are level with life today.

In these days too, when Superiors are doing their best to be dialogical, it is sometimes difficult to keep believing that congregations were not founded to cater for personal 'charisms' however well 'discerned'. The vow of obedience having usefully moved away from 'doing what you are told', as poverty has from 'getting permission', it must be rediscovered by active religious in its essential link with common vision and mission together — and this in situations which often call for a high degree of professionalism combined with courageous individualism. Can the Synod be aware of this and gather our experiences within an evangelical framework, but away from any suggestion that the Superior knows best about all things?

That the vow of chastity is now more often spoken of as the vow of celibacy shows, I think, that a deeper meaning for the virtue we are talking about needs to be enunciated by the Synod. More fundamental still is the need to stress that, without a healthy and mature psychosexual life-experience, one may survive as a celibate but chastity in its fullest sense would be impossible. This year, in a country of about ten million Catholics, about sixty religious, priests and bishops are under investigation on charges related to sexual misbehaviour. Is there any reason why this will not become a similar issue in other countries in the future? And may we ask why it is a growing problem? This is another reason why it would be good if the Synod said something profound about Christian celibacy as a charism which appears to be much rarer than we thought in the past, partly because of the healthy psychosexual life which it must presume.

FORMATION

Well considered steps have been taken in the difficult area of first formation, as pre-novitiates now play an important role in preparing postulants for the serious business of novitiate. Programmes of insertion and pastoral years are also making important contributions to priestly formation, but we must be careful lest apprenticeship get ahead of role learning; doing priestly things does not necessarily guarantee interiorization of priestly role-formation.

We continue the difficult search for formators with personal credibility, professional competence and the ability to witness to a faith community. And when we have found them, I suspect that these hardworking people would appreciate some words of encouragement in their efforts with the increasing number of applicants who come from dysfunctional families or who have already been through an unsuccessful marriage experience.

No professional person survives long today without continuous ongoing education, but the Church lacks any system which guarantees that priests and bishops must keep in touch with theological, catechetical, liturgical or pastoral developments; this is serious. Most congregations continue to invest heavily in programmes of ongoing formation and much good has been done by discussion days, journal reading, sharing groups and serious sabbaticals. Yet, is it not true that some theologically illiterate priests are doing more harm Sunday after Sunday to people's growth in holiness than many of the condemned theologians have done through their publications? Priest religious are no exception. What solution can the Synod offer us for the problem of motivating those most in need of change?

At least in words and on paper, most Congregations have rediscovered community as part of mission, wherein we should discern, support and challenge one another in faith. Yet, many men remain disinterested in any common mission even if they do change their places of ministry regularly at the Provincial's request. Others are both disinterested and immovable for any number of reasons. The modern person's option for a personal agenda and his difficulty with common vision have grown in men's congregations, due to the fact that almost any priest can find ministry on the edge of or outside his community. This eases a pastoral problem for bishops and often removes one for a Provincial, but it is hardly the stuff of which witnessing, apostolic communities are made; nor are parishioners' need for good priestly leadership being justly served.

I am convinced that it is in this area of renewal — praying, personally supportive, mutually challenging and truly discerning communities — that religious life is most urgently in need. Can the Synod assess if this is true and, if it is, give us a strong, inspirational call to move in this direction, but remembering all the while that active, clerical communities have very little resemblance to monastic or conventual ones? The movement towards district or local rather than 'same-roof' communities seems the only way to go.

At the annual meeting of Major Superiors of the USA as far back as June 1968, Fr. Felix Cardegna, SJ, then in charge of Jesuit formation at Woodstock, somewhat prophetically stated 'The thing to watch is not the numbers leaving but the numbers not entering.' It is through the vocation crisis that society is showing its lack of confidence in and support for religious life and, I might say, for priesthood. We are at a critical point in the future of most communities. Nor are the numbers alone important. Worse still are the indications that we are not attracting the leaders among youth.' The Synod might hear from all of us why this is still true. Leadership qualities are not prominent in most of those joining us and the surge of vocations in the Third World might not be altogether good news.

Listening to Major Superiors and seminary rectors in the developed world in recent years, I sense their malaise that far too many men seeking priesthood manifest three undesirable qualities; they are conservative, authoritarian and have a weak male identity; in many cases bishops seemed unworried about this trend. How to attract and keep faith-filled men capable of mission and leadership in the modern world is another question which we all might address during this time of consultation. The recent *Pastores Dabo Vobis* will help, but in my opinion, it did not stress enough the importance of careful selection, without which no formation programme can be successful. A strong word from the Synod on this score would help.

Another set of questions from the USG in preparation for the Synod asks our opinion on how religious life is responding to the challenges of mission in the modern world.

Clerical religious and missionary societies rightly thought of themselves as missionary, because until recently they manned all the front lines of our outreach to those outside the visible Church. However, we now know that to speak of mission in this limited way is not accurate, since as Redem*ptoris Missio* makes clear, mission is everywhere and *Pastores Dabo Vobis* stresses the missionary dimension of every priest's ministry. Yet, many priest religious belonging to missionary congregations have become maintenance men in somewhat static parishes, without hearing the call of *Christifideles Laici* to develop an apostolic laity. Nor do they reach out to inactive Catholics or to unbelievers around them. To repeat the call for the 'new evangelization' would seem opportune. Of course, parishes and mission stations cared for by priest religious suffer the disadvantage that a policy of lay-involvement begun by one priest may not be continued by the next one, since they are moved more often than diocesan clergy.

CAN WE ASK THE SYNOD FATHERS TO JOIN US

The challenge of mission is sharpened for all of us if we address the fact the modern person — the subject of the mission — is sensitively self aware, has constantly rising expectations, wants to control and consume, questions authority, is hesitant about commitment, has more choices available, is geographically and ideologically mobile, often feels disconnected, must be persuaded rather than pushed and is often searching anxiously for meaning. Can we ask the Synod Fathers to join us in trying to communicate with this new subject of mission, since in a way it concerns our identity as clerical religious. If we fail in this essential mission, the fundamentalists inside and outside the Church,[3] or the sects, will lead many away from the real Christ or out of the Church in search of him.

With modernity's call for continuous inculturation even in our own countries and the need for much more inter-religious dialogue in 'missionary' countries, most priests are faced with the need to develop a habit of reverent listening before they speak the good news anywhere today.

The movement of most congregations to the margin and to the poor in recent years must be encouraged, and may we hope that the Synod will not issue any warnings about our commitment, especially to the growing number of urban poor. Most local bishops appreciate our efforts, but not all are ready for prophetic activity which bounces back from some more comfortable Catholics through the diocesan newspaper. Let us experiment and learn through mistakes what we already know in theory, that evangelization must neither bypass social concern nor be swallowed up by it.

The emerging apostolic spirituality needs affirmation, since many front line missionaries are still trying to function on a quasi monastic one. Having shown the necessity of a new and deeper evangelical stance in order to work with the poor today, Guttierrez warns: 'Spirituality is a word coming from 17th century France; it can be used in a dangerous way in our Church today.' [4] The Synod could do well to ask if there is some truth in this observation and that of Secondin:

In my opinion there prevails in recent years, at least on the magisterial level, an attention to the intra-ecclesial perspective, with conventual or monastic versions (in the best sense) proposed a bit to everyone. The reflection on the historical-prophetic role is weak, or at least it is suspected and impeded :while it had notable developments in the 1970s, as shown by the courageous 1981 document: *Religious and Human Advancement.* [5]

In most countries, religious are losing effective control of universities, schools and hospitals and the trend seems irreversible. It has certainly freed us for other work but it has two disadvantages also. It removes high profile symbols of our identity and mission. It also means that we are losing potential sources from which to evangelize the more comfortable sections of society — an exercise which we may not have performed all that well while we had the advantage. The Synod might encourage us to ask if these sources of mission and symbols of identity can be replaced in another way, and perhaps at the same time encourage us to ask in what way the rich are also meant to be recipients of the Gospel.

Apart from the growing collision with financial and political interests in our own countries, a serious enough missionary problem is that more countries are closing to expatriate missionaries. Of course, it can be an advantage, calling local churches to be missionary at home. Expulsion, alienation or defamation of prophets is not new, whether it be pressuring the Major Superior's Justice and Peace branch in a Catholic country, the killing of Archbishop Romero and 7,000 catechists in Central America or the ruthlessness of the Shining Path anarchists against religious doing social work in Peru. Priests religious could be encouraged to take the lead in forming local lay missionaries when overseas sources are no longer available. It is good news to find lay missionaries even from Korea and Japan in other countries today, most of whom are inspired by and working with missionary societies and congregations.

Most congregations have rediscovered their charism, defined by *Mutuae Relationes* as 'the experience of the Holy Spirit, which includes spirituality and apostolate.' We all recognize that we have come from our founder's response to a perceived need and that each congregation became another updated presence of God's saving love in the world. Just as death awaits any organism which loses its roots or fails to adapt to its environment, religious life is now under pressure to make life-producing adaptations within itself and to a fast changing world.

This is taking place as we try to live and proclaim Jesus Christ in a world of unprecedented social change, growing secularism, structured oppression, forced migrations, hunger, tribalism and serious breakdown of family life. It is also a world in which so many good people search for meaning and a new world order. The questions are: following our founders' initiatives, how to become new missionary modalities in this modernizing, modern and postmodern world — all three of which often exist in the same country, parish, family or individual? Can the Synod gather our individual insights on this central question, helping us to combine continuity and creativity in our lives and mission at this moment in history? And can we help the Synod with our hard-earned experience while we journey into the 21st century as Church together?

I. Benito Blanco, SJ, President of CLAR in reply to a question at the USG meeting, May 27-29, 1992.
2. J. W. O'Malley, SJ: 'Priesthood, Ministry and Religious Life' in Theolog*ical Studies* (49), 1988.
3. See Patrick Arnold: 'The Rise of Catholic Fundamentalism' in *America* 11 April 1987
4. Gustavo Guttierrez, 'A New Evangelization' in *Sedos Bulletin* 4une-July, 1992
5. Text of 'Religious and Human Advancement' in *Vatican 11: More Postconciliar Documents* ed. Austin Flannery, OP, pp 260-284.

TWO
The Identity of Religious

SEAN FAGAN, SM

To collect information on the actual experience and views of religious themselves, the Union of Superiors General sent a questionnaire to the generalates of religious orders and congregations in 1992. Some congregations canvassed their provinces and synthesized the responses for submission to the USG. A congregation-wide consultation should provide a rich source of information on how religious today view the theology of religious life, on what they experience in relating to bishops, diocesan clergy, laity and other religious, on the missionary dimension of religious life in face of modem challenges, and on how the foundational charism of religious institutes becomes incarnate, grows and develops in different cultural contexts (these were the headings suggested by USG).

One wonders how the material collected will compare with what .Desmond O'Donnell, OMI, has to say in the preceding chapter. He is a priest-psychologist with long years of world-wide experience in helping religious, not only in personal counselling, but as resource-person to so many chapters and international seminars. A first reaction to his wide-ranging, indeed comprehensive paper, is to hope that it will be given all the attention it deserves both by the USG and by the secretariat preparing the 1994 synod. It is true that his primary standpoint is that of clerical religious, but much of what he says applies to all religious. Both congress and synod will benefit from the widest possible consultation of religious themselves, but the resulting documents will fall far short of what is needed if O'Donnell's perceptive comments are not heeded, or the questions he raises are not fully addressed.

He is right to warn against 'umbrella words' used to cover over important distinctions. Apostolic religious feel frustrated when they receive official documents exhorting them to fidelity in terms that apply more to contemplatives. But even more basic is the challenge to recognise the ambiguity of so many phrases used in Vatican II documents to describe religious life. The expressions listed by O'Donnell were common currency thirty years ago, but they are much more problematic today. This is not merely a question of words or literary style, but of theology, and the problem is central for religious because it is a question of identity. In a more stable society, with a fixed and static theology, most religious had a clear idea of their vocation and role. But in a more turbulent and questioning world, in a more secularised society and in a post-modernity culture, many individuals are no longer sure what it means to be a religious. It is significant that the most recent and most professional survey of religious in the United States (summarised in a later section of this book, qv) pin-pointed role clarity as a central issue. 55% of sisters, 65 % of brothers and 68% of priests reported high role clarity, but these percentages were linked to age, so that the older religious had the highest role clarity. It was much lower among younger members and among the better educated. Ambiguity regarding role can lead to anxiety, reduced ability to meet role requirements, decreased satisfaction in ministry, lower trust and self-confidence, and greater propensity to leave religious life. It would seem that this is one of the factors responsible for diminishing numbers in recent decades. In the Nazi concentration camps Viktor Frankl discovered that people could survive the most appalling deprivation, but without 'meaning' they lost interest in life and simply died. The meaning of religious life needs to be clarified for today's world, not only in the documents used to describe it, but in the personal conviction of those committed to it and in the shining testimony of their day to day living.

O'DONNELL'S GENTLE INVITATION

It would be a pity to underestimate the importance of Des O'Donnell's gentle invitation to the Synod Father to be humble and honest in their deliberations, and especially in whatever final statement they produce. In today's complex world, no statement can claim to be the last word, providing all the answers. Religious life is a mystery, sharing in the Church's own mysterious nature, but this does not justify speaking of it in mysterious terms or obscure language. Any discussion of it must take account of current theology and the discoveries of the human sciences, and be in touch with the actual experience of religious themselves. Official Roman documents remain largely unread by the vast majority of the faithful, by large numbers of priests and one suspects even by busy bishops. This is not simply from lack of interest or respect, but very often because they are written in a style that is totally foreign to most people's normal usage. It is significant that the Nygren-Ukeritis survey on the future of religious orders in the US mentioned above reveals that most American religious do not believe that reliance on external authority can favourably influence the future of religious life. There seems to be a widespread rejection of the tendency to seek help from outside sources such as church authority. This seems to be a reaction against the dogmatising approach of many Roman documents. The synod should be aware of this obstacle. Its statements need the moral authority of having the ring of truth rather than relying on the legal authority of their canonical status.

To have the ring of truth in whatever document is produced, it is essential that the synod have the fullest input from religious themselves. If the USG can get a really worldwide representative feedback to its questionnaire it may be able to produce a document that will not be dominated by one theology or confined to a single European culture. It is to be hoped that the various congregations will prepare their submissions carefully . Given the limited time available for consultation, however, few can be expected to compare with the recent US survey. This was begun in 1989 and most of its results were published last September. It was carried out by Fr. David Nygren and Sister Miriam Ukeritis. It is a highly professional survey reflecting the opinions of more than 10,000 religious sisters, brothers and priests, in turn reflecting 126,000 religious in 816 groups. Focused on the future of religious orders in the United States, it set out to examine the changes that are occurring in the experience and the understandings of religious life. It was based on the assumption that only religious themselves can describe their experience as religious, and the data collected is intended to help religious in their own self-direction . The authors claim that without significant change, religious life in the US will continue to decline and those who most need the help of religious will not be cared for. They stress that the generosity so evident in religious today remains a strong model of self-sacrifice, but this needs to be articulated and spread if others are to follow Jesus in this way. The survey very obviously reflects the American context in which it was carried out, but many of the problems it reveals will have their counterpart in other countries. It would be a pity if it were to be neglected or dismissed as a purely American phenomenon. No doubt it will be taken into account both by the USG congress and by the secretariat preparing the synod, although of course it needs to be complemented by contributions from other countries and cultures.

ROLE CLARITY

Both the congress and the synod have a daunting task even if they simply take the topics listed by Des O'Donnell. All of these need attention and he has highlighted most of the critical issues. It should be obvious from

his comments that for all of them a fresh approach is needed because of
the changed situation of today's world. As the US survey revealed,
perhaps the central challenge is role clarity, the identity question. As
O'Donnell points out, this is a problem for clerical religious particularly
insofar as so many focus on their priestly ministry and say that being a
priest is their way of being a religious. But the non-clerical members of
clerical institutes are a constant reminder that religious life has its own
identity, transcending clerical and lay. Although this awareness is growing, there are still large numbers of religious priests who are unsure of
their identity as religious and in practice function as diocesan clergy. On
the other hand, many religious sisters and brothers who have awakened
to the theology of baptism and realise the ecclesial and missionary role
of the laity wonder in what way they themselves are different. Some even
say there is little difference.

In so many areas of life we define ourselves by our differences, but
when the differences are blurred our identity suffers. Perhaps it is
unrealistic to expect the congress or synod to solve this problem with a
clarity that will convince all . This may be an area in which they could
heed O'Donnell's suggestion that they not try to do the impossible, but
rather join us in the journey as we search together for some pointers to
give meaning to our religious life. It is to be hoped that the mystery of
religious life will not be squeezed into some abstract, so-called classical
definition that takes no account of today's theology and psychology. Any
attempt at definition must recognize the difficulty and respect the
mystery. Rather than emphasize differences, however, perhaps we can
recognise the continuity and express our specificity in different terms.
Religious and laity are equally members of the Church, sharing in the
same baptismal grace and called to the same mission to spread the good
news. All are called to live the life of Jesus. But the Church is helped by
the presence of religious insofar as 'If there is no specialized concentration of what is important to everyone, in the long run the community
suffers as a result' (Schillebeeckx). Too often in the past laity were
defined as non-clerics, women as non-male. Religious do not need this
kind of definition. However, it would be a serious mistake to pretend that
there are no differences between religious and laity, as writers like
Elizabeth McDonough, OP, have rightly pointed out.

A MOVEMENT TAKES RISKS

The search for clarification of the role of religious must also keep in
balance the two elements of movement and institution. The Church itself

began as a movement, but it could only survive insofar as it developed the character of institution. It will always have to live with a creative tension between the two. The tragedy is that too often it seems to give precedence to the element of institution. The same is true of all religious orders and congregations. Each began as a movement, but those that survived could do so only by adopting the structure of institution, necessitating law and order, offices and procedures. There are considerable differences between the two. An institution is conservative while a movement is progressive. While an institution is more or less passive, yielding to influences from outside, a movement is active, influencing rather than being influenced. An institution looks to the past, while a movement looks to the future. An institution tends to be anxious and careful, guarding its boundaries, whereas a movement is prepared to take risks, to launch out and cross frontiers. It is the charismatic element at the heart of religious life that draws people to join it, but had there been no institutional framework to ensure survival there would be no congregation to join. The challenge to religious is to keep the two in balance. The tension can be painful at times, but it should be lived creatively. Any description of religious life must embrace both dimensions if it is to be faithful to genuine tradition. The Vatican II call to religious to rediscover and study their original charism has led to a new awareness of the charismatic element of religious life. The challenge is to see how this can be explained and lived in today's world. A congress or synod can give us some pointers in this area and remind us of the wider context, but ultimately it is up to each congregation, community and individual to find practical ways in which to bring it alive, so that religious will be recognised not primarily by what they do but by what they are and what they are committed to. Our prayers and good wishes go to both congress and synod; they need them.

THREE
Still Struggling with Renewal

FINTAN SHEERAN, SS CC

Religious congregations have been struggling with renewal for over twenty five years now with mixed results. This article is an attempt to appropriate some of that experience in terms of 'what have we learned?' The perspective is that of practical learning about human dynamics and change in the particular setting of religious life as we have been living it. A considerable fund of hard-earned knowledge is available to us. We have learned enough to know what must happen if significant renewal of our province or congregation or order is to take place. We now know quite a bit about why, so often, it is not happening. We have learned, for example, that we can submit ourselves to analyses of all sorts— socio-logical, theological, anthropological, psychological—and not budge an inch. We have learned that the principal obstacle to real change is not the recalcitrance of 'bad' religious but the intransigence of 'good' ones. We have learned just how profoundly loath we are to really question the appropriateness of our apostolic engagements. And, not incidentally, we know now that the material security assured by various institutional incomes will almost never be surrendered willingly no matter what the impact on our manner of life or brake on our sense of mission. And we have learned—or have we?— that the prospect of renewing our order, congregation or province in a way which includes all, or even most of the members, is a total and frequently, fatal illusion; 'bringing everybody along' is a journey to nowhere.

NEITHER IS IT TOO EARLY

It is not yet too late to benefit from what we have learned; much remains to be done. Neither is it too early; we are surely running out of time. There are those who say that it is already too late in the west, that the religious life has no future here. A roughly similar view says that religious life will so merge into the life of the general Church population that it will be indistinguishable as a particular way of life. Neither view seems justified. There are sufficient indications that the religious life will continue to be a vital and distinctive expression of Christian life even in the First World, though (some would say, because) it will be on a vastly reduced scale. There is one point upon which all observers seem to agree and that is: if the religious life does not submit itself to profound transformation it won't make any difference whether it survives or not; better in that case that it pass away. It must be said that history shows that religious groups can survive a long time without authentic renewal. As time passes, however, such groups become quite irrelevant to the mission of the Church.

The statements of 'learning' that follow are based on the experience of struggles for renewal within my own religious congregation and on extensive experience of working with other congregations as they engage in the same search and struggle. We have not learned the easy way; in these matters, probably, there is no easy way.

Let us begin with a hopeful assertion based on small realities: a renewed religious life is coming into being. There are some signs and stirrings; new commitments and new beginnings. This is not to say, however, that all existing orders and congregations will be part of that future. Far from it. For one thing, many groups are already passing away; other groups are disappearing in the First World while they are growing in the Third World. What about groups that are centuries old? Very large groups? The survival of orders and congregations is affected by their age and size, but history says that these are not determinative factors. Many groups, old and relatively young, large and small, will pass away. The renewal of religious in the Church will comprise the renewal of some existing orders and congregations, the founding of some new ones and the demise of many. All of these developments are already observably in process.

THE NEED FOR INTERVENTION

Can a province or congregation evolve gradually and naturally into a renewed state of life? Will the general good will of the members provide the momentum required to move the community forward? Can a movement of renewal begin, continue and come to fruition without any deliberate intervention? This is entirely unlikely. Renewal of a province or congregation does not just happen. It requires deliberate intervention which addresses renewal intentionally, explicitly. And the intervention in question is something more than a matter of analysis. It must be such that it moves the group beyond reflection to a confrontation with choice and action. Historical analyses, for example, can reveal movements of growth and decline in the life of a congregation or province; various psychosocial analyses can help to identify some of the dynamic patterns which are typical of various stages of growth and ageing and help us choose appropriate courses of response. Psychological profiles, attitudinal surveys and such, offer deeper insight into the human realities being dealt with, but analyses of themselves do not initiate any change. They may point to its necessity and urgency and suggest its character, but unless they are integrated into an over-all movement of renewal geared toward choice and action, even very well-designed studies can remain quite unproductive. The information provided can remain unapplied and the exercise itself leave people wondering where to go next. This sort of unfinished enterprise risks leaving disillusionment in its wake. To repeat, an intentional effort of communal renewal requires intervention in the life-processes of the group, an intervention which leads the group to decision and action.

At theoretical level this is nothing more than a truism. Which congregation, however, has not come to appreciate the truth of this statement at the level of practical reality. Renewal requires profound change; changes of attitude and of understanding, of orientation and of behaviour; of a way of living and of being in mission; of ways of relating and of praying; of being community. Interventions on behalf of renewal must never suggest that anything other than personal and communal conversion is in question.

DOES RENEWAL BRING DIVISION?

The fact is that in every community there are those who, for whatever reason, cannot or will not undergo change in any significant way. Nor will they accept that the community be changed in any real way; certainly not in the way or in the depth demanded by renewal. In fact, the community as a whole may be incapable of, or may refuse change This is one of those truths that most congregations are reluctant to accept; at least, we are reluctant to accept its implications. It is a truth that can be particularly difficult and puzzling for superiors. The role—and deep instinct—of every superior in religious life is to promote and cultivate the unity of the community. But every serious effort at congregational renewal arrives at that point beyond which one cannot go without accepting the possibility, indeed the likelihood, of a divided community. This is the Rubicon of communal renewal. Superiors and others can be confronted with a choice between pursuing renewal, with division as an apparently inevitable consequence, or deferring, for the sake of unity, to those who refuse the demands of change. For almost all congregations and orders it is the sheer dead weight of a dominant mode of life/mission which is securely in place and will not be interfered with that has defied or minimized all efforts at renewal. (In almost all cases, by the way, it is a way of life come into being since the Council.) It is the deadly inertia of good people who are rather content that stifles deep longing for new life and immobilizes groups. Those who want to commit themselves to finding a renewed expression of religious life must be given the psychological and physical space to pursue this goal. Renewal, after all, is not about the conversion of sinners but about the much more difficult business of the conversion of the good. We know this; what we cannot do is accept the implications.

Frequently it is when a process of renewal moves closer to making decisions that the reality of division becomes clear. Renewal does not so much divide communities as manifest already existing divisions. Everything possible must be done to invite all without exception to participate, to the degree that they can, in the movement of renewal, and everything possible must be done to secure the unity of all around this movement. These efforts must be sustained even when the initial responses are negative. But the renewal of the community must be pursued even if one consequence will be a split in the community itself. The work of renewal will sow seeds of division. Leaders very frequently—almost inevitably—have to choose to do this. It is always a source of very real pain. The goals of community renewal must be pursued even if those who respond positively prove to be a small minority and it becomes clear that the majority will not do so. This presents special problems which cannot be dealt with here but the point should be clear: the pursuit of renewal and refounding may well be a source of division in the community but it must not be abandoned or delayed because of this. To expect all to collaborate in the work of renewal is quite simply an unreal expectation. A unity that can be sustained only at the price of renewal is an obstacle to conversion.

IRRESOLUTE LEADERSHIP

Without the sustained, active support of official leadership intervention to achieve renewal will almost always fail of its purpose. This is not to say that congregations can never be renewed without the support of leadership. Still less is it being said that leaders must be the source of every renewal initiative or movement; far from it. Experience says, however, that congregational renewal without the sustained commitment and active support of the official leadership is highly unlikely. On the other hand, the experience of renewal stalling, or failing altogether, because of uncommitted or irresolute leadership, is all too common. Leadership for renewal requires commitment which is both 'official' and personal. Otherwise it will not be credible and will not have the conviction needed to sustain the inevitable difficulties and opposition. Can we be in any doubt that authentic leadership in our Church now demands deep commitment to renewal and a capacity to translate that commitment into leadership action? Leadership does not require the permission of the members to invite and challenge the community to renewal. It is a primary function of leadership to initiate and pursue efforts of renewal; it is not a matter which is subject to popular vote and it can be seriously misleading to seem to indicate that it is.

Without some 'grass roots' enterprise of renewed life/mission, either prior to or as an early response to deliberate intervention at congregation (or province) level, the effort at communal renewal will almost always fail of its purpose.

Interventions made on behalf of renewal can only stimulate and foster what is already alive or is coming to life; life is in the membership. But the movement of renewal needs some concrete, observable expressions

—a new community dedicated to creating a more authentic mode of life, a new mission among the poor, etc. The articulation of ideals and hopes is necessary and helpful but without some flesh and blood realizations a movement of renewal loses credibility and becomes a too easy target for the sceptic and those who resist change. More important: positive, concrete, observable realizations authenticate the desire for renewal and become powerful incentives and catalysts for further change. Leadership must vigorously foster and facilitate such realizations and, if necessary, be active in initiating them.

Sustained interaction has the capacity to open the group to profound change and to make change possible if the community decides that it wants to change. One central purpose of any plan or programme of renewal is to provide a suitable structure or scaffolding for this exchange. The members must speak and listen to each other; particularly, listen. An accumulation of information is not enough; the dynamic of personal interaction is critical. That is why such things as surveys and question-naires have a limited usefulness in renewal efforts. And it is also why the once-in-a-while get-together cannot generate the vision and energy required to initiate and sustain a movement of renewal.

Some groups have lost the habit of being together and have cast off the discipline it demands. Recovering this habit is no easy matter. In terms of focus, this interaction among the members must centre in some way around the community's identity and mission.

'WE HAVE ALWAYS DONE THIS'

Some communities focus their renewal efforts on a particular dimension of their life—community life, for example—while others take a more comprehensive approach. Whatever the direct focus may be at the outset, sooner or later the community will confront the reality that no radical renewal is possible without radical reappraisal of its apostolic works and orientations. This element is indispensable. Frequently appeal is made against the need for such revision on the grounds of 'tradition': 'we have always done this; it is a traditional work.' But, in fact, it can be said that the more long-standing, more dominant and established an apostolic work is in the life of a congregation or province, the more necessary it is that it be reappraised. And the more resistance there will be to such an appraisal. Efforts at renewal must deal seriously with apostolic revision.

The reality is that apostolates of long standing very often serve and function in a way far removed from the original intention and need. To put it simply: if, for example, we serve in schools, parishes, hospitals, etc., it is not enough to ask: how can we improve the quality of our services in these ministries?

Rather we must first ask: does our presence in these ministries make sense any more? Is the charismatic inspiration and societal need that moved us into these works and places many years ago still operative? Is this response still a valid one for us? The question to be asked about an apostolic work in terms of renewal is emphatically not: is this a good work? That is never the renewal question. Of course it is a 'good work'; we would not be about a work that was not 'good'. The fact that an apostolate is obviously a good work is not of itself a justification for our congregation continuing to do it in this place at this time. In some ways 'good works' and our inability to relinquish them constitute a crisis for religious congregations. For men religious recent developments have created another pitfall. With the decline in numbers of diocesan priests many dioceses ask religious to take on parishes and other tasks previously done by the secular clergy. If they were not forced to do so most dioceses would not entrust these ministries to religious. Communities must discern carefully. Further diocesan assimilation is not necessarily the road to renewal. It can create situations which mens' communities know full well are often entirely uncongenial for religious life itself never mind its renewal.

OPENNESS OF SPIRIT

For all apostolic evaluation the key element is the openness of spirit with which the evaluative question is asked. If those doing the discernment are not open to the possibility of a radical outcome then the evaluation will inevitably conclude by affirming that it is God's will that we continue what we are at.

'Renewal' (refounding) is what happens to an apostolic community which recognizes that its long-accustomed apostolic posture and works and accompanying manner of life, thought and behaviour are no longer adequate as authentic Gospel responses to reality. Accepting this, it struggles to make a corporate pastoral response to the world around it of a character and in a manner which are faithful to the originating inspiration of the group. This response is the axis around which the renewal efforts of the congregation must ultimately revolve.

(Some communities are beginning to identify those key ingredients which seem to be characteristic of the sort of apostolic endeavours which re-energize groups and enable deep and pervasive changes in their manner of life. They seem to provide the life-giving dynamism without which the apostolic enterprise does not materialize. I mention some of these characteristics briefly:

a) The province, or at least some members, are preoccupied with a sharply perceived state of significant human need. This perception arises from some form of solidarity with people in need.

b) These are people with a disposition of heart to give themselves entirely to the task of responding to the perceived need in union with others.

c) This perception and disposition generate a decision to subordinate all other demands, agendas and possibilities, including one's own life resources, to the task of responding to the perceived need. The response will be a particular one, not just a general intention to 'do good'.

d) The response is not predicated on the immediate availability of resources other than those already in hand.)

A radical reappraisal of the congregation's mission posture and works is inevitably at the heart of the whole endeavour. Mission reorientation will gradually and surely bring about a changed theology, a changed spirituality, a changed manner of life together and a new perception of how to dispose of our resources in mission. In short, our total pastoral orientation will have undergone change. It is not a matter of getting the theory right first, or the theology and/or the spirituality reasonably complete, and then moving on from there. No, the process of change happens in its various facets as the group submits itself to the need to be renewed, as it struggles with apostolic reorientation. No two groups will be the same as regards the rhythm, the pace, or the order of the elements involved. If it is authentic, in the end all will be affected and deeply changed—community life, prayer, authority, recruitment, spirituality, formation, theology, ministry everything. There will be a new living synthesis, a new apostolic religious life.

As a province or congregation (or small group) takes up this struggle it will of necessity experience itself going through, smoothly or awkwardly, slowly or quickly, a process comprising perception and appraisal, choice and decision, risk-taking and action. It will come to realize in the actual experience that the whole process is not just a transitional phase but that in time it will be the typical and permanent movement of the community's life.

The belief in question includes faith that the call to renewal is of the Spirit and that, as with all such calls, it is historic, meaning that it is for our time and that this time is passing. It is a faith which perceives the charism of the congregation as a particular apostolic impulse and initiative in the Church, having the capacity to give vision and power to the community, enabling it to make an appropriate apostolic pastoral response, here and now, to the reality of our world.

Four
About the *Lineamenta*

FLANNAN MARKHAM, SS.CC.

Footnotes, in any work, can be a good indication of the thrust and scope of that work and the reader is able to gauge the perspective from which it is written. All in all the *Lineamenta* has 130 footnotes. Apart from Popes the following are excluded, in the sense that nothing is attributed to them:

> All who have lived since 549 A.D. All women. All mendicants, clerks regular, nuns, sisters and apostolic religious. All natives of the Americas, Australasia, the Orient. All natives of African and European countries, except Egypt, Algeria, Italy, S.W. Germany. These countries merit one footnote each in the persons of Sts. Athanasius, Augustine, Benedict and Ambrose.

What is incomprehensible is the fact that Sts. Bernard, Francis, Clare, Dominic, Bonaventure, Catherine of Siena, Anthony, Thomas Aquinas, Ignatius Loyola, Angela Merici, Alphonsus Ligouri, Francis de Sales, Louise de Marillac, Vincent de Paul, John Baptist de la Salle, John of God, Francis Cabrini, etc., are omitted. Apart from these where are the insights of Mary Ward, Catherine McAuley, Ignatius Rice, Margaret McGillup, etc? One wonders whether the foundation of this approach is exclusively the monastic model of religious life.

All the Vatican II and post Vatican II documents are listed early on and yet one misses some of their major insights in the final product. Where is the outward thrust of the vows beautifully delineated by Paul VI in *Evangelica Testificatio?* In its place there looms an individual personalistic approach to the vows. Also missing is the dynamic approach to charism outlined in *Mutuae Relationes* and in its place is a rather vague understanding of charism. One notes immediately the difference in this approach to charism and that of John Lozano. Astonishingly the whole notion of charism of each religious institute is subsumed in one short paragraph (No 16). The idea that 'no charism ought to be altered or destroyed, but ought to be conserved and renewed' seems to fly in the face of history. How many orders over the centuries have ceased to exist? One is also reminded of the late Fr Arrupe's comment that the Society of Jesus had not been given the grace of immortality.

One is also amazed at the omission of any significant reference to the prophetic dimension of religious life. Authors on religious life since Vatican II have developed this, to the great benefit of religious. One recalls Lozano, Woodward, Schneiders, Boff and O'Murchu and their insightful approaches. The omission does not augur well for the expected document from the Synod. When one compares what Raymond Brown and Nadine Foley, OP have written on consecration with what is in the document, one has to wonder why there is a significantly different nuance. This has to be evaluated in the same context as the recognition of the new grouping of religious in the US. The emphasis on consecration here has that *fuga mundi* ring which may become a resounding peal in the final document.

GOOD QUESTIONS?

One final caution is related to the twenty questions interspersed throughout the document. Howard Gray, S.J. commented, a few years ago, that before one answers a question, one must be sure that the question is a good question. We could spend too much time answering questions which do not deserve answers.

The document states that the Synod will deal with the nature, identity and role (gift and mission) of consecrated life. 'The bishops want to help you to be Gospel leaven and evangelisers of the third millenium and social ordering of peoples.' One would hope that the religious representation at the Synod would be such as to help bishops in this task. Bishops, except religious bishops, have very little knowledge of what constitutes religious life and therefore need insights from those who live this way of life. If religious do not have a significant role in preparation for and input at the Synod, then the resultant document will suffer. Religious themselves then must try, with every means, to see to it that their voices are heard in preparation for the Synod. If we don't, then we will only have ourselves to blame.

The document makes easy reading and is set out in such a way that it lends itself to much discussion. Naturally it is biased in a certain direction and that is fine as long as readers are aware of other approaches. The introduction deals with the reason for the Synod, and the documents on religious life during and after Vatican II. This is basically the informative section. Part One deals with the nature and identity of religious life and, in turn, is divided into two sections. One deals with the fundamentals of religious life, while the other deals with the variety of charisms and plurality of forms of religious life. The first section reminds one of 'Essential Elements of Religious Life' [1983] (a 'domestic document about housekeeping' — Howard Gray) with which commentators had problems, both as to content and exact authorship. This section could have been written before Vatican II, which is not a fault in itself. However, the vows are dealt with as if *Evangelica Testificatio* had never been written. When one looks at the essential values and demands of the spiritual life, one sees 'renunciation of the world' heading the list. One wonders how 'God so loved the world as to send his only begotten Son' fits into this model?

The section on variety of forms of religious life is an historical approach and is well done. It is heartening to see the question of clerical religious life addressed here and also that of the brother in non-clerical institutions. The section on brothers can be expanded and addressed in depth in future preparations.

Part II deals with consecrated life in the Church and the world today and is excellent from the point of view of raising questions and it also reveals the stance taken by the document. It certainly does not have the pessimism of Cardinal Ratzinger as it surveys the years of renewal, and the listing of positive signs of renewal is helpful. As it recounts the new values of religious life it highlights the collaboration evident among religious and laity, as well as the increased sensitivity to the poor and marginalised. As it recounts the shadow side of renewal one is dismayed at the lack of nuance in the approach and unless this approach is changed, the analysis which is needed will not be forthcoming. One wonders whether Bellah's book *Habits of the Heart* had an influence here. Without a doubt the section devoted to 'overcoming the ambiguity and challenges of modern society' is excellent in that it concerns itself with very real issues. [N.21] I hope that the ambiguity will not be met by certainty but with 'helps' to live with it and that the challenges will spur to creativity. The document calls for a continuation of renewal but one shudders at the points outlined, not major points, but matters of detail. Why in 1993 has the matter of religious dress to be raised? One is reminded here of the Russian Orthodox Church discussing liturgical colours in Moscow in 1917.

OVER-STRESS ON LOCAL CHURCH

Part III deals with consecrated life and its role in Church and world. The section on the role of consecrated life in the Church is not only weak but exacerbates the role of religious priests. It is here that the prophetic role of the life should have been highlighted and the omission is due to an over-stress on the relationship between the religious life and the local Church. The section on collaboration with the laity is sound and yet that innate suspicion of the laity can be read in the very last sentence [cf. N.41].

The section dealing with religious life in Church Mission looks towards the needs of the present and challenges of the future. Points of note are, reference to mission *ad gentes* which is directed also towards 'countgries which have for centuries accepted the proclamation of Christ' [N.43], ecumenism, attention to young people, preferential choice for the poor and presence in culture, etc. One does not expect a very detailed approach in such documents but the lack of any reference to justice in the thrust towards the poor, a lack of understanding of the real financial demands in the education of youth and the total omission of the challenge of Christian feminism is disappointing.

The lack of an understanding of the different spiritualities undergirding the different expressions of religious life is the most surprising and most serious omission in this document. It really shows that, as the Council Fathers at Vatican II instinctively knew, the correct approach was to leave it to religious, with all their expertise and experience, to take on the findings of the Council and respond to them. Some people complain (see 'The Future of Religious Life in the United States, later in this volume) that Vatican II delineated very clearly the role of bishops, priests and laity but not that of religious. I rejoice that it did not delineate the role of religious. What the Council said to religious was, in effect: 'have your own council, delineate you own role' and that is what religious enthusiastically did in their chapters and special chapters. In a time of ambiguity insecure people look for certainties, and some may look to the Synod to provide such security. With God's help it will not go down that road. Religious life is too complex for simplistic answers. Religious are seeking from the Synod an understanding of what they are trying to accomplish, encouragement as they respond to new challenges, and above all life-giving words inspiring them to continue their great work for evangelisation. The last thing religious life needs is a return to the past; that is a death wish.

FIVE
Some Questions on the *Lineamenta*

JAN KERKHOFS, SJ

The following questions were prepared by Father Jan Kerkhofs, SJ, professor of theology at Louvain University, for the Union of the Conferences of Major Superiors of Europe. Father Kerkhofs's questions are a distillation from the *Lineamenta*, the preliminary draft document prepared for the Synod on religious life, which is printed elsewhere in this volume. Father Kerkhofs's questions were sent to all the member conferences of the *Unio Conferentiarum Europae Superiorum Majorum*, to give the union its official title. Father Kerkhofs is particularly well versed in the sociology of religion in Europe, having been chairperson of the guiding committee of the European Value Systems report, first published in 1984, and due to be re-published shortly, with considerably wider scope.

The authors whose contributions follow Father Kerkhofs' questions comment either on them or on the *Lineamenta* directly.

I, AN OVERVIEW:

(a) Of your country: what are the main features of the society in which you live?
(b) Of religious life:

What developments are taking place in religious life?
What social currents confront you?
What problems face you?
How has religious life tried to cope with them?

II, QUESTIONNAIRE:

(1) In your over-all situation, what features provide the best possibility of achieving the *vita evangelica*? It would be helpful to take into account what is meant by being a disciple of Jesus and the more or less general perception of the institutional Church — and therefore of religious life too, to some extent — as lacking credibility.

(2) Most religious institutes, with a few exceptions here and there, face the problem of an ageing membership. How can the coming generations of religious, sometimes very few in number, be assured of the spiritual, apostolic and material space which they will need if they are to follow

new paths, in keeping with the deeper identity of their institutes? Which space they will also need if they have to cope with the absence of this deeper identity. What must be done to ensure that the older generations (a) do not become discouraged and (b) do not impede genuine *aggiornamento* of spirituality and apostolic commitment?

(3) In your situation, do some of your commitments require new forms of collaboration — on a practical, spiritual and institutional level — between your members and lay men and women? Which of the existing forms of collaboration need to be more fully developed?

(4) What forms of community life can ensure both an authentic religious life and a serious commitment to today's world? And how can one preserve *communio* within an institute which has a great diversity of commitments?

When younger members are few in number, an institute can find that its commitments can lead to division among its members, with some living in very small communities and with older members living in large communities. Is preparation needed for life in a small community? What are the psychological consequences? How can one combine respect for privacy with life in such a community? What is being done to prepare for the abandonment of many places, such as hospitals and schools, where it has become impossible to continue?

(5) Very often, such developments make it necessary to enter into a new kind of relationship with the local, regional or universal hierarchy. What have been the main positive and negative experiences as such relationships have evolved? Is religious life seen as something valuable in itself, or merely as a useful apostolic resource?

(6) Is there something special about the ministry of religious priests and religious deacons in comparison with secular priests and deacons? How do people rate the vocation of religious brothers who are not deacons?

(7) What level of maturity do you consider necessary for accepting candidates (a) to the noviciate and (b) to perpetual vows? Are there differences of emphasis in comparison with previous generations? Can one visualise forms of religious life which permit membership for limited periods?

(8) There are religious women who by conviction and out of apostolic commitment feel called to some ministries in the Church, including the diaconate and priesthood. How does this strike you?

(9) The prophetic mission of religious life almost of necessity involves some tension between fidelity to the greater tradition and a creativity that goes beyond traditions. For the most part this happens where faith requires a special commitment to the promotion of justice. How can one ensure discernment without stifling the Spirit? Similar tension can exist also in ecumenical work.

(10) In a number of central and eastern European countries religious life

is beginning anew. What do you think of the possibility of "exchanging gifts" between eastern and central European communities and western European communities? What are the gifts which can be given and received, in an atmosphere of mutual respect and so as to promote a conciliar spirit?

(11) On reflection, as we approach the end of the second millenium in a Europe which seems to lack certainty and to distrust ideology and dogmatism, how would you re-define genuine consecrated life?

SIX

The Survival of Religious Life?

GERALD A. ARBUCKLE, S.M.

> Religious life is in such a state that only a radically new leadership
> approach and re-orientation will allow it to survive and authentically
> grow according to the values of Vatican II.

In the following comments I am unable to follow precisely the questions
based on the *Lineamenta*. Generally the questions, together with the
Lineamenta itself, convey the impression that though there are problems
in contemporary religious life, nonetheless with a few not too radical
changes the former dynamism and structures will return. Unfortunately,
that is not my experience. The fact is religious life is in such a state that
only a radically new leadership approach and re-orientation will allow it
to survive and authentically grow according to the values of Vatican II.
For many existing communities it is far from certain that they have the
inner resources for this profound revitalization to occur.

My aims in this brief commentary* are (i) to show why religious life
is at its most exciting stage in generations; (ii) to illustrate why the word
'renewal' used in the *Lineamenta* inadequately expresses the reality and
the challenge we face; (iii) to explain why the lack of appropriate
leadership in religious life together with other obstacles, including
contemporary restorationism in the Church, are obstructing the transforming or refounding of religious life.

My comments relate particularly to apostolic religious life and they
are of course personal, but they are based on a wide experience of
observing religious life in the First and Third Worlds over many years.
The *Lineamenta* says religious life must be viewed within the context of
the world and the Church and that is where I would begin.

I. THE WORLD AND THE CHALLENGE TO REFOUND THE CHURCH [1]

The Western world is in a liminal space, for its economic/cultural
superiority of centuries is being threatened, even undermined, with
alarming speed. And the shape of the new West has yet to emerge. The
symptoms of liminal chaos are evident. Among them are rising unemployment, violence, the breakdown of family structures, loss of traditional values through secularization and secularism, the growing gap

between the rich and poor. Within the Third World also the division between the rich/powerful and the poor/politically weak grows daily. While there are points of hope, the enormity of the problems gives no grounds for optimism.

And the Church? The process of finding and implementing new methods of bringing the faith-justice Good News to the contemporary world has to be more a matter of rebirth, Phoenix-like, than the gentle, refreshing breeze that the phrase 'renewal of the Church, its structures and pastoral methods' has come to connote. The word 'renewal' has lost its original sense of urgency and radicality. So daunting is the challenge that we must now speak of refounding (or transforming) the Church (John Paul II speaks of building 'anew' the Church), its pastoral methods and structures, in order to relate the Gospel to the contemporary world.

By refounding the Church I mean the process whereby the Gospel interacts with the most urgent and persistent needs of today; it means inventing entirely new pastoral methods and structures, because so much of the old simply will no longer work or fit the variety and complexity of the world's problems. Remember, we renew a car by replacing a flat tire with a sound spare, but we refound the car by inventing an entirely new form of transportation without wheels, e.g. by inventing the hovercraft. Metaphorically in the pastoral world that is the challenge we face! In brief, what we need are not more of the same pastoral methods, even if vastly improved, but creative 'quantum-leap' pastoral imagination and action, under the inspiration of innovative leadership at all levels. Certainly, we require good administrators, but the primary need is for prophetic leaders who imaginatively re-interpret the Gospel message for this age.

II. RELIGIOUS LIFE: IS IT RESPONDING PROPHETICALLY?

Religious life is in its own state of liminality, the betwixt-and-between stage, in which the irrelevant of the pre-Council days has yet to be fully let go of and religious life based on the Council's values has yet to be confidently born[2]. Its creation story or myth for the period immediately prior to Vatican II mirrored the ghetto state of the Church itself. Religious life had lost that prophetic passion that had so characterized the great founding figures of the past, e.g. St Francis of Assisi, Mary Ward. They recognized that religious by definition must challenge both society *and* the Church with the radical demands of the Gospel. Instead we had become exemplary supporters of the ghetto Church, remote from the turmoil of the world in change, the spiritual élite of the Church. We needed a revolution in thinking to re-discover our identity.

Vatican II was that revolution. It destroyed the prevailing vision of religious life the moment it stated that Christians must, with listening and compassionate hearts, enter into dialogue with a world in change. Religious had now to rediscover the heart of their mission by centering on Christ, the dynamism of their founding vision and the needs of the Church/humankind.

However, it is a primary axiom of applied anthropology that no founding myth or story can be interfered with, even for the right reasons, *without* cultural and personal catastrophes. In other words, when identities and a sense of belonging are undermined, people feel lost or rootless. This is the chaos of liminality, for the new founding story has yet to be articulated clearly and actioned in concrete ways.

AT THE CUTTING EDGE?

Theoretically, we religious admit that we must be at the cutting edge between the Gospel and cultures. But cultures of religious congregations in which the key symbols are stability, conformity to unchanging customs and flight from the world, cannot change quickly to a way of life demanding mobility, frequent change, prophetic challenging of society and the institutional Church. The *Lineamenta* does not refer in any significant way to the enormity of the Council's mythological or religious life paradigm change and the seriousness of its consequences, consequences which, typically, can follow any rapid cultural breakdown. Examples are unarticulated grief over the loss of identity, drifting without concretized/interiorized goals, individualism, addictive behaviour, lack of energy, denial, nostalgia for the past leading to restorationism, which is the effort to return religious life back to the attitudes and structures of the pre-Council years.

Hence, we also must speak no longer of renewal of religious life but of its refounding, with structures and attitudes that relate to the Gospel, not to the maintenance of a Church unconcerned with people's anxieties and hopes, but to a world in revolutionary change. Refounding of religious life is the process whereby the Gospel is brought into interaction with the most urgent and persistent problems of today. It is, and must be, painful and risky, because ultimately refounding is the ascetical entering into the paschal mystery for mission.

Is this refounding occurring? Yes, I am frequently seeing examples of it, but I believe that many religious communities have neither the resources, nor the will, to be involved in this process.

III. OBSTACLES TO REFOUNDING/TRANSFORMING

The following are obstacles to refounding that are not, or are only lightly, considered in the *Lineamenta*:

Confusion about the Role of the Vows: Especially from the eleventh century on most congregations were founded to render apostolic service to the world, not primarily for their members' individual sanctification. The commitment to the vows flows from this dominant emphasis on the consecrated mission with and to others; the vows are indispensable, but we do not enter religious life to live the vows for their own sake, but as signs of our prophetic stand for Christ's mission to the world[3]. In the generations prior to the Council the vows had become the centre of religious life, not the ministry to the world. As this approach fostered individualism and escape from the anxieties of humankind, we could be holy in fine houses in the midst of slums and without guilt — provided 'we kept the vows'. I sense that the *Lineamenta* still prefers this latter thinking, thus encouraging religious to repeat the mistakes of the past, e.g. living in comfortable houses in places like Africa, Asia or deprived inner suburbs of Western cities while the poor remain at the gate!

Poverty of Congregational Leadership: For refounding/transforming communities to emerge three groups of people are needed: skilled congregational leaders, radically innovative people and 'renewal' persons (that is, religious who cannot be prophetically innovative, but are open to co-operate with people in communities who are). I believe skilled congregational leadership is rare. Where a leader of the right calibre exists he/she, *inter alia*[4], (i) has the ability to create collaboratively, and to communicate, a realistic vision/strategies; (ii) empowers people to claim their own authority to act prophetically within the context of the congregation; (iii) consistently calls apostolates and communities to be accountable to the vision/strategies; (iv) places a priority on acquisition of leadership skills; (v) spiritually is prepared to rest in the Gethsemane or Golgotha of uncertainty, actively waiting on the Spirit; (vi) recognizes that refounding is a gift of the Lord, to be accepted or rejected and that, while the order of pastoral planning is necessary, far more is required, such as imaginative risk-taking under the inspiration of the Spirit.

Community Models Confused: At present there are three major community models: monastic, conventual and apostolic; when they are confused with one another all kinds of unnecessary tensions emerge and energy for corporate mission is lost. The primary emphasis in each model differs. For example, the primary concern of the apostolic model is the pastoral needs of people beyond the community; apostolic religious are to be open to move with short notice to the more urgent pastoral needs. Community structures must therefore be flexible. To impose uncritically the community structures appropriate to the monastic model is evangelically unjust. Yet, there are religious who are attempting this, all in the name of 'authentic renewal'.[5]

A new type of religious life community, which I term the 'therapeutic' or 'me-istic' model, has emerged diametrically opposed to the values of religious life.[6] The primary function of community, according to this aberrant model, is to serve the individualistic and narcissistic or self-fulfilment needs of members. Collaborative action for mission is impossible in this situation. The harsh truth is that active communities ministerially/religiously die, when they turn aside from their primary task of evangelizing outwards.

Passive and Active Internal Opposition: Refounding religious congregations is a co-operative community process involving congregational leaders, refounding and renewal people (in the sense already described). However, I commonly find that many religious, because they have become locked-in on the therapeutic, even neurotic, model of religious life, do not want to be renewal people and participate in the refounding process. In fact I generally find therapeutic religious passively and actively obstructing the process.

The only way forward is to adopt boldly the axiom: 'the new belongs elsewhere'. By this strategy the refounding process is given structural space to by-pass the neurotic congregational sub-culture. Recall the instruction of Christ: 'And if anyone does not welcome you or listen to what you have to say, as you walk out of the house or town shake the dust from your feet.'(Mt.10:14) That is, if people are not interested in refounding for mission, even more so if they seek to subvert it deliberately or otherwise, then following Jesus' advice congregational leaders must encourage energies to be unequivocally directed to points of apostolic potential. Go wherever there is life, not death or persistent resistance: 'Leave the dead to bury the dead; your duty is to go and spread the news of the kingdom of God'(Lk. 9:60). This requires a boldness and courage in leadership to withstand the pressures from those unwilling to participate in collaborative action for refounding.

Clericalism and Ecclesiastical Restorationism: Restorationism is an ill-defined, but nonetheless powerful, movement within the Church towards the *uncritical* reaffirmation of pre-Vatican II structures and attitudes[7], in reaction to the stress resulting from the theological and cultural turmoil generated by the changes of the Council and the modern world at large.

It takes many forms, some fanatically aggressive and others less so. It is marked by degrees of intolerance to any form of opposition, an anti-world ethos, suspicion or condemnation of people involved in social justice ministries. Restorationists fear disorder or malaise, because they cannot cope with the unpredictability and messiness that are the inevitable accompaniment of the anxiety-evoking new and bold pastoral endeavours of religious and others, who take the mission of Christ to the world seriously. Within the hierarchical structures of the Church restorationism is a powerful and well orchestrated force, as is evident, for example, in the official support for right-wing movements and conservative appointments. Though restorationism is less powerful within religious congregations, the pervading restorationist ethos in the Church at large is making it more and more difficult for religious to be pastorally and prophetically creative.

WOMEN RELIGIOUS LEAD THE WAY

In the refounding of religious congregations, women religious are commonly leading the way. Widespread participation over many years in all kinds of ongoing formation programmes has produced in many religious women a prayerful, yet restless, creative apostolic zeal for the Lord's work. I meet sisters in their sixties and seventies who are preparing for their fourth or fifth career in the service of local Churches at home or in the Third World countries. Retirement is a rarely mentioned word. Generally sisters are far more theologically and pastorally updated than their male counterparts.

Their faith and courage, however, are being increasingly tested and purified. Not uncommonly members of the hierarchy, clergy and laity criticise them or even treat them as social and apostolic outsiders because 'they have stopped looking and acting like true religious sisters'. For these critics being a 'true' religious sister means wearing the veil, being involved in the traditional apostolic works of teaching or nursing, being unquestionably submissive to a patriarchal leadership. Congregations of brothers, especially teaching ones, sometimes experience problems of adjustment whenever an apostolate is perceived incorrectly to be integral to the charism. For example, for some communities of brothers the withdrawal from a school in order to experiment with other forms of reaching the poor may evoke identity crises and hesitancy in risking the new. However, clerical ignorance, fear and intolerance prevent many sisters and brothers from initiating prophetic pastoral action.

The reasons for the hesitancy of clerical religious to develop comparable prophetic leadership are complex. Ultimately, however, I believe it is the failure to integrate priesthood with religious life within clerical congregations over many generations that has significantly led to this crisis. After Vatican II clerical religious could rely on their priesthood for identity; they could allow the chaos of religious life revitalization to pass them by. Now, however, the traditional status of the priesthood within the Catholic culture is under attack from many sides: the feminist movement, the theological and professional qualities of sisters, the growing involvement by lay people in areas originally set aside for priests. Little wonder that many clerical religious feel lost, without apostolic energy and hesitant to join with religious women and others in collaborative ministries.[8]

Confused Formation Programmes: Inevitably, recruitment and formation strategies in congregations mirror the wider chaos in religious life and the Church. If the primary aim of religious life is unclear to leaders and religious, then candidates will be allowed in and formation programmes developed that conflict with the prophetic function of congregations.

Since prophetic action is at the very heart of religious life, candidates must not be recruited unless there is the well-founded hope that they can fit in and contribute to the development of communities marked by faith interdependence and mutuality. Apostolic communities cannot survive unless their members are prepared to share with one another their own journeys in faith with the Lord, but without a realistic hope of spiritual and human maturity this is impossible. One cannot be a community 'escapist' or 'refugee' and be actively committed to prophetic corporate action at the same time. I find congregations accepting this view, even articulating it in mission statements, but in reality they ignore it. Therapeutic community life is fostered, candidates with above-average needs for security and affirmation are accepted, in the hope that eventually miracles of maturity will occur. They don't! Appropriate screening and formation is a justice imperative — justice for the candidate, the congregation and the Church.

And in the Third World — in Africa and the Philippines, for example — one still finds formation houses with many candidates and no trained formators. Criteria for entrance and stages of formation, if they exist, are not adhered to. Often a pre-Vatican II model of religious life is imposed, even with restorationist zeal. Formation houses provide candidates with upper-class accommodation making a mockery of the congregation's rhetoric about faith/justice, poverty and the preferential option for the

poor. Congregational leaders seem to became mesmerized by the vocation potential, thus losing touch with reality, believing that God wishes
their institutes to survive at all costs.

CONCLUSION

Religious life is refounding, when it is prophetically challenging the anti-
Gospel values of society and the pastoral inertia of the Church or its
dangerous accommodation with the world. That is the lesson of history.
It is the second prophetic imperative, the challenging of the Church to pull
back from its present restorationist zeal, that is surely the more painful.
It is a martyrdom of prophecy for committed religious, who, inspired by
a deep respect for Christ's Church, are bound to be misunderstood, even
marginalized.[9] Yet they approach this task with the gifts of the Holy Spirit
testifying to their prophetic authenticity: 'love, peace, patience, kindness,
goodness, trustfulness, gentleness and self-control.'(Gal.5:22)

*References are given to publications where some points are explained at greater depth.
1. See Arbuckle, *Earthing the Gospel: An Inculturation Handbook for the Pastoral
Worker* (London: Geoffrey Chapman, 1990), pp. 208-220.
2. See Arbuckle, *Out of Chaos: Refounding of Religious Congregations* (London:
Geoffrey Chapman, 1988), pp. 65-87.
3. See J. M. Tillard, *A Gospel Path: The Religious Life* (Brussels: *Lumen Vitae*, 1975),
p. 101, and J. Lozano, *Discipleship: Towards an Understanding of Religious Life*
(Chicago: Claret Center, 1980), p. 207.
4. See Arbuckle, *Refounding the Church* (London: Geoffrey Chapman). (Due for
publication Oct. 1993), Chaps. 4, 5, 7, 8. Also *Grieving for Change* (London: Geoffrey
Chapman, 1991), pp. 140-164.
5. See Arbuckle, 'Clarifying Community Models', *Review for Religious*, Vol. 50, No. 5,
1991, pp. 697-704.
6. See Arbuckle, 'Suffocating Religious Life: A New Type Emerges', *The Way
Supplement*, No. 65, 1989, pp.26-39.
7. See Arbuckle, *Refounding the Church*, op. cit., Chaps. 1-3.
8. See Arbuckle, *The Tablet*, 12 Jan. 1991, pp. 42-43.
9. See *Mutuae Relationes*, Congs. for Religious and Bishops, 1978, par. 12, apud
Vatican II: More Postconciliar Documents, ed Austin Flannery, OP., pp. 217-218.

SEVEN
Religious Life
in a Time of Turbulence

SEAN O'RIORDAN, CSSR

The chapter 'Clerical Religious: Taking Stock for the Synod' from the able pen of Fr. Desmond O'Donnell, OMI, has sparked a new and searching discussion in Ireland and elsewhere on the identity of religious life today, since it first appeared in in *Religious Life Review*, January/February 1993. True, the specific problem addressed by Fr. O'Donnell was that of the concrete identity and mission of clerical religious in this day and age. His article however ranged more widely and raised various issues that concern religious life as such in today's world. It was logical then that it should be followed in the same journey by Fr, Seán Fagan's contribution which directly focuses on 'The Identity of Religious' [and which is also contained in this volume. Ed.]

The purpose of the present article is not to comment on preceding ones or to add new points to those made by Frs. O'Donnell and Fagan. I fully agree with what they have written and could in some ways carry their line of thought further; but to me it seems more pertinent at this juncture to look at some important surveys of religious life which have appeared outside Ireland, noting how these indicate some general concerns which have surfaced far and wide in the contemporary Church.

In particular it seems important to me to look more closely at the *Lineamenta* (Outlines) issued by the Council of the General Secretariat of the Synod in 1992. The declared purpose of this document is to 'present the topic of the next synodal assembly ('The Consecrated Life and Its Role in the Church and in the World') in a complete organic manner, indicating the topic's precise content and its necessary limits' (Preface, p, 3).

What 'precise content' emerges in the *Lineamenta* and how does it relate to the content of the surveys and studies of religious life that have appeared in various countries? This is a more important and significant aspect of the document than the series of questions which it appends to each of its sections. These questions or a selection of them have been circulated in religious communities with a view to eliciting responses from the members. To discern the real import of the questions themselves, however, one must first discern the import and orientation of the *Lineamenta* as a whole. To grasp this rightly it is not enough to examine the document by itself. Rather the document has to be seen in the context of a broader Roman policy bearing on the life of the Church as a whole and on the 'consecrated life' as a special form of Christian life, which is defined as 'a more complete configuration to the mystery of Christ, chaste, poor and obedient' (art. 6).

The first part of this article, then, will briefly consider the re-evaluation of religious life which is going on in the Church of the 1990s. The second will consider the salient points of the *Lineamenta's* appraisal of it. The third will consider the actual impact of the *Lineamenta* not only on preparations for the Synod but on the way in which the Synod will deal with and decide on the subject assigned to it.

Perhaps the most detailed study of religious life in the present-day socio-cultural context of a particular country is *The Future of Religious Orders in the United States* compiled by two psychologists, Fr. David Nygren, CM and Sr. Miriam Ukeritis. [See summary of it later in this volume. Ed.] What interests me here is not the study as a whole but some significant emphases to be found in it. I list these, basing myself on the fuller text of the study published in *Origins,* 24 September 1992.

1) 'Only religious can describe their experience of faith as religious.' The point here is that outside authorities cannot prescribe the faith-experience that religious have or should have. Hence 'while maintaining a clear church identity, the structures of religious life will be based on mission rather than canons and the unique charism of religious life will remain largely distinct from hierarchical functions. An inclusive atmosphere will be marked by multiculturalism, a clear inclusion of women and the feminine, and a genuine respect for diversity.' Hence too, 'the abuses of authority in the past make individuals reluctant to endorse authority in any way. Religious, in particular, are clear in their lowered respect for the magisterial authority of the church and the U.S. hierarchy in particular.' There is question here of a specific reaction on the part of U.S. religious but, though in a less pronounced form, it is surfacing also in other countries among religious, including women religious.

2) 'The 30 years since the Second Vatican Council have been turbulent ones for Roman Catholic religious orders in the United States.' That word 'turbulent' suggested to me the title I have given to this article. But the 'turbulence' is not confined to the U.S. In various ways it shows itself among religious men and women in all Western countries and, slowly but

increasingly, in African and Asiatic countries as well. Fr. Desmond O'Donnell is referring to the same thing when he writes of "the present psycho-historical dislocation' and Fr. Seán Fagan too takes it for granted that religious life is going through a rough passage today.

Many of the particular features of the present 'turbulence' of religious life that are catalogued and analysed in the Nygren-Ukeritis study recur regularly in other studies of it, even if under different names. Thus Nygren-Ukeritis dwells at length on 'role clarity for religious' which is defined as 'the individual's perceived level of understanding regarding his or her purpose and function within the current structure of the church.' Confusion and dislocation in the area of role clarity leads to a crisis of 'identity' in religious life.

LOSS OF CONVICTION AND CLARITY

It is under this heading that the negative phenomena listed by Nygren-Ukeritis (anxiety, reduced ability to meet role requirements, decreased ministerial satisfaction, lower trust and self-confidence, increased sense of futility and greater propensity to leave a religious order) are usually discussed in European studies of the current problems of religious life. It all adds up to anomie, the term devised a century ago by the French sociologist Durkheim to characterise the situation of socio-cultural disintegration and breakdown. Nygren-Ukeritis applies it to the present malaise of religious life. 'Anomie, defined as a state in which normative standards of conduct and belief are weak or lacking, is characterised by disorientation, anxiety and isolation. The loss of conviction about the vows, lack of clarity about the role of religious, reaction to authority, lack of corporate mission and ministry, and disillusionment with leadership pose significant threats to the future of religious life.'

3) Of course the picture is not all bleak. Nygren-Ukeritis emphasises the presence in religious life of many men and women of profound spirituality. 'Their profile includes a radical dependence on God, whom they see as a benevolent authority, and a capacity to enter the life of another for the sake of the other and not to meet their own personal, even though seemingly altruistic, needs. They also possess a deep desire for oneness with God and with others. They are deeply committed to their congregation where, by objective standards, the costs of their work and membership are very high.'

A conclusion for the future is drawn from this fact. 'The research suggests that religious orders of the future will derive their mission and their life in common from a firm relationship with the person of Jesus, grounded in communion with the Word.' There is, however, a gap in the extrapolation from the present to the future of religious life, both in the Nygren-Ukeritis study and in most other studies of the kind. What is wanting is a careful consideration of how the truly dedicated religious of today might constitute the foundation on which a 'revitalized religious life, rooted in Jesus Christ and the Gospel's values' might be built up in the future. Projects of revitalisation for the future are still generally framed on the supposition that all members of the community must be involved in the process, even when it is obvious that many of them have been smitten by the malady of incurable anomie.

I would like to comment briefly on the document 'Male Religious Life: a Self-Portrait with Light and Shade' which is printed later in this volume, singling out some significant elements in it.

1) On the positive side there is rejoicing that 'a predominantly monastic understanding of religious life, even apostolic religious life, has been left behind and that a new and better 'manner of being and working' has been embodied in new religious constitutions. This reminds me of Fr. Desmond O'Donnell's words: 'May we ask the Synod Fathers to hesitate well before even hinting at a return to a quasi monastic spirituality?'

THE REMEDY FOR ANOMIE

2) The 'crisis of identity' of masculine religious life today is dealt with at length and the exemplifications of it correspond closely to the Nygren-Ukeritis study's exemplifications of the lack of 'role clarity' among religious. The name 'anomie' (equated with 'apathy') is again given to the resultant disorientation and disintegration.

3) 'We do not even have a satisfactory theology of the religious priesthood,' says the USG document. 'What is the relationship between the diocesan priesthood and the priesthood of religious?' Here a concern is expressed similar to that put forward in Fr. Desmond O 'Donnell's article .

4) What is the remedy for anomie? Nothing less than a decisive 'conversion on the part of religious to Christ and to the Gospel.' They need a 'transparent experience of God.'

5) This report has an original paragraph on the deviations to which men religious are prone when they are bereft of a truly evangelical spirituality, Among them are withdrawal into privacy (a new form of *fuga mundi*, 'flight from the world'), joining in 'crusading' movements, pursuing 'restoration' policies (what in this country we would call a 'right-wing' option) and going for quick-fix solutions to social and

personal problems.

The USG report, like the Nygren-Ukeritis study and the O'Donnell and Fagan articles, see no quick-fix solutions in sight to the problems of religious life today. The process of renewing that life will inevitably be a slow and difficult one, calling for much patient toil and a constant waiting on the Lord.

The *Lineamenta* (Outlines) for the 1994 synod have already been well summarised (and commented on) by Fr. Flannan Markham, SS CC. Examining the 'precise content' of the consecrated life as presented in the *Lineamenta* I observe many striking 'biases' (the word in Fr Markham's) over and above those noted by him. I would-in particular note the following:

1) The whole subject is treated in strongly magisterial and canonical terms (cf. the official documents, including the Code of Canon Law, listed in art. 4 and the frequent references to such documents all through the *Lineamenta*). The Nigerian-Ukeritis study puts its faith in 'mission rather than canons' but the *Lineamenta's* faith is put in canons embodying and formulating consecration and mission. In art. 15 we read that the evangelical counsels or charisms 'are ordered to the upbuilding of the Church, to the good of humanity and to the needs of the world...' 'Nevertheless,' it is added, 'the discernment of charisms and their proposed juridic approval belong to the *Pastors of the Church*' (emphasis in the original) . Again in art. 24 there is a paragraph on 'new communities' which 'are being formed today with special features similar to those of the consecrated life, but in reality are not such, because they lack due canonical recognition or because they do not meet the established requirements of a form of consecrated life recognized by the Church.' Canonical structure, then, is seen as inherent in and essential to the consecrated life,

2) Great emphasis is laid on the inherent bond between the consecrated life and devotion to the person of the Roman Pontiff. 'The ecclesial character of the consecrated life,' says art. 36, 'is expressed and realized through a special bond with the petrine ministry, which ought to be concretely manifested in a relationship of loving communion and obedience to the Roman Pontiff.' Later in the same article we read: 'This special relationship to the Holy Father of those living the consecrated life ought to be translated into a *deep spiritual communion with his person* (emphasis in the original), submission to his magisterium, total and ready acceptance of his directives and a generous cooperation in his ministry as Pastor of the Universal Church, which he exercises through the competent Departments of the Apostolic See.'

What lies behind these special stresses on the canonical status of the consecrated life and on the 'deep spiritual communion' with the person of the Holy Father that should characterise consecrated persons? Here we touch on an implicit but very real objective of the coming synod, namely to bring religious fully into line with the requirements of the present Pontificate and with the 'directives' (to use his own word) of John Paul II in person. The Roman authorities have been concerned for a long time about 'dissident' religious (e.g. the many religious theologians who propound one form or another of the Latin-American theology of liberation) and, more recently, about some 'dissident' religious bishops (e.g. Archbishop Weakland of Milwaukee, formerly Abbot-Primate of the Benedictines, who has openly queried the official position on the status of women in the Church). It is hoped that the synod will make religious once more a model body of obedient men and women in the Church, characterised by a 'relationship of loving communion and obedience to the Roman Pontiff.'

German writers on the papacy of John Paul II frequently speak of him as a 'visionary". He has, it is claimed, a splendid vision of what the Church should be and of what the world, evangelised by the Church, might be and this vision governs the whole of his pastoral activity. Others speak of his 'Utopian' ideals and aims. In so far as he is a man of 'vision' and of 'Utopia', the underlying model of it is Poland — the land of his fathers and the land of his faith. A Polish friend of mine in Rome was the first to point out to me the omnipresence of Poland, even when there is no explicit mention of it, in all the Pope's statements and declarations The *Lineamenta,* in the preparation of which John Paul II was personally involved, show this background in various ways in the passage — in religious dress, for example (art. 31.b: 'Why in 1993 has the matter of religious dress to be raised?' asks a puzzled Fr. Markham). More importantly, in art. 19.a on the consecrated life for women we are told of their presence 'in the area of the missions and the apostolate of education, social action and charity.' There is not a word here about the very large number of religious women now active in the parish ministry. This has reached such proportions in Brazil that the alienation of these women from religious life in its true identity is now becoming a problem — the kind of problem examined by Fr Desmond O'Donnell in regard to clerical religious men. It is, however, a kind of problem that is unknown in Poland where the diocesan clergy have as yet no need of outside helpers in parishes.

Will the programme for the synod outlined in the *Lineamenta* be significantly revised and altered by the synod itself? The short answer to this question is No. Analyses of the many synods held under the present Pontificate show that the essential lines of the *Lineamenta* for each synod come forth again in its final document, with minor modifications made to show that the synodal discussions have had some impact on it.

Briefly, the *Lineamenta* contain what John Paul II wants to say to religious today through the synod as intermediary. This does not mean that discussions by religious or others on the theme of the synod are pointless. On the contrary they are a valuable contribution to the consideration of the future of religious life — a future that will still be there when the 1994 synod has ended.

EIGHT
Religious Life Today: Response to Kerkhofs

JOAN D. CHITTISTER, OSB

OVERVIEW OF THE U.S. AND OF RELIGIOUS LIFE

The United States is a highly affluent, swiftly changing society where violence has been made a business, creature comfort is a given and insularism — social and political, cultural and global — has been raised to high art. It is a society that is to a large degree complacent, unaware and growing more frustrated every day.

Women religious, in particular, have in the last twenty-five years opened multiple new ministries in the country, despite criticism from both the church and the public, with few resources and at great cost to themselves. Nevertheless, this loss of identity, confusion in spirituality and change of roles and life-styles has brought with it a loss of defined spiritual life and a breakdown in cohesion among the groups themselves. Some groups have made few changes whatsoever and are becoming more and more anachronistic. Some groups have made cosmetic changes but have done little with the spiritual life of the group. Some groups are well on their way to high-level renewal at every level.

The woman's question in the church has led to wholesale disaffection among women religious for the structures that formed them and provide the basis. The Eucharist, most of all, has become a source of tension.

With these serious internal agendas, there has been little definition of the life to offer the next generation. Though the new works have been creative and highly successful and groups are beginning to get new members again, vocations are slim, candidates are older than in the past and groups are getting steadily smaller.

What social problems confront us? The US society is being inundated with an entirely new wave of immigrant population, both legal and illegal. The service-economy is plunging people into unskilled, low-paying jobs. The rich are getting richer; the poor are getting even poorer.

What problems face you? Religious communities are plagued by loss of personnel, reduction of resources and the difficulty of bringing members formed in a 'withdrawal' theology of religious life to an understanding of the impact they could have on a changed society.

How has religious life tried to cope with them? Religious communities have undertaken massive re-education programs, and given individual members a great deal of latitude to scout the Promised Land in hope of finding the painless way in. They have, in other words, done a great deal to foster the prophetic individuals in their midst. At the same time, they have done very little to function as prophetic groups. They are aggregations of good people who have nowhere near the impact on this society that they had on the last one when they set out as groups to address themselves to major social issues.

QUESTIONNAIRE

1. *How achieve vita evangelica?* Immersion in the scriptures and a new appreciation of the power of community witness is key, I think, to living the evangelical life in a world that is highly materialistic, structurally oppressive and fragmented to the breaking point. We are going to have to commit ourselves out of a faith perspective and as groups to the achievement of social justice rather than simply to individual ministries, good as they may be, and the dispensing of charity and catechisms. We are going to have to become signs of global concern rather than simply local agents of a local church whose own commitments are often perceived as either basically parochial or, in the case of the nature and role of women, for instance, as highly questionable. As it stands right now, we seem to be 'muddling through' without a bright ideal to make it worthwhile.

2. *The young a minority in an ageing community.* In times of great social change and ambiguity, prophetic leadership is a staple of transition. It is highly unlikely that large numbers of elderly members will either see or embrace a totally new way of living, being and responding to the world around them. It is the role of leadership in these situations to provide the space, the encouragement, the vision and the resources to enable younger members to re-root the community in different demonstrations of its basic charism. The important element in this process is that the relationship of these new activities to the founding charism be made continuously so that the elderly can come to see that the spirit that drove them drives the congregation still. Then they will neither despair not impede.

3. *Collaboration with lay people.* Collaboration is absolutely essential in this day and age if for no other reason than that the replacement rate of

religious communities cannot sustain the works begun by these groups. If these good works are to continue, they will have to be assumed by the laity. Education and catechesis is a prime example. At the same time, works of justice and peace which require different skills than those present in religious communities at the present time mean that we will have to reach out for the writers, scientists, activists, strategists, economists, and lawyers it will take to impact these new social arenas.

4. *Community life and apostolic commitment.* Most congregations and communities have a history of mission convents away from the central mother house or monastery. So, the notion that the whole congregation does not live in the same place is clearly not the contemporary question. The fact is that two major changes have taken place in these situations:

(a) What ties small groups together is no longer a single work. All the members of the small, local community do not work in the same place at the same time. This affects horariums and personal interaction.

(b) In communities of declining numbers of active members or in congregations attempting to open new lines of service to society, it has become more and more common for religious to live alone or in communities not of their own spiritual tradition.

In each of these cases, the identity of the community itself is both expanded and threatened at the same time. 'Community' requires very serious attention. In some instances, prescriptions of time may be the answer. Persons may be given only so many years to engage in ministries that take them out of their own community. In situations where whole institutions have grown up around the good works of various individuals, however, that is obviously neither possible nor desirable. It may, in fact, be a very artificial use of the term 'community', especially in apostolic congregations. What these circumstances may really require, then, is some clear, attainable, regular and defined community presence, participation or renewal periods that reimmerse a person in the group, its spiritual tradition, and its corporate identity.

At the same time, life in a small group requires a great deal of self-giving, a high level of interdependence, great sensitivity to the needs of others and serious spiritual discipline. It can also alienate a member from the larger, more impersonal style of the large group. The spiritual rigor of a defined prayer schedule, respect for silence and opportunities for private space make small group living every bit as responsible a vehicle of the spiritual life as large, robotizing facilities that wind up being places where people live alone together.

Far too little planning is being done to make the transition from large corporate works dynamic entries into new public arenas rather than simply the death of an old one. This is a time for beginnings, not endings. We seem to specialize in life by default right now.

5. *Relations with bishops and dioceses*. Few dioceses see religious life as a witness in its own right. Diminishment is regarded as treason. This relationship of religious to corporate works is precisely what has led to its present decline. We clung to works long after they were no longer what society needed from the charismatic and prophetic presence of religious orders.

6. *Religious priests and religious brothers*. The clericalization of male religious is itself a major question and, perhaps, an obstacle in the renewal of religious life. Until male religious ask themselves how and if priest-hood is necessary to the charism of the order, then ordination may be what makes the contemporary expression of the charism impossible. They will simply be secular priests living together outside the full jurisdiction of the local bishop. The question is, what is the prophetic role of their commu-nities to society and the church and how are they expressing that through priesthood or exclusive of priesthood. The denigration of religious Brothers by the church itself in its traditional refusal to permit non-ordained superiors in clerical communities makes the male religious vocation more a clerical than a religious one.

7. *Level of maturity demanded*. Candidates are now coming to religious life much later than in the immediate past. The culture around them with its long-term educational systems and multiple job opportunities has prolonged adolescence and provided a new kind of rite-of-passage into full adulthood. This will require an entirely different kind of formation program geared to the questions, needs and expectations of older mem-bers of society. Chastity will be seen as a process rather than an event; poverty will require that the community be seen as serving the poor rather than simply requiring dependence; obedience will be demilitarised in favour of discerned decision-making on all sides.

We are already developing a kind of temporary membership. More and more people enter and leave a few years later. The only question is, will there be such a thing as a core group of perpetually committed religious to sustain this. But if religious life is really 'a way of life,' then the answer seems obvious.

8. *The ordination of women* is a necessity if we are to maintain the internal consistency of the faith. The theologies of incarnation, grace, redemption and baptism require a rethinking of a 'tradition' that remains a tradition

simply because we do not change it. We have argued 'fit matter' before — in the case of Indians and Blacks, for instance — and come to our theological senses in the face of scientific data. We must now do the same thing again in regard to women. What theology has taught about women in the past is simply wrong. To save the church, we have to face these questions. The fact is that the church is about to have to choose between maleness and the sacraments.

9. *Creativity and fidelity to tradition*. If the charism of a community is from the Spirit, then the Spirit and the 'greater tradition' can never be at odds. It is the immediate past history of a congregation that too often passes as its 'tradition' and confuses its mission with its ministries. If a community and its individual members stay steeped in the founding spirit of the order, that will become the criterion for both discerning new ministries and evaluating past ones.

10. *Eastern and western religious exchanging gifts*. Western communities may be able to give Eastern European communities the theology of renewal and a sense of the charismatic traditions of religious life. New religious life in Eastern European communities could give us a model of looking at life afresh and asking where we fit in it at this time in history instead of attempting to recreate the 17th century in the 21st.

11. *Defining consecrated life*. Consecrated life is a commitment to living the ideals of the Christian community of *Acts* in a way that speaks truth to our time. It is a conscious attempt to hear the Word and to live the Word prophetically, to say the Word of God to power, to lay down our lives for our friends, to witness to cosmic Truth in a global village. It transcends the local and calls the local to the truth of the Beatitudes – whatever the cost.

NINE
Religious Life Today: Response to Kerkhofs

SEAN O'RIORDAN, CSSR

PREFATORY NOTE

The questions about religious life formulated by Fr. Jan Kerkhofs, SJ, are clear and logical. They do however raise a difficulty. Questions of this kind are appropriate when the subject under discussion is on the whole in a condition of stability and clear identifiability. The questions then relate to a well-defined subject, bringing out both its strengths and its weaknesses, its potential for the future and impediments to that potential.

The problem is that religious life today in the so-called First World no longer presents the features of stability and well-defined objectivity. It is in a state of flux, major change and considerable confusion. This comes out strikingly in several recent reports, notably in *The Future of Religious Orders in the United States* by Fr. Davis Nygren, C.M. and Sr. Miriam Ukeritis (summary, *RLR*, Jan-Feb., 1993) and in the Italian report *Vita religiosa maschile: autoritratto con chiaroscuri* published in the periodical *Testimoni* (Bologna), 30 January 1993 (translation, next issue of RLR). In such circumstances a strictly logical analysis of religious life as it is today is difficult to achieve. One should perhaps have recourse rather to 'chaos theory' which, beginning in the field of mathematics, is now being extended analogously to other sciences. Chaos theory accepts the confusion and unpredictability of things as they are and then aims at constructing a framework of order within which the confusion can be flexibly contained and coped with. The logical processes called for in such an enterprise have to be much more 'lateral' (to use Edward de Bono's word) and elastic than the usual ones.

In replying to Fr. Kerkhofs' questions I will of course take them as they are; but my replies will to some extent be conditioned by a chaos-theory approach. They will circle round the subject rather than try to find a linear trajectory through it. They will be of an indicative rather than a prescriptive character, aimed at showing how we might cope with the existing situation rather than at providing a clear and definite solution to the array of problems that confronts us.

I should like to make another preliminary comment on Fr. Kerkhofs' terminology. His questions were framed in the first place for the Union of the Conferences of Major Superiors of Europe. Consequently they deal with religious life as commonly understood, which is a canonical as well as a spiritual reality (cf. can. 607 ff). In some questions, however, a different terminology is used. Thus q. 7 asks: 'Can one visualise forms of religious life which permit membership for limited periods?' Canon Law envisages no such possibility (cf. can. 654—658). Accordingly, the word 'religious life' in q. 7 must be understood in a sense different from the ordinary one.

In q. 1 Fr. Kerkhofs speaks of the *vita evangelica*. Historically this is different from the *vita religiosa*. The first people to commit themselves to an ascetico-mystical life based on 'the following of Christ as this is put before us in the Gospel' (*Perfectae Caritatis* art. 2.a) were the solitaries of the early Church (cf. *Lumen Gentium* art. 43, *Perfectae Caritatis*, art. 1). They lived the 'evangelical life' (alternatively called the 'apostolic life') without a canonical structure and without the specific three vows that much later in history came to be seen as characterising 'religious life.' When Fr. Kerkhofs uses the term *vita evangelica*, is he using it as a synonym of religious life as now understood in the Church or in the older sense of a way of life based on Christ's way of life 'as this is put before us in the Gospel?' In the latter case the 'evangelical life' can be lived, not only in community but also individually, without formal community bonds, without a formal canonical structure and without the three vows of canonical religious life, though of course it will still be a poor, chaste and obedient way of life. In answering q. 1, I will assume that Fr. Kerkhofs has religious life in mind; but I shall be returning to the *vita evangelica* in the older sense in answering q. 11.

Q 11, however, introduces yet another term into Fr. Kerkhofs' questions. 'How,' he asks, 'would you re-define genuine consecrated life?' In Canon Law the term 'consecrated life' includes religious life but also other forms of life based on 'the profession of the evangelical counsels' (can. 573 ff). Is Fr. Kerkhofs referring to the consecrated life in the broader canonical sense or is he using the word as a synonym for religious life? Since he is writing for religious superiors in the first place, I will assume that he is referring to religious life.

I now address myself to the two parts of Fr. Kerkhofs' 'Questions on Religious Life', Part I. *An Overview* and Part II. *Questionnaire*. My answers will be on the whole brief, indicating what I think are the essential points in regard to each question.

AN OVERVIEW

The main features of the Irish society in which I live are rapid change, considerable confusion and much depression, caused in great part by the high rate of unemployment in the country. Add to these the political violence that plagues life in Northern Ireland

Religious life too is going through a vast process of change, some details of which will come out in my answers to the questionnaire. As for the social currents that confront us, there are new waves of secularism and consumerism in the air. At the same time many Christians, including younger people, are coming to a deeper appreciation of genuine Christian life and rising above the conventional religion of an older, more traditional and more static society

All this confronts religious life with new problems: falling numbers, far fewer entrants and far less appeal than it enjoyed in the past. At the same time it is still, on the whole, a respected way of life and the services it gives to the general community are appreciated.

Religious in Ireland both male and female have to a large extent coped well with rapidly changing conditions and with the problems that spring from them. They are not beset by nostalgia for the past. They accept the new situation in which they find themselves and try to cope with its demands and challenges. They are as a body a cheerful, enterprising group of people in the Irish Church.

QUESTIONNAIRE

1) If we take *vita evangelica* to mean a genuinely spiritual living of religious life, much progress can be seen in this over the past twenty years or so. Thanks to a variety of good educational programmes in Scripture, liturgy, theology and the like, religious have on the whole a much better understanding of what it is to be 'a disciple of Jesus' and many live up to this ideal in an exemplary manner. At the same time we have quite a number of religious whose better theoretic knowledge of the *vita evangelica* is not matched by their commitment to it. They have become, at least in part, 'secularised' in their outlook and way of life. Such people need a genuine *conversion* 'to Christ and to the Gospel', says the Italian report. In many, if not most cases of this kind, however, the problem goes very far back in their lives. They were never *deeply converted* to Christ even when they were, by conventional standards, 'observant' religious and continue to keep up some measure of 'observance'.

In Ireland the institutional Church has lost some measure of credibility, though it has gained some also by its championing of the cause of the poor and the dispossessed in our society. The credibility of religious life is in a somewhat similar position. Most people greatly respect dedicated religious but relatively few young people want to enter religious life, largely because of the *lifelong* commitment it calls for. Many young people here gladly join Christian or other idealistic groups, sometimes at great cost to themselves, as when they go to work in the deprived and even dangerous conditions of the Third World; but they know that they can always opt out of such groups and they need to retain that freedom.

2) The problem of ageing membership has on the whole been very well dealt with by Irish religious. Large and now useless properties have been sold; apostolic work of one kind or another has been reduced to a measure of feasibility, lay people taking over much of it; appropriate 'spiritual, apostolic and material space' has been created for the living of religious life in new conditions. The older generations for the most part are quite happy about this and readily fall in with it. 'Discouragement' is not really a problem with them nor do they impede the *aggiornamento* of spirituality and apostolic commitment.

3) My own Irish Redemptorist community has for a long time been using the collaboration of lay men and women. So have many other communities, some of which are training lay people to take over much, and eventually perhaps all, of their work. The form of the collaboration varies from case to case (in accordance with good chaos theory) and I would not favour any standardisation of it.

4) Where there is a genuine spirit of conversion to the Lord in a community, whether it be of a larger or smaller type, it will successfully combine 'an authentic religious life' with 'a serious commitment to today's world.' Nor will 'a great diversity of commitments' be a serious obstacle to *communio*. When serious obstacles do appear, they are usually the consequence of the psychological, personal and spiritual immaturity of some of the members — an immaturity that generally goes back for years and is not the consequence of modern changes in religious life. How is this problem to be dealt with? There is no straightforward or, in conventional terms, 'logical' way of dealing with it. It has to be seen as a problem of chaos and must be 'managed' in the best available way in each case.

Small communities of religious are fast increasing in number in Ireland, generally in response to local apostolic needs. The question is asked: 'Is preparation needed for life in a small community?' The first thing to be checked on is *personal capacity* for such a life Some religious have this capacity, others do not Those who have it can then be given some detailed preparation regarding the practical aspects of the life (the closer psychological interaction involved in it, the reduced space for privacy and so on).

I have already dealt with the question of what is to be done about hospitals, schools and other such institutions which religious can no longer operate. There have been few problems about this in Ireland. First of all, religious have always had lay collaborators in such works and it was relatively easy to hand on to them the greater part or even all of the functions previously exercised by religious. The State system of education and health care that prevails in this country and into which religious schools and hospitals have long been integrated greatly facilitates this transition.

5) The Church hierarchy in Ireland certainly sees religious life as valuable in itself but, naturally, looks to it in practice mainly as a useful apostolic resource. In regard to new developments in Irish religious life (creating small communities, handing over schools and hospitals, and the like) there have been few strains in the relationships between religious and the hierarchy. The hierarchy has on the whole left religious free to work things out for themselves as best they can.

6) The ministry of religious priests and religious deacons witnesses to the *vita evangelica* in the life of the Church in a way that does not normally happen in the ministry of secular priests and deacons. At least it *should* give this witness and when it does the apostolic fruits of it are very considerable. As for religious brothers who are not deacons, we have a number of outstanding men of that category in Ireland but their excellent service of the People of God attracts hardly any vocations to that form of religious life today.

7) A *good* level of personal maturity is surely necessary for candidates to the religious novitiate and a *high* level of it for those desiring to take perpetual vows. It has become customary in many religious institutes in Ireland to have candidates assessed by qualified psychologists whose collaboration in religious formation has over the years proved to be very valuable. This is a great advance on pre-Vatican II formation when few institutes availed themselves of professional psychological help.

It is at this point that Fr. Kerkhofs asks the question: 'Can one visualise forms of religious life which permit membership for limited periods?' As long as the present canonical structure of religious life is kept in place — and it is once again reiterated in the *Lineamenta* for the 1994 synod — the question has no practical significance. It is different if we ask whether there could be forms of the *vita evangelica* in its original sense which would permit the living of it for limited periods. Here the answer would be Yes. For long centuries men and women lived the *vita evangelica* in one form or another, often in association with a religious order but without their becoming members of the order, for a limited period of time. This practice still survives in the Eastern Churches. Even in the Western Church, as the *Lineamenta* for the synod, art. 24 notes, 'new communities' are arising 'with special features similar to those of the consecrated life.' In fact, however, adds the article, though in themselves laudable, such communities do not live the consecrated life 'because they lack due canonical recognition or because they do not meet the established requirements of a form of consecrated life recognised by the Church. ' This is, if you will, something of a put-down for communities of the *vita evangelica* in a flexible, non-canonical form; but the significance of the re-emergence of the *vita evangelica* as such in the life of the Church is something that I shall be returning to in my answer to q. 11.

8) As a theologian I have a quite open mind on the subject of women and priestly ministry in the Church. A number of religious women in Ireland, some of them theologically well-trained, are of the same opinion. There is however no demand for such ministry among our religious women at present. Our situation in this regard is quite different from that of other countries, notably the United States.

9) Good work is being done by various religious groups and bodies for the promotion of justice in Ireland. Their work comes across as Spirit-moved but also well balanced. It evokes some criticism from reactionary economists but not from the bishops whose own position on these issues is one of great social concern. As for ecumenical work, it too is being developed in Ireland. The bishops are often criticised for not giving it more active help; but at least they do not hinder it or create tensions for those engaged in it.

10) In the matter of 'exchanging gifts' between Western European Churches and those of central and eastern Europe, liberated after 1989, the original hope was that the Western Church would contribute financial help, theological learning, organisational skills and other resources which it possessed in abundance. In return the Churches of central and eastern Europe, especially of strongly Catholic Poland and Croatia, would infuse new energies of faith and dedication into the debilitated Catholicism of the secularised West. This hope has failed to materialise on the massive scale that was originally envisaged. However, there has been a real 'exchange of gifts' between the religious communities of the West and those farther to the East, particularly between communities

belonging to the same religious institute. The *communio* of a shared religious life has facilitated this process and will without doubt continue to do so.

11) 'How would you re-define genuine consecrated life?' The question is a logical and reasonable one, but I do not think it is radical enough. At the spiritual core of the consecrated life, which I take to mean religious life, there lies, as I have emphasised above, the *vita evangelica* in its pre-canonical form. The revival of the *vita evangelica* today, in a variety of forms ranging from the solitary life to different community embodiments of 'the following of Christ as this is put before us in the Gospel', is a significant phenomenon which religious life should carefully observe and from which it has much to learn. In short, we need above all a better *theology* of religious life in terms of the *vita evangelica*. Then we shall be in a better position to examine afresh the *structures* of religious life as they exist canonically at present and to see how they might be revised and renewed to make them more effective instruments of the living of the *vita evangelica* in religious institutes.

TEN

What Hopes for the Synod?

HELENA O'DONOGHUE, RSM

The announcement that the topic for the forthcoming Synod would be 'Consecrated Life in the Church and the World' was an exciting moment for me. I felt that we religious were being brought out of hiding at last, and that the light of day was going to warm and brighten our way of life. It seems as if we have been shoved into the Church's closet in recent decades and that all the joy of life has been beaten out of us. The idea of a Synod focusing on religious life was a marvellous ray of hope; it was like being invited to take a deep breath, to expand our lungs and take in the much needed oxygen of affirmation and development, of renewal and revitalisation, and to get ready to be relaunched and remissioned as one of the essential sources of life in the Church.

Hundreds of possibilities crossed my mind — perhaps we could expect a *Gaudium et Spes* for this in-between liminal form of Church-life, set in today's world; perhaps even a *Dei Verbum* or *Lumen Gentium* which would articulate in a positive way the revelatory and sacramental nature of the vowed life; or perhaps something utterly new and inspirational might emerge which would evoke, encourage and proclaim the human richness of the religious woman/man/congregation fully alive to the glory of God. I imagined the assembly — Pope, bishops, numerous *peritae* and *periti* from all shades of consecrated life, working together on the threads of a new tapestry to be woven during that Synod — a work of the Church at large, revaluing, discerning and refining one of its most precious dimensions.

HOPE DIMINISHED

Then the *Lineamenta* or preliminary document about the scope of the Synod was published. Initially I was energised by just taking up the document, recognising the familiar terms, and feeling how long it was since any core treatment of our way of life was top of the agenda. But concern and unease soon replaced my optimism. The document sets the scene, the agenda and the questions — like markers on a runway which channel and guide the incoming and outgoing planes. There was a feeling of being programmed, if not to some extent hijacked, made to follow a set route. I'm sure this was not intentional on the part of the Roman Congregation but the text does give the impression of being drawn up by persons who are not religious themselves or who are very removed from the ordinary lived experience of many religious today, especially women religious. My comments here are from the perspective of apostolic religious life as women experience it, though I recognise that we are just a part of the wide spectrum included in consecrated life.

I feel that the *Lineamenta* presents a vision of consecrated life as a kind of package, staid and static, a disembodied one-format way of life, seen through a narrow lens and described in saw-dust language. Examples of what I mean are terms like the following:

In par. 1: 'precise'. While some rearticulation of the nature and role of consecrated life is sorely needed, can there ever be anything 'precise' about something so organic, so charismatic and so worldwide?

In par. 8: 'perfection'. As a description of growth in holiness such terminology has been singularly harmful psychologically in the past. It leads to suppression of weakness and of all that is not 'perfect', and is out of sync with our common experience that struggle is inherent in the path to love, service and wholeness.

In par. 11, the concept of 'community' struck me as modelled on what was appropriate to monks or cloistered orders back in the era of uniformity and regularity. The superimposition of that model on active apostolic religious is no longer possible and is very far from the lived experience of most religious today.

In several places throughout the text the phrase 'while not belonging to the hierarchy of the Church' appears (pars 14 to 36). To say it once begs the question 'to whom or to what do we belong?' and there is no satisfactory answer. But to say it several times conveys some need to be constantly distinguishing and distancing, and to be setting hierarchy as the core norm of what it is to be Church. Why the need to describe consecrated life with reference to the hierarchy at all or so often?

The *Lineamenta* refers to positive and negative developments in religious life in recent years. These are true as far as they go, but the document fails to acknowledge the virtual explosion of creativity and initiative which has been the experience of congregations and members over the past two decades. The treatment of other aspects of modern society in a tone which denotes derision or at best cynicism was disturbing — for example, 'the cult of freedom' or the 'drive towards democracy' or 'a mistaken idea of feminism' (Par. 29). It gives the impression that human dignity and rights are to be lesser values in consecrated life.

Other examples abound, giving the picture of a one-dimensional phenomenon which needs to be 'controlled' and guided into its set place in the ecclesial scheme of things. I think I am right in suggesting that such a vision would not be shared generally at membership level, that such a model belongs to another time! Having examined the document I felt uncomfortable and fearful for the outcome of the Synod.

HOPE RECLAIMED

What I would have liked to see in the *Lineamenta*, and which I sincerely hope will yet reach the desks of the Synod members, was a more in-depth treatment of the new features of post Vatican II religious life. Yes, the essence of the life and its key components need to be articulated clearly in a contemporary Church which has begun to value the Christian commitment inherent in the baptised lay person. The document, to be fair, focuses on this need — the Synod intends to deal with the identity and role of consecrated life — though the language used is anything but people-friendly! But taking that task as a given, there is a more serious need to recognise and value the validity of, and variety of, new expressions within the traditional orders in the present Church. No one format will encompass this way of life any longer. Congregations have experienced the marvellous wind of the Spirit shattering many of their patterns, are deeply humbled before that Spirit and are searching for the wisdom to be faithful and responsive. Because the new Code of Canon Law has not allowed for this development it is imperative that a body such as the Synod would address it and affirm it, while setting necessary and adequate criteria for evaluation and discernment.

Many of the new insights distilled from recent experience need a more comprehensive theological treatment in the context of religious life. The need for a greater cultural harmony for this life-style is one which stands out, as the stereotypes commonly held by people have made the way of life unintelligble today, especially to the young. Life in society and life in the convent must not be so polarised that there is no real meeting between them, thus cutting off the person from his or her anthropological life lines. Only where there is an appropriate cultural harmony can consecrated life be a true witness to higher values, and a prophetic challenge to the unredeemed dimensions of a harsh and unjust society.

Another critical insight has been the shift in the understanding of obedience and authority, as a result of a heightened adult consciousness which finds itself called to be participative and active rather than a passive recipient of decisions which affect the life of the individual or the group.

The question of religious obedience after the mind of Jesus is a most neglected area in the contemporary theology of consecrated life.

Other areas of critical concern are the developments in communal patterns of prayer, interaction, and mission .... the possibilities are myriad. The valuing of these as new fruits from the old tree is vital. So too is the recent phenomenon of religious communities as incarnational 'presence' among the people, especially among poor people in public housing estates. The format of religious life here is very different from that presumed by the *Lineamenta.*

Finally, while the document does deal with religious life for women (Par. 19), it does no more than reiterate common platitudes about the gifts and achievements of religious women over the centuries. More is needed! The critical contribution of women's perspective to the reshaping/ renewal of consecrated life is not anticipated. The fact that women can live with multiple expressions within the one congregation is not noted or envisaged. The history of women living male-shaped patterns has left serious scars and an impoverished life-form. This has been changing — but it must be acknowledged and welcomed for the sake of a fuller renewal in the future. If given freedom and responsibility, women, responding to the Spirit, will affect religious life down to its foundations and will give rise to further expression of the unending richness of God's grace in consecrated life in the Church.

What can we hope for from the Synod? It is good that a Synod on consecrated life is happening at all. But the preparatory *Lineamenta* leaves a lot to be desired. I pray anxiously for the Synod and the Church, that it will not fail us in evoking our hope once again.

ELEVEN

The Synod Lineamenta:
European Religious Respond

JAN KERKHOFS, SJ

Father Kerkhofs' questions (see chapter 5) were submitted to the member conferences of the Union of the Conferences of Major Superiors of Europe earlier in 1993 and replies were received from women religious of Flemish-speaking Belgium and from religious, women and men, of French-speaking Belgium, of France, Greece, England and Wales, Spain, Austria, Portugal and Ireland. The German Conferences did not reply to Father Kerkhofs' questionnaire, but sent him their statements on the *Lineamenta*. He analysed the replies — adding the German Conference's comments — and on 2 September laid his findings, published below, before the General Assembly of the Union of the Conferences of Major Religious Superiors, in Prague. The translation from the French, as supplied to the Prague Assembly, is our own. The statements of the German conferences are published in the documentation section of this volume.

The questionnaire asked, first of all, for a brief, general, socio-cultural description of each member country. We shall come back to this at the end of the report.

The second question had to do with the state of religious life in general. We shall summarise here the more important details of this over-all description. What do the replies tell us about religious life in general? This short summary does not contain information about individual countries which is true only of them.

Almost everywhere the need to accept the challenges posed by injustice is emphasised. These challenges are often spelled out: there is a rapid increase of direct involvement — of women religious especially — with the poor and the marginalised (drugs, AIDS, immigration, misery in all its forms). In a climate marked by individualism and competition, religious opt for solidarity. This option to be with people presupposes an authentic life-style both at the human and at the religious level. One tries to forge links with the surrounding milieu, to open oneself to truly human values, increasingly to share with lay people one's community's spiritual life and its apostolic commitment.

This more radical commitment demands that one focuses on what is essential in religious life: following Christ, *sequela Christi* (not to be confused with imitation of Christ), a solid and authentic prayer life, a sisterly and brotherly quality in community life, an unremitting reading of the signs of the times, an ongoing formation which takes into account the accelerating socio-cultural changes (the 'world' sets the agenda for apostolic religious). All are agreed that 'without the suffering of Jesus Christ a flourishing religious life is impossible in a world which has become secularised'.

Many obstacles are listed: first of all, inside the institutes themselves. On the one hand, there is the rapidly ageing membership, one of whose consequences is a shortage of capable superiors. On the other hand, many young religious have a fear of definitive commitment. A tentative search for a reinterpretation of the vows is under way, a reinterpretation which is necessary but which is a delicate matter. Too many religious are either too dependent on their superiors (a lack of human maturity) or are too independent (a lack of community loyalty).

WOMEN OFFERED LITTLE SCOPE, PRIEST-RELIGIOUS OVERSTRETCHED

Many obstacles originating from outside religious life are mentioned. Involvement in parishes (because of the shortage of diocesan priests) tends to weaken communities. The lack of credibility of the institutional Church (patriarchal, centralised, too 'traditional') has repercussions on religious life, being regarded all too often merely as an ecclesial conduit.

The Church entertains too many stereotypes of religious: either as people who, in popular parlance, 'have left the world', or as cheap labour, without prophetic liberty. The complaint is voiced that there is a lack of openness to women on the part of the Church. They are not offered enough scope by the pastoral structures of the Church, while priest-religious are over-stretched. The Church envisages religious life too much in terms of canon law rather than in terms of the Gospel (and the counsels).

In this context, many replies were severely critical of the *Lineamenta* for having focused, it would appear, on the monastic rather than on the apostolic life. The *Lineamenta* reflects anxiety, fear of the world rather than openness (there is little in the way of subsidiarity, ecumenism and collegiality, dialogue with other religions and their followers). One has the impression that the 1994 Synod will be the termination of reflection, rather than the commencement of an ongoing process (the final text of the Synod ought not to be a 'definitive text', nor a copy of the preparatory text). Many replies comment on the *Lineamenta's* negative view of the world (number 29 is cited as an example: fear of liberty, fear of the advancement of women, fear of the modern world, judged *a priori* to be 'profoundly inimical to gospel values'). The Church and religious life are presented as closed systems. One reply ended with: 'We refuse to allow ourselves to be imprisoned in the past.' Secularisation is constantly identified with secularism.

Quite frequent was a demand that the Synod permit free and frank dialogue during the sessions, on condition that there be present a sufficient number of truly representative men and women religious (brothers, especially). The German women superiors were especially insistent on this. They very much deplored the use of outdated terminology in the *Lineamenta* ('consecration', bridal relationship with God).

A third obstacle comes from the general ambiance. One can cite the climate of indifference, continuing dechristianization, questionable attitudes towards religion portrayed in many television programmes, the fanaticism displayed in countries where there is a state religion is helpful neither to religious life nor to apostolic activity. Consumerism reigns in cities, stress and individualism are obstacles to interior silence.

REPLIES TO INDIVIDUAL QUESTIONS

1, *The Challenge of Ageing Membership*: There are indeed countries where there are many people entering religious life, where the pyramid of ages has not yet been upturned (at least in certain institutes). In general, however, ageing is everywhere the greatest institutional challenge facing institutes. The phenomenon evokes differing reactions. 'The elderly are not discouraged, provided that they do not feel neglected, that they are prepared in time for ageing, that they are kept well informed about programmes of renewal and that superiors behave courageously in the face of possible polarisations (in houses or in provinces). The demand is frequently voiced that superiors be truly caring (that at the appropriate time they be part of the social security systems, that the caring personnel be suitable)'.

It has been established that it is becoming more and more difficult to find superiors who are both capable and available for the (large) establishments housing retired religious. The fact that there are so many elderly people can prove a hindrance to young religious and superiors are thus faced with a dilemma with regard to the composition of a commu-

nity. Certain suggestions have been offered: to encourage the drawing of
a distinction always between what is essential and what is accessory, to
promote tolerance and assimilation, but to accept the existence of
differences, to avoid isolating young religious (by establishing small
communities which include some older religious who will not obstruct
the younger ones), to avoid burdening the young with existing apostolates, to maintain contact, so essential, sufficient for the transmission of
an institute's values and charism.

It is often said that there are greater tensions in sisters' and brothers'
institutes than in priests'. The group aged sixty plus or minus pose greater
problems than do older age groups, this group being still active but not
very capable of renewal. For young religious, the presence of a large
number of elderly members poses quite a serious problem: what is the
present identity of the institute? New candidates have the right to know
what they are being formed for, and the formation ought to be both human
and spiritual, which means that they are afforded space for freedom and
for experimenting.

NEED FOR MIXED COMMUNITIES

2, *Collaboration with Lay People*: For many reasons, such as the quest for
spirituality by lay people, new forms of co-operation and even of
integration with lay people are being sought and developed. Two reasons
in particular must be mentioned: (1) the ineluctable transfer of many
works to lay people and (2) the desire that the profound inspiration of an
institute would not be lost because of the very small number of full-time
members. In many countries it is stressed that the affiliation of lay people
as associate member has to be encouraged, even to the extent of establishing mixed communities, composed of religious and lay people. Such a
partnership can take many forms (sharing the charism, in-depth study of
a renewed theology of ministry, association for a limited period, for quite
a long period, or definitively. In one country, one found that many
communities are moving towards types of formal association with lay
people (which is not to say that such partnership would be canonically
structured). Elsewhere it is pointed out that a founder's charism is not
confined to religious; as a result, communities with young people set
themselves up as groups or centres of invigoration. Sometimes communities take in the aged relatives of women religious.

In any event, many countries see in this 'a sign of the times', they
consider research of this sort very profitable and an encouragement to
allow themselves to be further challenged by lay folk. Sometimes

traditional experiences are recalled, such as those of the Third Orders.

3, *Community Life*: The present evolution is well summarised in the Irish report: a community of friends focused on the apostolic ministry and based on agreement with regard to (a) prayer, ministry, form of presence and (b) real commitment by each member in those three domains.

There is need to form all members for a life in small communities. This presupposes respect for privacy (easier in large communities) and special attention to the changeover from a system of corporate commitment (large institutional apostolates) to a system of small communities. To be able to achieve this, it is necessary to equip oneself with the true charism of the institute and to take account of the challenge and the sadness implied in the abandonment of collective institutional commitment.

In general, this kind of evolution is acknowledged elsewhere. The recommendations which have been added are wise. While acknowledging the need for flexibility and creativity, the need for 'clear and concrete agreements' is emphasised (otherwise the communities would break up for want of a real identity). For many, life in a small community is seen as too demanding, both psychologically and even materially. For the moment, coexistence with large communities seems sensible. They are a necessary refuge for some people.

In any case, neither respect for privacy nor the common life should be made into absolutes. The ideal seems to be communities of seven or eight people; smaller groups should be joined to others, using weekly meetings to supply the need for relaxation and communal reflection. Major superiors will be watchful lest one person prove dominant in the (small) community.

MUTUAE RELATIONS NOT YET FULLY OPERATIVE

For many, life in a small community promotes the human and spiritual growth of the members. Interpersonal relationships, both internal and external, can be more authentic — provided that one accepts differences, that joint decision-making is flexible and that one achieves participative government, that individual projects do not become divorced from the community and that communication between communities is encouraged.

4, *Relations with the Hierarchy*: Reading the replies, one soon forms the impression that *Mutuae Relationes* has not yet achieved its objective. Friction and tension continue, much more at higher levels than at local. The replies show that all too often the institutional Church regards religious merely as personnel to be used, while failing to acknowledge that religious life has value of itself. Often, too, the needs of dioceses deprive communities of their best members. Many replies, it is true, point to positive, if limited, relationships with the hierarchy, but there are numerous complaints: over-centralisation, anxiety about possible abuses, insufficient information on both sides with regard to appointments, little or no respect for women religious in positions of responsibility.

All too often the hierarchy see apostolic religious life in the guise of the contemplative life, or they identify religious obedience with obedience to the bishop. The fear of competition still survives in regard to religious vocations. In one country it is pointed out that the bishops do not like religious to say how life is lived in the diocesan community; the majority of bishops do not want dialogue with the people, unlike the religious who engage in it. And yet, we are told in another country, there is more and more call on finances and personnel from religious institutes.

5, *The Ministry of Religious*: This subject — at least in the replies — produced fewer reactions than that of relations with the hierarchy. The urgency of the problem is acknowledged, but not many details are given.

It is accepted that, increasingly, priest religious are involved in diocesan apostolates, a fact which has persuaded many institutes to develop 'pastoral communities' of religious, each of whom, as a team, take on responsibility for a territory. In Holland, half of the parishes are served by religious priests. This creates many problems at present. In the past, a small community used to serve a Dutch parish, but very often nowadays only a single religious remains, which means that the religious identity has disappeared. The present policy is not to appoint young priest religious (at least in principle) and to concentrate the religious of one institute in a regional team. In Holland teams of women religious or brothers take charge of parishes where there is no resident priest.

MINISTRIES FOR WOMEN, BUT NOT NECESSARILY ORDAINED MINISTRIES

On the other hand, in many clerical institutes, the tendency is to put the emphasis on the religious life, rather than on the priesthood. It is even said that priest-religious suffer from their ambiguous status.

The nature of the problem of the brothers is well known. It was even said that, in the questionnaire, no account was taken of the difference between brothers in clerical institutes and those in lay institutes, these latter having more contact with the lay sphere. At the same the vocations crisis among the brothers is everywhere in evidence. It is stated as a matter for regret, but only in Portugal and Germany, that when women religious do pastoral work their contribution is not always acknowledged. Elsewhere the situation has much improved. The feminist debate has opened. It comes up in the context of current discussions on the ordained ministry in general. However, it would seem that while few women feel called to the ordained ministry, many feel concern about the place and role of women in the Church.

Reactions are very nuanced. There is on all sides the desire that ministries be open to women, but not necessarily ordained ministries. 'In France we are not aware of a ground-swell in favour of calling women to the ordained ministries, but very much in favour of their performing accessory ministries — with the dying, in retreat houses and in spiritual direction. All in all, we feel more called to sharing the spiritual life with lay people than to the quest for ordained ministries. We feel more impelled to defend ourselves against clericalism.'

In Austria and in Flemish-speaking Belgium a prudent approach has been chosen: avoid fanatical attitudes, accept a progressive development, invite dialogue with the hierarchy. One must have confidence in the Holy Spirit who will indicate the path to be followed. In the meantime we must continue with our experience with non-ordained ministries. In Greece, mention was made of the long tradition of deaconesses. That approach would be well received, but opening the way to the presbyterate would not be welcomed, because of the attitude of the Orthodox Church, which is very closed and very anti-Catholic.

6, *Choice of Candidates and their Formation*: Everywhere the need for human and affective maturity is underlined. Mature development in solid faith and a balanced integration in celibacy probably need a longer time in formation and direction than in the past. A pluralist and mixed society makes new demands, requiring at once both flexibility and firmness. Individual religious need to be formed for a life less protected and more independent. A great deal of discernment will be needed to find one's own identity and to accept that of one's institute. This presupposes that from the noviciate a really good spirituality and a solid theological formation would be given.

In effect, more than in the past young people need to be guided towards maturity, balance, openness, a taste for the things of God, a sense of justice and of co-responsibility. For young people in the post-modern world all this cannot be taken for granted. While Ireland is not keen on commitment to religious life for a limited period, in France and Belgium temporary commitments are not ruled out *a priori*. One ought perhaps to see here a sign of the times. We have the example of the Copts. Not a few vocations are, in actual fact, for a limited period — members leave after a number of years, but they have been formed. Association for a limited period could be beneficial. *To be continued.*

It is remarkable that many countries have not replied to this question, which is so important. Why this failure?

7, *The Prophetic Role of Religious*: We have had few responses on this subject. Mention was made several times of the danger posed by 'traditions'; these could put a brake on the creativity and the liberty of the Holy Spirit. We live at a time when tension between the 'Great Tradition' and a large number of socio-cultural and historical 'traditions' is strongly in evidence. Religious have to accept that tension — in the realm of justice, for example, human rights and the rights of women — and must accept the risks involved. It is pointed out that in this area the *Lineamenta* is revealed as being over distrustful. Nevertheless, tension between the institutional Church and communion in the Spirit is real — for example, the place of women and male authority, or the danger of viewing religious as clerics, apostolic religious as contemplatives, or the Kingdom of God as coterminous with the institutional Church.

Everywhere it requires courage to allow oneself to be guided by the Holy Spirit, which supposes a good deal of discernment. This last cannot be realised unless one shares the spiritual and social needs of our world as it is, seeks responses suited to the charism of one's institute and enters into supportive dialogue with one's religious superiors. One must avoid unilateranism in attempting this — every prophetic choice must be based on the scriptures. One must not close one's mind to the choice made by other people and must avoid locking oneself into one problem — dangerously reducing everything to one problem which has but one solution. German superiors acknowledge that a return to the charism of the founder is not often sufficient for an authentic renewal. Dialogue with today's world, with its real questions, openness to the paths traced by new movements of lay Christians, the challenge posed by the many poor people today — all these could help reveal the types of prophetic presence that are needed now.

8, *Collaboration between Religious of East and West*: Let us simply note that inspiration was lacking here. Replies were either non-existent, or there were vague replies such as 'aid between abbeys', theological and spiritual aid to make up for forty years of 'isolation', 'sensible and discreet material aid', no 'massive' projects, 'dialogue within institutes', 'collective support for pilot projects', 'twinning of parishes'.

Only once was it said that the West could learn something, especially from the faithfulness and courage which the brothers and sisters in the East have shown.

9, *How Religious Life is Conceived Today*: In general, it is felt that there is no need to redefine the religious life. One country in particular is very brief and very clear: 'It is sufficient to examine thoroughly the texts of the Council.' Otherwise, how can a synod of bishops redefine the religious life, so rich in history, and so complex?

Ireland risked a definition: 'religious life is a life involving a total offering of oneself to God, lived in a community based on the evangelical counsels and made up of a group of people sharing the same motivation.'

Elsewhere two traits are underlined: to implant oneself in Christ, to live the sisterhood/brotherhood (Austria). In Portugal, three axes are mentioned: a solid evangelical life, the cultivation of values in depth, openness to social problems, especially on 'the frontiers'.

Since the replies come in the main from apostolic institutes, one is not surprised to see the accent placed on openness. Austria underlines the need to be a sign, one that is credible and is nowadays intelligible, of the love of God in the world, the need for a service which corresponds to the charism of each institute and which applies both to preaching and to works of mercy.

France develops this vision with regard to the *Lineamenta*: 'What we want is not so much a definition of the religious life as an opportunity to re-think this in the world in which we live.' One hopes from the Synod 'a text which encourages a quest and a conversion, rather than a text which idealises the consecrated life and places it outside today's world, a world portrayed negatively. This would make religious life difficult, it not impossible, to live.'

German superiors emphasise the need for dialogue between contemplative and apostolic religious, so that all might be better able to integrate action with contemplation.

Should one end with an abrupt summary by the Conference of England and Wales? It is a judgement which will not fail to invite reflection: 'It is the end of institutional religious life and its refounding in contemporary culture.' 'Without risk, there is no future', add the German superiors.

REFLECTIONS IN THE GUISE OF A CONCLUSION

1) Many 'Europes' are missing: Central Europe and Eastern Europe, the Nordic countries and, in Western Europe, Italy and Germany. For

Germany we received a very rich document emanating from the Conference of German Superiors, not by way of replies to our questionnaire, as such, but to those of the *Lineamenta*. (The statements by the German conferences are in the documentation section of this volume.) All the reflections and suggestions touch on the themes of our questionnaire and we used them for our synthesis. For Flemish-speaking Belgium the male religious did not reply. Austria was not fully represented: male and female monasteries and contemplatives were missing.

Another limitation: Conferences replied, but how is one to determine whether or not their contributions reflect the average view held in the institutes? Further, an average view tells us nothing about extreme views. Totally moribund institutes, which are numerous, and newly-founded institutes, which are rare, are not in the picture. One could conclude that our enquiry is not at all, or only to a limited extent, representative. This would be a false conclusion. Those in charge of the Conferences know well the situation in their respective countries and those which have replied represent many tens of thousands of male and female religious. 2). The great majority of the replies underline four main preoccupations: (a) thorough investigation, (b) openness, (c) the need for creativity and liberty, (d) great reservations with regard to the text of the Lineamenta and serious doubts about the Synod's ability to meet the present hopes of the institutes. The institutes seem to want to encourage new forms of partnership with lay people and to avoid all forms of clericalisation. They want to be in the world of today without being 'of the world' (and in this context 'the world' has two different senses). The confidence in the Holy Spirit, so frequently expressed, is striking. In a final conference (which follows this paper) I will endeavour, in my personal and therefore limited capacity, but in accepting criticism, to explain how I see the future.

TWELVE

Confidence in
the Spirit of Jesus

JAN KERKHOFS, SJ

With the possible exception of a few phrases, the two preceding conferences are objective and as honest a summary as possible of the two
surveys.[1] In this final conference I am on less certain ground, or, as the
English say 'I am skating on very thin ice.' Which means that anybody
can put a question mark after many of my interpretations and suggestions.
This is not true of everything I have to say, however, for I am in no doubt
about the truth or the importance of certain matters. As in every good
democracy, everyone has the right to dissent.

This talk is divided into three parts. First, a brief look at the situation
as I believe it can be understood. This is followed by an analysis of the
reasons, deep down, for our present situation. Finally, an attempt at a
vision of the future with some suggestions in the form of questions.

THE SITUATION

One cannot now and one will not in the future be able to talk about men
and women religious in general terms. All through the history of the
Church the 'religious life' and, in a larger context, the *vita evangelica* or
vita apostolica have always shown that the Spirit leads freely those
women and men whom he touches with his energising gentleness. We see
this in the ancient foundations with centuries-long traditions and in new
communities founded in recent decades.

The prophetic quality of religious life is as pluriform as was that of the
first apostles and the four evangelists. It is not only all the great founders
and foundresses who have identified at the very heart of their order or
institute an opening to the newness of the Spirit: they have known that a
personal God calls and guides each one along a special path, respecting,
within the framework of the community, the uniqueness of every human
person and their need to live freely their vocations. Great superiors have
always claimed for their institutes and inside them a way of reconciling
loyalty with freedom. This rediscovery of the strength and of the freedom
of the Spirit is without doubt the clearest sign of the very radical change

which religious life has experienced in the brief post-conciliar period.

However, we are not naive. History shows that many institutes die, often a lingering death and that those who start up again after an unavoidable crisis are precisely those who have had the strength to be able to change and the opportunity to do so, to discern deep down what is essential and to sacrifice the accessory, who have been influenced by what takes place in the world and in the universal Church. This is still the case for every local Church, and for all the great Churches from time to time called upon to distinguish between the living Tradition and the historically determined socio-cultural traditions. These changes are inevitably accompanied by crises of growth, by polarisations, by flights to a sterile past or towards a too utopian or chaotic future.

In the phase of the acceleration of history through which we are living and which is unique in the course of the long pilgrimage of 'the human phenomenon' (Teilhard de Chardin), births and deaths accelerate also. And as is the case for the entire demographic biology of Europe, with the strange exception of Sweden, deaths now are more numerous than births. In spite of this, European religious life is by far the most important, in terms of numbers, in comparison with the other continents. However, when one compares the ages-pyramids, the southern hemisphere would seem to be the principal location for the development of religious life in the third millenium. At the same time, because of the spread of the modern way of life, imported models will force those religious to achieve much more profound inculturations.

LARGE INSTITUTIONS WEIGH HEAVILY

Within Europe, there are without any doubt differences of varying importance between regions and cultures. At the same time, the global tendency seems to be the same throughout. In Poland itself — the only country in Eastern Europe in which religious are numerous — one notices a decrease in the number of entries. Elsewhere, massive numbers entering noviciates and seminaries have not been the tradition norm, in comparison, for example with the impressive numbers which were to be found in Ireland, Holland, Belgium and France. These latter were the missionary countries *par excellence*.

Consequently, almost every European country is now experiencing an inverse ages pyramid — and this is true also of the United States and Canada. The older religious and the large institutions in which religious are involved weigh heavily on the chances of renewal and inculturation which one expects from the younger religious.

Sadly, it cannot be denied that in some institutions the very quality of the few candidates entering has diminished — soundings taken in many masculine institutions bear this out. To traverse the desert one needs strong personalities, well balanced and capable of facing solitude, tension and doubt. More than ever, the virtue of discernment is needed and young superiors who are sufficiently solid to carry all the burdens cheerfully, are becoming increasingly rare.

HOW HAVE WE COME TO THIS JOURNEY ACROSS THE DESERT?

Let me say again that, from country to country, the rhythm of the evolution and its deep-seated causes will vary, as the countries' socio-cultural history, far-off or recent, has varied. Everywhere, however, one finds confirmation of what Karl Rahner liked to emphasise when he defined our situation as an *ungleichzeitige Gleichzeitigkeit* (a non simultaneous simultaneity). In other words, our situation involves the co-existence in the same country, the same group, the same family, of a number of phases of the historical evolution and of its different interpretations. There are, for example, communities which continue to be inspired by the traditionalism of Mgr Lefebvre, there are other which are impatient to practice a thrusting ecumenism.

In bringing together the main traits of the acceleration of history in the second half of the twentieth century, we must first acknowledge the general perception of the end of 'traditional Christendom' — with the exception of Greece, which is schizophrenic. Education, hospitals, art, popular culture and the media (with the exception of tourist pilgrimages) and organisations involved in the Third World, all of these are secularised. Even certain great Christian social organisations, Christian trade unions, political parties calling themselves Christian, all of these are in that situation. The great modern humanitarian organisations — such as the Red Cross, Amnesty International, Green Peace, *Médicins sans Frontiers* — no longer have a religious colouring.

At the start of the century, in many countries one had to be religious or celibate in order to teach, nurse or do voluntary work in 'the colonies'. Even many groups of university professors still lived in a climate which was explicitly religious or Christian. And in the Church itself the statement 'outside the Church there is no salvation: *extra Ecclesiam nulla salus*' was widely (and in a very material sense) accepted. At least for the Christians, still clearly in the majority, the world deemed 'profane' was still solidly oriented towards what one can in sociological terms call 'the ecclesial system'. Here are two striking examples: in Holland in 1901 only 1% of the population stated that they did not belong to any religion. In 1990, that figure had risen to 51% (for those aged 18-24 it had risen to 61%). In 1990 in Belgium 32% said that they did not belong to any religion, while this was true of 41% of those aged between 18 and 24. Nevertheless, these two countries are known for Christian educational and hospital systems unique in the world, Christians succeeded one another as prime ministers, tens of thousands of religious and thousands of missionaries emerged from schools and parishes up to 1950. Global organisations, Christian trade unions as well as Christian managers of firms set up their headquarters there. These two countries have more Catholic universities than all other European countries put together. The end of a war was the end of a period. Nowadays, in the capitals of both countries more than half of all infants are no longer baptised — and this is also the case for all major cities of North-West Europe.

Meanwhile, two great legacies of the French revolution, liberty and equality, have spread among the populace, with definitive results in education, in promoting the emancipation of women. In a parallel development, post-war socio-economic progress has contributed to a very great improvement in the living standards of the majority of the population of western Europe and even of many parts of central Europe.

NO LONGER NEED A PERSON BECOME A PRIEST TO GET AN EDUCATION

The consequences for religious life are obvious: the old sociological supports of the three vows have disappeared. It is no longer necessary to become a religious in order to secure an education, nor need one become a priest in order to climb higher up the social ladder. Sexuality is prized — to the extent that love is reduced to eroticism. Even the Council has changed the enumeration of the ends of Christian marriage. Everywhere people set about updating their understanding of the three vows, in worthwhile or in questionable fashion. The ideological change, however, has had a more profound influence than have the socio-cultural changes, which in large part have resulted from scientific, technological and economic changes. One can describe the main characteristics of the ideological change as follows: Rationalism prepared the way for liberal Protestantism, on the one hand, and, among the educated in Catholic countries, for positivism — and sometimes for a virulent anti-clericalism. Later, nationalist and totalitarian ideologies filled the ideological void which had been created among the masses. In the west, after the second world war a practical materialism invaded all social categories, while so-called scientific materialism manipulated the search for meaning in central Europe. The findings of our survey of values show how wide-spread have been the repercussions on traditional beliefs.

In the meantime, during the long period which began with the Renaissance, the Church chose to go the way of interdict and fear, and of compromise with States whose leaders, in general, professed nothing more than a benevolent agnosticism. It did not pursue a frank dialogue with what one might call 'modernity'. 'Rationalism' was condemned, but the importance of rationality was not accepted. In consequence, a credible attempt at discernment was lacking. One can cite for the crisis in theological reflection the great French Catholic historian, Jean Delumeau — *La Peur en Occident*, Fayard, Paris, 1978 — and Giuseppe Alberigo in Bologna, a specialist on the Councils — *La Chrétiente en Débat*, Cerf, Paris, 1984. Not without reason did Hans Urs von Balthaser speak of a time when the Church was confined to a fortress (*Die Schliefung der Bastionen*).

Vatican II put an end to that dim period. To an extent, however, the Council came too late. Unfortunately, it did not have enough time to undertake sufficiently deep analyses, especially with regard to the relationships between the Church and the Kingdom. A theology of history, by now a world history, was lacking, as were, in practice, the keys to the difference between the great tradition and the traditions. The Council was concerned above all with the *aggiornamento* of the Church. The debate nowadays, however, is about the existence of God and the meaning of existence. Europe and the Churches face an immense challenge: how to convey meaning to this 'post-modern' man, who is less and less convinced by rational responses, who remains 'religious' but understands less and less the language in which the Christian message is conveyed — look at the reactions to the new catechism, the Drewermann phenomenon,[2] etc. Basically, neither Marx nor Freud have survived, but Nietzsche has. It is he —with Dostoievski — who has best expressed the experience of nihilism, man's radical confrontation with his direction-less freedom. (See Marcel Gauchet, *Le Désenchantement du Monde*, Gallimard, Paris, 1985). All of this has had profound repercussions, on exegesis especially, and then on the handing on of the faith. In this context, Christians will be they who have had a personal experience of the Spirit of Jesus, placing their hope in him and setting off on their way through the desert. They will share humbly with those who are searching in the Church or outside the Church.

From this very rapid sketch we can conclude that where Christians themselves have become a minority in a culture where 'Christendom' has left many vestiges — frequently ambiguous — religious life, or the *vita evangelica* can be the way only for Abrahamic nuclei. They will have to be in the world without being 'of the world', must love creation, while refusing to accept any one-dimensional and fruitless interpretation. Neither Christianity nor religious life have ever faced a like situation.

WHAT KIND OF RELIGIOUS LIFE IN THIS CONTEXT?

In a world closed in on itself — something to which even the 'New Age' wave testifies, since it is man alone who has given it meaning — a religious life, however little institutionalised, must first of all be an authentic vita *evangelica*. By this title it will be for it to make real the 'following of Christ': *sequela Christi* in the context of a Europe at the end of the second millenium after Jesus Christ, where the entire context is different from the time of the historical Jesus and where all needs to be reinterpreted if we are to be faithful to the 'today of the Spirit'.

This vocation must, firstly, be rooted in the Spirit, who alone guarantees its authenticity; it will be essentially prophetic, a critical presence, that is to say, swimming against the current. At the heart of this evangelical life will be eschatological hope. There are two aspects of this hope. First of all, it is historically located, limited to one cause, in spite of Somalia, Bosnia, AIDS, suicides, corruption, drugs, people's many betrayals, and even the weakness of the Church. Then, and more radically, this this-worldly hope is taken up into another dimension of hope. In other words there is always the horizon of the presence of the living God and the light of his infinite tenderness. Religious will thus be universal brothers and sisters, animated by hope in the midst of people they meet along the way, people experiencing a brutal or refined despair.

To explain what I want to say, permit me to quote from a tribute which appeared in the newspaper, *La Croix* (28 June 1993) to Jacques à Pierre Bérégovoy, one-time prime minister, who committed suicide in France:

> The President of the European Commission, M. Jacques Delors, would discern behind the Bérégovoy drama 'the veritable earthquake which has devastated industrialised societies ... undermined by the erosion of traditional values which have not yet been replaced by anything durable and positive.' Towards the end of his reflections, ruminating about 'other dimensions of destiny besides political, economic and social action', Jacques Delors began to speak again about this 'dark anguish into which our societies are often plunged.' Instead of this anguish he offered 'the hope which Christians possess ... and which bids us look beyond the sea's horizons, beyond our own

existence.'

It is true that to take on this perspective is a hazardous adventure, but it is at the heart of the *vita evangelica*. Without it, religious life has no meaning.

For the future, a return to that *vita evangelica* is a *sine qua non* of all renewal. We are not primarily contemplative, monastic or apostolic, nor are we primarily Benedictines, Dominicans, Jesuits or anything else. We are primarily men and women seized by the God of Jesus Christ who takes us and pushes us along the path of humanity — 'follow me'. Everything else is secondary. Very great flexibility then becomes possible.

Let us now proceed a little further along that route of the possible. Let us take as patron St Thomas More, whose utopian approach is capable of stimulating the imagination and thus the necessary creativity.

Vita evangelica means, first of all, service of the gospel and obedience to the Spirit of Jesus. Jesus looked forward to the Kingdom. The community of the apostles, the embryonic Church which he formed, is primarily at the service of the Kingdom, it may not be self-regarding. All Christians are called to that *vita evangelica*. A religious *vita evangelica* must therefore seek first the Kingdom — which means courageously living the historic and current dialectical tension between Kingdom and Church. This has never been easy, and it is not easy just now when nostalgia for a reassuring past has reappeared everywhere. It follows that one cannot wall up the Spirit in traditions, not even in canonically-approved traditions. Not that one wants to neglect the wisdom which has also been inspired by the same Spirit and is on offer in these traditions.

By way of example, one could visualise certain concrete possibilities.

1. *In a Church which has turned its face towards ecumenism, why not encourage the creation of truly ecumenical communities?*

Religious life offers a space *par excellence* for an endeavour to live the communion of the Churches. Without appealing to great theological theories, prayer and apostolic commitment make further developments possible.

2. *In a Church which rejects class structures and where all are first and foremost brothers and sisters, why not have many more possible patterns of membership?*

One can devise varying kinds of formulae for lay involvement: for a limited period, for a single form of apostolate, for a long and not pre-determined period. Lay people who, obviously, would be carefully selected, could benefit from the spirituality, the period of formation, certain facilities of hospitality, etc. One could even consider prolonging the collaboration of members who wish to continue their involvement, but more after the fashion full members — for example, those who after a long period with temporary vows accept that they have a vocation to the *vita evangelica*, but not after the pattern of religious life with the three vows.

3. *Though they belong to their respective communities, can religious not operate in collaboration with other religious and lay people, in joint undertakings, while being members of different institutes?*

Such enterprises could be: centres for combatting AIDS, organisations caring for migrants and drug addicts, Pax Christi networks, parishes, universities. Many Christians of this kind already belong to basic communities. A certain number of organisations are developing into new forms of religious life.

4. *Is it not possible to have religious communities which would provide space for meetings of members of different religions, thus facilitating mutual enrichment while avoiding a facile utopian syncretism?*

Such places would help to the institutional Churches to integrate better into a world which is growing increasingly multi-cultural. The fact that many religious institutes are international in membership is a guarantee that such meetings would be serious and balanced.

5. *What about solitary people?*

Religious communities have a special mission to people in our anonymous and fragile society who are alone, people who are celibate by force of circumstances, widows and widowers, divorced persons ... who want to experience the 'sacrament of friendship'.

6. *What initiatives are needed in order to give concrete expression to the link between faith and justice?*

It is for religious, especially, to launch all kinds of ideas: with regard to unemployment, for example, the on-going structural problems facing rural populations, migrants, prostitutes, people engaged in regional, national and European economies, in trade unions and in high finance. Personal contact on the ground must be complemented by work on the structures, work which is fully warranted on scientific grounds, but is guided by a true hierarchy of values.

It goes without saying that all this needs an adequate and on-going formation, very great freedom, combined with a mature asceticism — taking care lest one become the prisoner of a desire for power — and whole-hearted collaboration with competent and incorrupt lay people. Since many such enterprises have international ramifications, one should consider the possibility of collaboration across the frontiers of different provinces and even of different institutes. Experience shows that this is difficult and that many religious remain, unconsciously, nationalist and the prisoners of prejudices which militate against an attitude of openness and tolerance towards the otherness of the other person.

7 *Is it not foreseeable that, in the near future, ministries will be given to lay people, men and women, including women religious, and that we will get round to assigning ordained ministries to them?*

Such people, vitally necessary for the Church, will need resource centres and centres where real dialogue can take place and where people can live in brotherly and sisterly fashion, free of traditional inhibitions — in other words, where the male members will not feel obliged to appropriate the hierarchical functions. Religious communities formed to render this service will be extremely important in continuing to guarantee the quality of this new ecclesial tissue and in enabling it to be truly part of today's human community — in other words, discerning real needs and speaking a language which can be understood.

8. *Will these new conditions not affect community life itself?*

With fewer members of apostolic communities and with many of them doing specialised work, one will not any longer find many communities where all the members do the same kind of work — only communities of retired religious will still be large. This change will need (a) a much more thorough psychological formation to ensure that each member develops a deeper personal relationship with his or her brothers and sisters in the community; (b) a formation which allows for a truer respect for each one's privacy; (c) a more authentic faith dialogue to make up for the fact that religious will be members of 'communities characterised by dispersal' for multiple commitments in the world — *communitas ad dispersionem*, to use the phrase of the late Pedro Arrupe, who had been General of the Jesuits. This will mean that the content of the vow of obedience will evolve towards a vow of solidarity and dialogue, implying much more evangelical *correctio fraterna*. Religious communities could thus give an example to the Church at large, which finds it so difficult to enter the 'synodal' phase of its history.

This list could be lengthened and could be made more precise in many ways. The object is to stimulate your reflections. Let us finish with an important remark. Nothing will be done without a large measure of mutual confidence within institutes. Such confidence will make possible the necessary opening. Neither can anything be done without the intelligent involvement of superiors gifted in dialogue, capable of discernment and courageous. Where such qualities are lacking, it is more honest and more Christian to accept courageously the death of an institute or a province, rather than make impossible promises to the few candidates who offer themselves. For the others, may the Spirit of Jesus guide them, according to the word heard by the prophet Isaiah:

Look, I am doing something new,
now it emerges, can you not see it?
Yes, I am making a road in the desert
and rivers in wastelands. (Is. 43:19)

1. Of the two talks to which Father Kerkhofs refers, one is a report of an on-going survey of religious beliefs and practices in Europe and elsewhere and which will appear in the Ocober issue of *Doctrine and Life*. A part of it, however, is in 'This & That' in this issue, q.v. The other is printed in this issue of Religious Life Review, pp 285-293.
2. On the Drewermann issue, see 'God and the Unconscious Mind: The Eugen Drewermann Case', by Moya Frenz St Leger, *Doctrine and Life*, July-August, 1993.

THIRTEEN
The Shape of the 1994 Synod

PETER HEBBLETHWAITE

What the Synod is in general terms is described in the Code of Canon Law (Nos 342-348). It is a meeting of Bishops who "by their counsel, assist the Roman Pontiff in the defence and development of faith and morals, and in the preservation and strengthening of ecclesiastical discipline" (Canon 342). This is somewhat more restrictive than Paul VI's description in *Apostolica Sollicitudo*, the founding document of the Synod: "By its very nature the task of the Synod is to inform and give advice." It is the Holy Father who seeks (and needs) advice and information.

The emphasis on *Bishops* should be noted. The Synod On Religious counts as the ninth in the series. The seventh in 1987 was on the Laity and the eighth in 1990 on the Priestly Ministry; but that did not mean that the laity or priests had any right to be present. Twenty religious women will be present at the 1994 Synod. Their presence is a "concession", and they will not have the right to vote.

The synod has a permanent Secretariat headed by Belgian Archbishop Jan Schotte C.I.C.M (a Scheutist). He is aided by a Synod Council consisting of twelve members elected by the 1990 Synod (three per continent) and three named by the Pope. It does not seem that they play a very significant role. For the key decision — the choice of theme — belongs to the Pope "after extensive consultation" (*Lineamenta* 1).

Once the theme had been assigned, Archbishop Schotte then set about the preparation of the working-paper or *Lineamenta*. Its purpose, he explains in the covering letter, is "to stimulate an in-depth reflection on the topic by the pastors of the Church and by all other interested parties." It is not "an anticipation of any possible conclusions of the Synod."

CONTROVERSIAL POINTS COULD GET LOST

So the *Lineamenta* is neither exhaustive, definitive or normative. It is not intended to steer the Synod in particular directions. Comment on it is free. The widest possible involvement of everyone concerned is urged. Answers must arrive in Rome by November 1, 1993. Religious should send "any contribution they might wish to make either to the Union of Superiors General (USG), the International Union of Superiors General

(USIG), the World Conference of Secular Institutes (CMIS) or the Congregation for Institutes of Consecrated Life and Societies of Apostolic Life."

This is the first of the many filters through which upward communication has to pass. There are several stages in the "processing" of the information in which controversial or even merely interesting points could get lost.

Anyway, on the basis of this consultation to which the episcopal conferences and the dicasteries of the Roman Curia will also have contributed, Archbishop Schotte and his team will devise the *Instrumentum Laboris* or working-paper proper. It might loosely be described as setting the Synod agenda.

At the start of the 1990 Synod on Priestly Ministry Archbishop Schotte reported that 19 out of the 29 Roman dicasteries had replied, 6 out of 13 Oriental Churches and 68 out of the 106 episcopal conferences had made their views known. Only religious gave a 100% response — but since they had only one respondent, the USG, that was hardly surprising.

When the Synod gathers in October 1994 it will have its own officials appointed for its duration. The most important of them is the relator who opens the Synod discussions by highlighting features of the *Instrumentum Laboris* he thinks appropriate. The relator is usually a cardinal. At the Synod on priestly ministry, the Dominican Cardinal Lucas Moreira Neves was relator.

The two best-known religious in the college of Cardinals are Basil Hume O.S.B. of Westminster and Carlo Maria Martini S.J. of Milan. However, it is unlikely that either will be relator. They would not be content to read out words written by others. This criterion would *a fortiori* rule out the two Brazilian Franciscans, Paulo Evaristo Arns of Suo Paolo and Aloisio Lorscheider of Fortaleza.

A BETTER POINT OF INSERTION OF IDEAS

But whoever the relator, the most exciting stage of any Synod comes next. It involves listening to speeches (not more than ten minutes long) from representatives of episcopal conferences. This panorama of experiences always gives a good sense of the universality of the Church. Moreover, for many religious, these speeches will be a better point of insertion for their ideas than the previous carefully controlled consultation on the *Lineamenta* — provided, that is, they can find a sympathetic bishop among those going to the Synod from their country. Bishops who wish to talk sense on this universal stage are usually ready to listen. The US

Bishops will have carved up the topics between them.

If the bulk of the *Lineamenta* pass into the *Instrumentum Laboris* (which is possible but not certain), one can see grounds for some stirring speeches. Bishop A is sure to deplore the way the definition of religious life is based on Canon Law when *Perfectae Caritatis* offers a much better approach: "Since the fundamental norm of the religious life is the following of Christ as proposed by the Gospel, such is to be regarded by all communities as the supreme norm."

Arcbishop B is bound to pounce on the fantasy that "a mistaken idea of feminism has laid claim to the right to participate in the life of the Church in ways which are not in keeping with the hierarchical structure willed by Christ" (29d).

Bishop C will find very droll the idea that the "option for the poor" can be a danger to religious life, not because it exposes religious to the risk of martyrdom but because it exposes them contamination from worldliness (44c).

These are just imaginary speeches. But speeches along similar lines will undoubtedly be made. The texts of "good speeches" will be handed out to the press, replacing the banal summaries offered by the press office. Everyone will have a great sense of freedom and openness. Everyone will be enriched. Cardinal Myroslav Vlk from Prague will speak of the underground sisters of the Czech lands (though not of the ordination of women or married men). There will be revelations from the Baltic Republics, Belorus and the Ukraine. All of which will create a mood of optimism. Journalists who go home after the first week will report that the Synod is a remarkable success.

A BOTTLE-NECK DEVELOPS

However, the next stage invariably is a let-down. As it passes from week 1 to week 2, the Synod resembles a funnel: the broad scope of the first week narrows down to a thin bottle-neck. The *relator* reappears and replies to the circa 120 speeches and written interventions that have been made. That, at least, is what he is supposed to do. But the *relatio altera* as it is called rarely fulfils its promise. This is partly because its function is forward-looking: it has to prepare the questions to be discussed in the *circuli minores* or small working-groups.

The 1987 Synod on the Laity, for example, was broken down into twelve language-based groups: three French, three English, three Spanish-Portuguese, one German, one Italian and one Latin. The twenty religious women invited for 1994, passive so far, can intervene at this stage. Each group elects a president and a *rapporteur*. Their task is to discuss the questions raised by the *relator* in his concluding remarks to the first week. But often they range far and wide. The groups come together by hazard of the alphabet. By the end of the second week they complete their synthetic reports on the *quaestiones disputatae*. In 1987 these texts were published or rather leaked. They are the best clue to the real mind of the Synod; but it is not yet a united mind.

All the material hitherto produced — the speeches and written interventions of the first week, the discussions in the *circuli minores* in the second week — now disappears into the maw of the Synod Secretariat. Two "special secretaries" are appointed for this purpose — though they have a plethora of special assistants and other helpers. The purpose now is to turn the material into a series of *propositiones*. These are not usually proposals for action — though they may be — so much as theological statements, often a paragraph long. They are supposed to deal with the major issues that have been raised so far. And they are intended as the "counsel" given to the Holy Father by the Synod.

So by the middle of the third week the *propositiones* come before the language-groups who debate them and, finding their own cherished ideas not reflected therein, proceed to amend and cut them about. In a faint echo of conciliar procedure, the amendments proposed are called *modi*, and they have to be justified in the same way: only amendments going in the general direction of the *propositiones* can be entertained.

The Synod secretariat now burns the midnight-oil. The Synod fathers and their guests — in this case the religious — will have little to do and can see going-home time coming. It feels like end of term.

To occupy this interval the usual practice is for curial cardinals to dilate on matters of common interest. In 1990, at the Synod on Priestly Ministry, Cardinal Joseph Ratzinger gave news of the state of *The Catechism of the Catholic Church*; Cardinal Bernardin Gantin explained what had happened to the document on episcopal conferences (it was stuck); and there was an introduction to the Oriental Code of Canon Law.

These diversions allow time for the Synod secretariat to complete its work of amending the *propositiones*. These have usually numbered between 40 and 50. But there is no rule. The penultimate act of the Synod is to vote on them: *placet* or *non placet*. Massively approved, they will not be published (though they may be leaked) on the grounds that they constitute the Synod's "advice to the Holy Father" and are therefore properly reserved to his eyes.

Some cultural even will mark the end of the Synod — say a new musical setting of St. Francis Canticle of the Sun or something similar. Then there will be a final concelebration in which the Pope will quote the Psalm about 'how good it is for brothers to dwell together in union' adding, no doubt with a twinkle in his eye, 'and the sisters too' (applause).

The 'message' of the Synod will be unveiled and immediately forgotten. The function of the 'message' appears to be to permit a bishop to have something to say to the journalists on arrival at his home airport. 'What did the Synod achieve?' asks the reporter. 'Read this message,' says the Bishop, hastily departing.

Some months later, sometimes a year-and-half later, the Pope will publish his synthesis of the work of the Synod. The post-synodal exhortation, *Christifideles Laici* on the Laity was published in April 1989.

It was disappointing in two respects. The reconsideration of the 1972 document *Ministeria Quaedam* on lay ministries, recommended by the Synod, was entrusted to a special, anonymous commission with no clear indication about whether its brief was to *extend* lay ministries (including those of women) or cut them down. (It has still not reported). Second, the Synod's recommendation that 'new movements' (such as Communion and Liberation) should be in the first place under the local bishop or episcopal conference was simply ignored.

But in other respects *Christifideles Laici* was a much richer document than the Synod Propositions on which it was based; though that was not, admittedly, a very remarkable achievement. Its key-word was *participation*. It urged the participation of lay women and men in all consultative bodies from parish councils to diocesan councils, and in the preparation of documents. But there was no machinery for its implementation.

Much the same can be said of *Pastores Dabo Vobis*, the fruit of the 1990 Synod on the Priestly Ministry. It left few questions unresolved, and trounced those who had had the temerity to raise the possible ordination of married men. Thus by 1998, if the usual pattern is followed, a post-synodal apostolic exhortation on religious life will be published. It might be called *Vos estis Amici mei*.

The *Lineamenta*:

The title of the *Lineamenta*, or Outline, is 'The Consecrated Life and its Role in the Church and in the World.' Our translation is based on that of the Vatican Polyglot Press. In most instances I have substituted the word 'religious' for the ubiquitous word 'consecrated' (as in 'consecrated life'), even though the *Lineamenta* extends the word 'consecrated' to members of secular institutes and members of institutes of apostolic life — see below, paragraph 5 of the Preface. The substitution has a practical advantage: it is simpler to speak of 'religious' than to have to use cumbersome phrases like 'those in consecrated life', or 'members of institutes of consecrated life'. I have retained the word 'consecrated' however where the sense of a passage required it. Because it is the more common English usage, I have substituted the word 'religious' for 'the consecrated life' in sentences attributing a role or activities to 'the consecrated life'. I have also substituted 'local Church' and 'local Churches' for 'particular Church' and 'particular Churches.' I have made other changes too in the interests of clarity or of closer conformity to English usage. I have replaced translations of Vatican Council and other Vatican documents with those from my own edition. I have also omitted many of the footnotes, as being of interest only to those with access to the *Acta Apostolicae Sedis*. [Editor]

PREFACE

On 30 December 1991 the Holy Father Pope John Paul II called for the convocation in autumn 1994 of the Ninth Ordinary General Assembly of the Synod of Bishops to treat the topic: *De vita consecrata deque eius munere in ecclesia et in mundo* ('The Consecrated Life and its Role in the Church and in the World').

Following established procedures, the Holy Father chose the topic after consulting the Oriental Churches, the episcopal conferences, the heads of the departments of the Roman Curia and the Union of Superiors General. He also asked the advice of the Council of the General Secretariat, who evaluated the information received in the consultation and discussed the pastoral urgency, the interest world-wide and the timeliness of discussion of religious life. On the instructions of the Holy Father the Council of the General Secretariat of the Synod continued to examine the topic before drafting the text of the *Lineamenta*. The pages which follow present the topic of the next Synod in all its parts, indicating its content and its limits.

The *Lineamenta*, with questions at the end of each section, has a twofold purpose. First the intention is to promote, in preparation for the Synod, an in-depth reflection on the topic by the pastors of the Church and by all other interested parties. Secondly, it is hoped to obtain information and pointers which will be helpful in preparing the agenda of the Synod. In this way aspects of the topic will emerge which point to the pastoral needs of the Church for the future.

It is useful to recall once again that the sole purpose of the *Lineamenta* is to introduce the topic and to promote a preliminary study of it. Consequently the document should not be seen as anticipating any possible conclusions of the

Synod, much less as an exhaustive treatment of religious life. Instead the *Lineamenta* represents a precise phase in the Synodal process, the reflective phase, and helps to make the Synod's discussion more responsive to the expectations of the People of God and more effective in its service to the Church.

The *Lineamenta* defines the topic in broad terms. Strictly speaking Canon Law applies the title 'consecrated life' to the religious life and to secular institutes only. However in this document the term 'consecrated life' [in this version, 'religious life': Editor] is used in a wider sense to include also the societies of apostolic life, for obvious reasons and in accordance with *The Code of Canon Law* (hereafter CIC). Even though the societies of apostolic life do not belong to the canonical definition of the consecrated life they are so treated because they are 'comparable' to the institutes of religious life (see CIC 731, § 1). Therefore the reference to the consecrated [religious] life in the *Lineamenta* text is meant to include religious orders and congregations, secular institutes as well as societies of apostolic life, except in those cases where a single group is explicitly named because of a feature specific to that group.

It is hoped that the Church community at all levels will try to ensure the widest possible response to the *Lineamenta* from clergy, religious and laity. Answers to the questions, it is hoped, will provide information about religious life in general and about individual institutes.

The responses to the questions are to arrive at the General Secretariat of the Synod of Bishops no later than 1 November 1993 from the customary ecclesial bodies: the Oriental Churches, the episcopal conferences or similar episcopal assemblies and the departments of the Roman Curia. The institutes of consecrated life and the societies of apostolic life are invited to send any contribution they might wish to make to either the Union of Superiors General (USG), the International Union of Superiors General (UISG) the World Conference of Secular Institutes (CMIS) or the Congregation for Institutes of Consecrated Life and Societies of Apostolic Life, who will take this information into consideration in drafting their responses.

The preparations for the Ninth Ordinary General Assembly in autumn 1994 begin with a period of reflection, meditation and prayer for everyone at all levels of the universal Church so that all those who have responded to the call of the Lord in the institutes of religious life and the societies of apostolic life might more profoundly take to heart the mission of the Church for the salvation of the world and become more authentically committed to its service

JAN P. SCHOTTE, CICM   GENERAL SECRETARY

INTRODUCTION A SYNOD FOR THE RELIGIOUS LIFE

1. *The Consecrated Life and Its Role in the Church and in the World* is the topic which His Holiness Pope John Paul II, after extensive consultation, has chosen for the Ninth Ordinary General Assembly of the Synod of Bishops.

The choice is an indication of the Church's esteem for the religious life and serves as a grace-filled moment for all those called to follow Christ through the evangelical counsels of chastity, poverty and obedience. On the threshold of the year 2000 the words of Christ resound with special force: 'If you wish to be perfect, go sell what you have, give to the poor and you will have a treasure in heaven; then come and follow me' (Mt 19:21) (See St. Athanasius, *Vita Sancti Antonii*, 2)

The Synod is also of great interest to the entire People of God. The Second Vatican Council treats the theology of the religious life in chapter VI of the constitution *Lumen Gentium, hereafter* LG (F1, pp 350 ff). The document mentions that the state of life constituted by the profession of the evangelical counsels 'while not entering into the hierarchical structure of the Church, belongs undeniably to her life and holiness' (ibid., p. 405). It says: 'All the members of the Church should unfailingly fulfil the duties of their Christian calling. The profession of the evangelical counsels shines before them as a sign which can and should inspire them to do so' (ibid., p.404).

The aspects of the topic to be treated at the Synod are the nature (identity) and the role (gift, mission, m*unus*) of religious institutes in their many Church-approved forms. Nevertheless, the societies of apostolic life, because they are comparable to the institutes of religious life (See CIC, 731), are also to be included in the topic chosen for the Synod, but the particular character of their life and apostolate is to be borne in mind.

On 2 February 1992, at a Eucharistic liturgy in St. Peter's basilica for women and men religious, Pope John Paul II, spoke about the approaching Synod and invited everyone to respond generously: 'In lighting these candles which signify the light of Christ, we are also beginning to prepare for the next assembly of the Synod of Bishops which, as you know, will deal with the religious life and its involvement in the Church and world. On the threshold of the year 2000, then, it will deal with your life, your consecration, your way of participating in evangelization and, thus, in the Church's missionary activity. Support the preparations for it with your prayers and respond when consulted.'

The preparations for the Synod and its celebration ought to provide the entire Church with a providential opportunity for becoming more aware of the nature and role of the religious life. Even though the Synod's specific task is reserved to the pastors of the Church in communion with the pope, the entire Church is called to work together in the period of consultation preceding the Synod. Bishops, priests, lay people and especially members of the institutes of religious life and the societies of apostolic life are invited to devote themselves to prayer, study and discernment. They will thus be contributing to the renewal of religious life in its spiritual, communal and apostolic aspects, under the guidance of the Holy Spirit, who continually renews the Church and guides it towards the fullness of the Kingdom of Christ.

2. Religious have contributed to previous Synods in the study of justice in the world, evangelisation, catechesis, the family, penance and reconciliation. In fact, some post-Synodal documents make explicit reference to the religious life and its specific contribution. A case in point is a statement in the Apostolic Exhortation *Evangelii Nuntiandi*, issued after the Third Ordinary General Assembly, which spoke of the presence and role of religious in evangelisation. Placing the religious life in the context of the mystery and mission of the Church, Pope Paul VI said: 'In this perspective it is easy to appreciate the role played in evangelisation by religious men and women dedicated to prayer, silence and works of penance. Some, indeed very many, religious devote themselves directly to the proclamation of Christ. They have made and continue to make an inestimable contribution to the work of evangelization. By virtue of their religious consecration they are

particularly free and willing to leave all things and go to the ends of the earth to preach the Gospel. They are always full of courage in their work and their apostolate is often outstanding in its admirable resourcefulness and initiative. They are generous and are often to be found in the most remote mission stations where they may have to endure great dangers to health and even to life. The Church is undoubtedly greatly indebted to them' (Paul VI, EN 69: F2, p. 746). Even today these words stand as an appeal to religious for a stronger presence in the new evangelisation.

The recent Synods on the laity and on priestly formation also saw the presence and contribution of members of religious institutes and societies of apostolic life. Explicit references to them are made in the post-Synodal documents, *Christifideles Laici* and *Pastores Dabo Vobis*. With the religious life being treated at the next Synod the presentation of the three major vocations in the mystical Body of Christ will be complete: the ministerial priesthood, the laity and the religious.

IN THE CHURCH AND IN THE WORLD

3. The Synod is specifically concerned with the mission and role of religious in the Church and the world of today. On the one hand, religious life is set in the mystery of Church communion as a special gift of grace to the People of God; on the other hand, because of the richness of its charisms for service of the Kingdom, it is called upon today to make an ever more generous contribution to the new evangelisation of the world, granted the variety of situations and cultures in which the religious life is to be found and the diversity of its membership.

On 2 February Pope John Paul II, in explaining the meaning of the Synod on religious life had this to say: 'The successors of the apostles will meet to discuss your life, the contribution which your founders and their respective spiritual families have made to the Church's mission in the past, and are making at the present moment. They want to understand the breadth and depth of the plan of the Lord who sanctifies, enriches and also guides his people by means of the gifts and charisms of the communities of religious life and societies of apostolic life. The bishops want to help you to be Gospel leaven and evangelisers of the cultures of the third millennium and the social ordering of peoples' (John Paul II, address on 3 February 1992).

The Holy Father's words are an invitation to engage in discernment and renewal within the context of a profound shared dialogue, for the purpose of making the religious life shine forth in accordance to God's plan. This discernment should not be unmindful of the road which religious have already travelled with the Church in the course of time, nor should it forget the precious nature of their presence in the Church's life and ministry, nor the ongoing need which the Church has of charisms inspired by the Spirit. Religious, for their part, ought to continue to strive for perfection within an increasingly close-knit ecclesial communion.

The two-fold perspective of the Synod — 'in the Church and in the world' — indicates the concrete way in which the presence and role of religious institutes and the societies of apostolic life ought to be approached. Religious live in this Church and in this world. They are present in the Church with the saving testimony of Christ. And from this Church and from this society come today's vocations. After a suitable initiation, those who are called are sent into this Church and into this society on an apostolic mission. Therefore, it must not be forgotten that many of the problems of the religious life today, are a result of contact with and opposition to the world of today. The growing socialisation and secularisation have significantly affected the balance between spiritual values and apostolic works. Religious life, although not of the world, cannot distance itself from the world nor from the concrete experience of its cultural, economic and social settings. It is impossible to ignore the influence exercised on the development of the religious life by the profound changes which have taken place in society in the last decade. On the other hand, the very condition of today's world sets in stark relief the perception and witness of the age-old values of the Gospel.

TEACHING OF THE MAGISTERIUM

4. In the last decade the Church's Magisterium has treated the religious life in a rich body of teachings contained in documents from the popes, episcopal conferences and individual bishops. The constitution *Lumen Gentium* (F1, pp. 350 ff) and the decree *Perfectae Caritatis* (ibid. pp. 611 ff) of the Second Vatican Council serve as the Council's 'magna carta' of the theological and pastoral renewal of the religious life. These documents contain many authoritative interventions by the Supreme Pontiffs, Paul VI and John Paul II. Among others it is well to recall the Apostolic Exhortation of Paul VI *Evangelica Testificatio* (ibid, pp. 680 ff) and the Apostolic Exhortation of John Paul II *Redemptionis Donum*.

The Apostolic See, acting through the appropriate Roman congregations, has followed and guided the path of the religious life in the last decade with documents of great doctrinal and normative value. Among them are the following documents from the Congregation for the Institutes of Consecrated Life and the Societies of Apostolic Life: *Mutuae Relationes* (F2, pp 209-243), *Religious and Human Advancement* (ibid., pp. 260-284)*The Contemplative Dimension of the Religious Life* (ibid., pp 244-259). Authoritative statements on the religious life have been recently presented by the same Congregation in the document *Essential Elements on the Teaching of the Church on Religious Life in the Institutes Dedicated to Apostolic Works* and in the instruction *Potissimum Institutioni* which contains *Directives on Formation in institutes of Consecrated Life* (1990)

To these texts one must add the doctrinal and normative synthesis of *The Code of Canon Law* (CIC) and *The Code of Canon Law for the Oriental Church* (CCEO), which constitute a point of reference for the life and legislation of the different institutes.

Furthermore, it is well to note to what extent the life and role of religious in the Church and in the world is at the centre of the Magisterium of Pope John Paul II, in his apostolic visitations and in the various meetings with individual religious families, especially on the occasion of their general chapters, or when he addresses specific geographic areas.

All this doctrinal material, accepted and incorporated in the basic documents of religious institutes and of societies of apostolic life, approved by the Apostolic See, constitutes the legacy and essential content of the Church's thought in our times. and therefore ought to guide the process of reflection in view of the next Synod. Not needing to repeat again all that has been taught authoritatively by the Magisterium on the subject, in what follows we will keep in mind the essentials of that teaching. They will guide the reflections of the Lineamenta and whose purpose it is to assist the reflection on the nature and identity of the religious life (part 1), its present state (part II) and its role (part III).

The Nature and Identity of the Religious Life

1. FUNDAMENTALS OF THE RELIGIOUS LIFE

5. For a proper understanding of the role of the religious in the Church and in the world one needs to recall the essential elements found in all of its forms, so as to clarify from the start its specific nature and identity.

'Life consecrated through the profession of the evangelical counsels is a stable form of living by which the faithful, following Christ more closely under the action of the Holy Spirit, are totally dedicated to God, who is loved most of all. By a new and special title they are dedicated to seeking the perfection of charity in service to the Kingdom of God, for the honour of God, the building up of the Church and the salvation of the world. They are a splendid sign in the Church, foretelling the heavenly glory' (CIC, 573).

The above theological and canonical definition of the religious life in the Church sets out the fundamental traits of the religious life in terms of the teaching of the dogmatic constitution Lumen *Gentium*. In considering the essential characteristics of the religious life and what distinguishes it from other vocations in the Church, one must pay particular attention to certain aspects, especially the unity existing between vocation, consecration and mission, the contents of virginity and sacred bonds, the communal and eschatological dimension, and the basic requirements of an authentic spiritual life. Added to these features is the charism proper to each institute, which will be treated later.

VOCATION, CONSECRATION AND MISSION

6. The religious life bears the Trinitarian imprint of a divine vocation which originates in the Father. It is manifested in dedication to God, who is loved above all things, and is expressed in the following of Christ, the Lord and Master, through the profession of the evangelical counsels of chastity, poverty and obedience. Furthermore, it is guided by the constant action of the Holy Spirit, who moves a person to accept the call and to remain faithful to a life of more perfect conformity to Christ and to total dedication to his service in the Church.

In imitation of Jesus, the beloved of the Father, who lived consecration to its perfection, religious consecration is a true covenant with God or *homologhía prós Theón*, to use an expression dear to the early Church. This consecration 'is deeply rooted in their baptismal consecration and is a fuller expression of it' (PC, 5: F1, p. 614). Through the public profession of the evangelical counsels religious try to take on more fully the likeness of the mystery of Christ, chaste, poor and obedient. In this way consecration by means of the evangelical counsels expresses the grace of the call and the anointing of the Spirit by which God himself chooses and empowers people to give themselves totally and to dedicate themselves effectively, freely and totally to the Lord as the one supremely loved, and to his service. The Church authenticates the vocation and accepts the profession of the evangelical counsels, and through a liturgical celebration associates with the Eucharistic sacrifice the total offering of life made by those who are consecrated.

Consecration, as God's choice and a person's dedicated response involves mission. Both are aspects of the same reality. When the Lord consecrates people, he gives them a special grace so that they can obey his loving will. As Christ 'whom the Father consecrated and sent into the world' (Jn 10:36), and in imitation of him, all religious, each according to the charism of the institute, are necessarily engaged in mission. In fact, 'Being means to and instruments of love, the evangelical counsels unite those who practice them to the Church and her mystery in a special way. It follows that the spiritual life of such Christians should be dedicated also to the welfare of the entire Church. To the extent of their capacities and in keeping with the particular kind of religious life to which they are individually called, they have the duty to work for the implanting and strengthening of the kingdom of Christ in souls, and for spreading it to the four corners of the earth' (LG: , p. 404).

THE EVANGELICAL COUNSELS

7. Not only are the counsels of chastity, poverty and obedience based on the words and example of the Lord, they represent in the Church the form of life which the Son of God chose for himself when he came into the world to do the Father's will. It is likewise the same form of life embraced by the Virgin Mother, and the one presented to the disciples who became his followers (See LG, 42, 44, 46: F1, pp 400-402, 404-405, 406-407). They carry the grace of being made like to Christ, who was himself consecrated and sent, and require a personal and spousal love for him, the basis and ultimate reason which enables a person to live in communion with the Lord and, in union with him, to live in virginal chastity, voluntary poverty and total obedience to the Father and to his plan of salvation. The meaning and motivation for 'following Christ", source of inspiration in the religious life for the Churches of both the East and West, can be summarised in an old saying quoted by St Benedict in his rule: 'Do not prefer anything to Christ'. Among the evangelical counsels there is the precious gift given to some who dedicate themselves more easily to God alone through an undivided heart in virginity and celibacy. The evangelical counsel of chastity, assumed on behalf of the Kingdom of God, and which is a sign of the future life and the source of abundant fruitfulness brings with it the duty of perfect continence (See LG, 42; PC, 12; CIC, 599). In the religious life it sets in relief the spousal character of one's gift of self and consequently the primacy of a lively fruitful love of God and of others.

The evangelical counsel of poverty, in imitation of Christ, who was rich, yet for our sake became poor, so that by his poverty we might become rich (see 2 Cor 8:9), requires of all, individuals and communities, a life of poverty—in spirit and fact—which is serious and fruitful, and which limits the use and disposition of goods, according to each individual institute's laws (See LG, 42; PC, 13; CIC, 600).

The evangelical counsel of obedience makes a person like Christ who for our sake made himself obedient to the Father's will unto death even death on a cross (Phil 2:8). It implies submission in a spirit of faith and love to the will of God as it is expressed through lawful superiors according to the various Church-approved constitutions, for the purpose of collaboration according to the design of God for the building up of the Body of Christ (See LG, 42; PC, 14; CIC, 601).

8. The demands of the evangelical counsels of chastity, poverty and obedience touch the human person in its very being and in its relationship with others. The practice of these counsels in a spirit of faith, hope, and charity and a constant striving towards the perfection of charity, leads to maturity of life in Christ. It promotes purification of heart and spiritual liberty and it makes religious ready to serve the Gospel, it leads to love for others and helps them to collaborate in building up the earthly city, in accordance with their charisms.

The evangelical counsels make plain the radical meaning of the Gospel and bear testimony to it, in that they are a "total yes" to the love of God and neighbour, and stand in marked opposition to the negative tendencies of the world and sin, as witnessed in many sectors of society today. People today labour under an excessive quest for pleasure, and selfishness, the opposite to chaste and universal love. They worship possession and indulge in consumerism which is contrary to the seriousness of evangelical poverty and the sharing of goods. They try to assert power to the point of oppressing others, which is so remote from the fellowship of communion and obedience to God's design. The evangelical counsels are an affirmation in our world of the primacy of the love of God and neighbour—on a personal and social level—in the construction of an authentic civilisation enlightened by the love of Christ. The counsels, grounded in the teaching and example of the Master, demand that the Gospel be lived in its fullness, the supreme rule for all institutes (See PC, 2).

COMMUNAL AND ESCHATOLOGICAL DIMENSION

9. One of the characteristics of the religious life, almost from the beginning, has been community life. In addition to following Christ, the religious life looks back to the life of the primitive Jerusalem community (see Acts 2:42-47; 4:32-35); it is an expression of a desire to live that apostolic life style, which has been a constant point of reference down the centuries. It is the ideal pursued by the early coenobites of the East and explained in the Rule of St Augustine: 'The primary purpose for which you have gathered together in one community is to live in this house with but one mind and one heart in the service to God' (Rule of St. Augustine, 1).

Referring to the example of the early Church, the Second Vatican Council has highlighted the profound evangelical meaning and requirements of the common life, especially for religious (See PC, 15). Brought together by the love of Christ in community all members form one single family. United in the name of the Lord and for love of him, they seek to fulfil their vocation, consecration and mission through the common profession of the evangelical counsels. The common life, rooted in the same vocation, consecration, mission and charism, is nourished by the members coming together at the one table of the word and of the Eucharist and in common prayer. It is expressed in the sharing of spiritual and material goods; it grows with daily perseverance in charity and reciprocal service; and it makes for perfect unity of hearts and minds. As a family united in the name of Christ, the community enjoys his presence (see Mt 18:20), according to the age-old monastic ideal and becomes a symbol of the Church, which is 'a communion of life, charity, and truth' (LG, 9). Furthermore, this unity points to the coming of Christ; it is a source of great apostolic dynamism and is a sign of the call to universal reconciliation (See PC, 15; CIC, 602). The life of brothers and sisters in community, a school of the Lord's service and of the evangelical virtues, is founded on the new commandment of Christ, to love one another as Christ has loved us, even to the extent of giving his life (see Jn 15 12-13). Placed under-authority, which is responsible for safeguarding its unity and encouraging everyone to share enthusiastically in consecration and mission, community life should itself express and should achieve its project: the realisation of life in common in the concrete and in the particular, according to the possibilities and circumstances of the situation and in keeping with each institute's charism (CIC, 607, S2). As a reflection of the Church-communion, community is not an introspective entity, rather is it open to the multiplicity of relationships with others which are provided by prayer, apostolic service, and collaboration with other members of the Church, all of whom share in the same baptismal consecra-tion and are called to holiness and mission in the variety and complementarity of different vocations. In its communitarian aspect, the role of the religious life is to offer to all members of the People of God the supreme value of the charity of Christ's disciples, lived in perseverance in brotherly and sisterly communion.

10. The religious life, as well as expressing the pursuit on earth of the mystery of Christ, has an unmistakable eschatological dimension. It is to be 'a very clear symbol of the of heavenly Kingdom' (PC, 1: F1, p. 611) which can and ought to attract in effect all members of the Church to fulfil with renewed effort the duties of the Christian vocation, and to lead them onward towards the heavenly goods which are present even in this world. This is so because the religious life testifies to the new and eternal life acquired by the redemption of Christ and 'preluding our future resurrection and glory of the heavenly Kingdom' (LG, 44: F1, p. 404). In Church-communion and mission, through which the diverse states and vocations express the universal call to holiness in a complementary and reciprocal manner, 'the religious state bears witness to the eschatological character of the Church, that is, the striving towards the Kingdom of God that is prefigured and in some way anticipated and experienced even now through the vows of chastity, poverty and obedience' (John Paul II, *Christifideles Laici*, 55).

ESSENTIAL VALUES AND DEMANDS OF THE SPIRITUAL LIFE

11. The decree *Perfectae caritatis*, number 5, sets out clearly the fundamental elements which all forms of religious life have in common and which require a special spiritual commitment to put them into practice. According to this document the essential aspects are:

a) *renunciation of the world and fundamental choice of God alone,* based on baptismal consecration as well as on a religious consecration which is a fuller manifestation of it;

b) the *Christo-centric meaning of consecration* which is expressed in follow-ing the Master, leaving all to seek the one thing necessary for life, so as to listen to his word and put it into action, in total dedication to everything which is the Lord's;

c) *the paschal dimension of consecration,* in as much as it is conformed to the person of Christ, who died and rose, and is the ideal model of perfect charity towards God and neighbour. Such participation in the mystery of Christ, crucified and risen, should manifest itself in every form of the religious life, in union with his voluntary emptying of self, his fullness of life according to the Spirit, in humility and obedience, in fortitude and charity, and in joy and newness of life, in view of an authentic witness to the resurrection;

d) *total dedication to the service of the Lord in his Church.* It is not possible to choose Christ without choosing all that is his, that is to say, the Church and the Kingdom. For this reason the apostolic dimension of the religious life is marked through and through by the very mystery of salvation in Christ and is expressed, after to the example of the Master in the proclamation of the Gospel, in prayer, works of charity and mercy.

e) *unity of life in contemplation and action.* The religious life is, at one and the same time, a permanent commitment to seeking God above all things, cleaving to him with all one's mind and heart, and a generous dedication to apostolic love so as to be one with him in the work of redemption and the spread of his kingdom.

12. So that these elements might be more clearly in evidence, the Church invites religious to develop more fully their personal and communal spiritual life under the constant guiding action of the Holy Spirit, the source of all interior renewal (See PC, 6; CIC, 663). The main elements of such a life are:

a) *The primacy of perfect charity towards God and neighbour.* This is manifested through the evangelical counsels of chastity, poverty and obedience, as a special commitment to love by Christ's disciples. This love, in turn, ought to enliven and enflame the actual practice of the evangelical counsels.

b) The religious life should be renewed daily *at the authentic sources of Christian spirituality,* especially the Church's liturgy. This ought to be done, in keeping with the tradition and custom of each institute, through the celebration of the Eucharist, the summit and source of the Church's life, and centre of the community, and through communal liturgical prayer.

c) Furthermore, the spiritual life ought to be nourished constantly by *diligent reading, meditation, contemplation and a lived experience of God's Word,* which is the pure and perennial source of the spiritual life, in accordance with the legitimate traditions of *lectio divina* and other forms of contemplation, and personal and communal prayer. The exercises of piety proper to each institute should likewise be given their due place in the programme of personal and communal life.

d) The *commitment to continual conversion,* proper to consecration, demands self-denial in accordance with the Gospel and a corresponding ascetical way of life. It also implies the frequent celebration of the sacrament of Penance and the practice of making retreats, which is needed to recover strength of body and spirit.

e) *Devotion to the Blessed Virgin Mary, Mother of God,* model and patron of the religious life, occupies a unique place in the spiritual life and ought to be nourished by the liturgy and the pious exercises approved by the Church.

These make up the essential values of consecration to be confirmed and lived in the Church according to the charism of each type of religious life and of each institute.

13. The faithfulness of religious to the essential values briefly described above is a guarantee of fruitfulness within institutes themselves as well as within the universal Church and the local Churches. At the same time, this witness serves as a sign and incentive for all members of the People of God, and is a lively

testimony for society of the truth and strength of the Gospel of Christ. Obscuring these values cannot but cause harm to the very life of the Church and to her mission in the world today. For this reason, the celebration of the Synod is a timely occasion to examine carefully the values which determine the specific nature of religious life in the Church. In this regard many questions immediately come to mind: How are these values of the religious life lived and perceived? How can a new vigour be acquired in witnessing to the Gospel and in the missionary spirit called for in the new evangelisation? What means are needed to keep religious life fruitful, given that it essentially depends on the fervour of charity and the effective pursuit of holiness?

Variety of Charism and Forms

14. In the mystery of the Church, the mystical Body of Christ, 'there is a variety of gifts, but the same Spirit; and there are varieties of service, but the same Lord; and there are varieties of activities, but it is the same God who activates all of them in every one' (I Cor 12:4-6). The charisms are given for the common good, and for the communion and mission of the Church. The apostle Paul exhorts the community to aspire to the higher gifts, pointing to the way of charity (see I Cor 12:31).

As mentioned above, the religious life, while not belonging to the hierarchy of the Church, belongs unquestionably to the Church's life and holiness. In this sense one speaks of "the charism of the religious life" as a gift of God to his Church. One speaks of it as a universal reality and as a special vocation and mission in those called to follow Christ by professing the evangelical counsels. One speaks of religious life too in all of its different forms recognised by the Church in the course of history.

To understand the charismatic nature of the religious life it is necessary to turn again to the teaching of the Second Vatican Council and post-conciliar documents. These documents refer to the charismatic character of the religious life as a special gift of the Spirit to his Church and as a grace which was manifested in the course of history through foundational charisms.

To understand better the rich character of charisms, it is necessary to examine the variety of forms of religious life recognised by the Church, instancing some which deserve particular attention, and view them from a theological and canonical perspective.

THE CHARISM OF THE CONSECRATED LIFE

15. The constitution *Lumen Gentium* teaches that total dedication to God in the celibate life for the sake of the Kingdom of Heaven and in the evangelical counsels, is 'a precious gift of divine grace'(LG, 42: F1, p. 401). More specifically: 'The teaching and example of Christ provide the foundation for the evangelical counsels of chaste self-dedication to God, of poverty and obedience. The Apostles and Fathers of the Church commend them as an ideal of life, and so do her doctors and pastors. They therefore constitute a gift of God which the Church has received from her Lord and which by his grace she always safeguards' (Ibid., 43: F1, p. 402).

As gifts of the Spirit, these charisms are ordered to the building up of the

Church, to the good of humanity and to the needs of the world, and are to be accepted gratefully. However, the discernment of charisms and their eventual legal approval is the responsibility of the pastors of the Church. This is why the Second Vatican Council says of the evangelical counsels: 'Church authority has been at pains to give a right interpretation of the counsels, to regulate their practice, and also to set up stable forms of living embodying them' (ibid).

At the root of the many charismatic experiences in the religious life is a special gift of grace which brings to light an inner aspect of *the mystery of Christ and a particular dimension of the Church's life*. These experiences, in effect, in the interior of the mystical Body, make manifest the multi-form grace of Christ, the head of the Church. 'Let religious see well to it that the Church truly show forth Christ through them with ever-increasing clarity to believers and unbelievers alike — Christ in contemplation on the mountain, or proclaiming the kingdom of God to the multitudes, or healing the sick and maimed and converting sinners to a good life, or blessing children and doing good to all, always in obedience to the will of the Father who sent him' (ibid 46: F1, p. 406). Furthermore, through the providential action of the Spirit the extraordinary variety of communities makes the Church ready and equipped for every good work, embellishes her with the variety of her children's gifts as a bride is adorned for her spouse, and manifests the manifold wisdom of God. (See PC, 1).

HISTORIC DIMENSION OF FOUNDATIONAL CHARISMS

16. To help us understand better the historic development of these diverse forms of the religious life, the Second Vatican Council stated: 'From the God-given seed of the counsels a wonderful and wide-spreading tree has grown up in the field of the Lord, branching out into various forms of religious life lived in solitude or in community. Different religious families have come into existence in which spiritual resources are multiplied for the progress in holiness of their members and for the good of the entire Body of Christ' (LG, 43: F1, p. 403). And the decree *Perfectae caritatis* says: 'From the very beginning of the Church there were men and women who set out to follow Christ with greater liberty, and to imitate him more closely, by practising the evangelical counsels. They led lives dedicated to God, each in their own way. Many of them under the inspiration of the Holy Spirit, became hermits or founded religious families. These the Church, by virtue of her divine authority, gladly accepted and approved' (PC, 1: F1, p 611).

In the differing inspirations and characteristics of the various institutes, the Church acknowledges 'the charisms of founders' (See *Evangelica Testificatio*, 11: F1, p 685). Each charism 'is seen to be an experience of the Spirit transmitted to their followers to be lived by them, to be preserved, deepened and constantly developed, in harmony with the Body of Christ continually in a process of growth. "It is for this reason that the distinctive character of various religious institutes is preserved and fostered by the Church"' (MR, 11: F2, p. 217; LG 44: F1, p. 404)

Without taking from the essential characteristic of the religious life, which is to endeavour to achieve the perfection of charity, each charism involves a special way of living the evangelical counsels faithfully and fully. In addition, it implies a particular style of spiritual life and type of apostolate, a specific experience of community life, and a particular involvement in the world. Each religious family's charism is enriched by that family's patrimony of life, history and spirituality, in communion with the spirit of the founder and is given flesh and blood in the lives of his or her disciples. No charism may be altered or destroyed, but ought to be conserved and renewed, in perfect docility to the legitimate authority of the Church, which oversees its authenticity and ratifies 'the intention and plan of the founders' (CIC, 578).

17. The different kinds of religious life and the different institutes owe their origins to a particular experience of the Spirit thanks to which each founder gave expression to the essential elements of consecrated life centred on an aspect of the mystery of Christ, a fundamental Gospel value and a particular apostolate. Their vitality and the service they render the Church are in proportion to the faithfulness to the gift of grace which had given with the original charism.

The history of the religious life repays study. From the beginning of the Christian era to the present day the religious life has witnessed the birth of individual and communal forms of following Christ and consecration. Over the centuries these continued to flourish and to be approved. Thus one had the different forms of Eastern and Western monasticism, the flowering of the mendicant and contemplative orders, of the clerks regular and the apostolic communities, the great diffusion of congregations and institutes of apostolic and missionary life for both men and women, and the secular institutes, a development peculiar to our century. Even in these days the Church is continuing to experience the establishment and renewal of various forms of religious life.

In the course of history various institutes have known periods of splendour and decline. Some forms which prospered in former times have disappeared. Other forms, after an interval of deep crisis and suppression, witnessed a rebirth. Many institutes have undergone reform and division. The Church has always kept watch over the genuineness and vitality of the religious life. This is displayed in the call of the Second Vatican Council to renewal through a continual return to the basics of the Christian life, a re-evaluation of the original inspiration of each institute and adaptation to the changing conditions of the times (See PC, 2).

THE DIFFERENT FORMS OF CONSECRATED LIFE

18. In the Church today there are many forms of religious life. The decree *Perfectae caritatis* deals with these in some detail, describing the essential characteristics of contemplative institutes and of the many families engaged in various apostolic activities. The document speaks of institutes of canonical and monastic life, the mendicant orders, lay institutes, and secular institutes (See ibid., 7-11).

These unique Church-recognised forms of religious life are described more precisely, however, in *The Code of Canon Law* and *The Code of Canon Law for the Oriental Churches,* which divide them into certain fundamental categories:

a) In the first place, *The Code of Canon Law* describes a religious institute as 'a society in which, in accordance with their own law, the members pronounce public vows and live a fraternal life in common. The vows are perpetual or temporary; if the latter, they are to be renewed when the time elapses' (CIC, 607, § 2). *The Code of Canon Law for the Oriental Churches,* in keeping with the ancient tradition in the East, puts particular emphasis on monks and various kinds of monasteries. Religious institutes include a great variety of forms: 1) orders (canons regular, monks, mendicant orders, religious clerics); 2) religious clerical congregations: and 3) religious lay congregations. Among these, one must also mention religious institutes who through a special vow are bound either to the contemplative and monastic life or to evangelisation and the foreign missions.

b) Listed among the forms of the consecrated life are secular institutes in which the Christian faithful 'living in the world strive for the perfection of charity and endeavour to contribute to the sanctification of the world, especially from within' (CIC, 710)

c) 'Comparable to institutes of consecrated life are societies of apostolic life whose members, without taking religious vows, pursue the particular apostolic purpose proper to each society. Leading a life of brothers or sisters in common according to a particular way of life, they strive for the perfection of charity through the observance of the constitutions' (ibid., 731, § 1)

d) The Church today acknowledges the eremitic or anchoritic life with which the faithful, more strictly separated from the world, in silence, solitude and continual prayer, dedicate their lives to the praise of God and the salvation of the world, under the guidance of the bishop (See CIC, 603).

e) Similar to these forms of consecrated life is the order of virgins, who, answering the sacred call to follow Christ more closely, are consecrated to God by the diocesan bishop according to the approved liturgical rite. They are mystically espoused to Christ, Son of God; and are dedicated to the service of the Church. They can form associations to help each other observe their commitment more faithfully and together to serve the Church in ways which are in harmony with their state (See CIC., 604).

f) *The Code of Canon Law* provides also for the existence of new forms of consecrated life which the Spirit inspires in the Church. These may be approved by the Apostolic See, in co-operation with the diocesan bishop, who should endeavour to judge their suitability (See CIC, 605).

Institutes of consecrated life are of pontifical right or diocesan right, depending on whether they are established and approved by the Apostolic See or solely by the diocesan bishop (See CIC, 589). Some of these forms, as in the case of hermits and virgins, have a need of special discernment and guidance by the pastors of the Church.

The preparation for the next Synod and its celebration should be viewed as an opportunity to give all of these renewed attention.

SPECIFIC ASPECTS INTERNAL TO THE CONSECRATED LIFE

19. While the basic divisions of consecrated life are as described above, there are further classifications, arising from other factors, which deserve particular attention.

a) Today in the light of the changing role of women in society and in the Church, *the religious life for women* has become a matter of considerable importance. There is a very great number of women both in the contemplative life and in the active life. The Church owes much to religious women in the missions and in the apostolates of education, social action and charity. The role of religious women and their increasing evangelising potential merits close attention, especially in the light of the apostolic letter of John Paul II, *Mulieris Dignitatem.* The Holy Father emphasises a woman's dignity and mission, in reference to virginity for the sake of the Kingdom and motherhood according to the Spirit. Their valuable apostolic contribution has many times been emphasised: 'Women religious therefore, faithful to their calling and putting to good use the inborn qualities of their womanhood, should respond to the concrete needs of the Church and the world, by seeking out and contributing new forms of apostolic service' (MR, 49: F2, p. 236)

b) *Religious clerics and lay religious.* While by its very nature the religious life is neither clerical nor lay, some institutes are made up entirely of either clergy or the laity (CIC, 588). At the same time, there are certain institutes which have both clerical and lay members. Their common religious vocation and the diversity of participation in the life, administration and apostolates of these institutes is determined by the institute's particular charism and laws. Religious priests and deacons are associated in the Church's ministry in the manner proper to each institute. Today, it seems necessary in both lay and clerical institutes to examine thoroughly and evaluate the dignity, formation, participation and apostolic service of lay brothers within the community and the Church's apostolate. Their presence and work is esteemed both because of the testimony they give in living the religious life, and because of the fundamental character and variety of their apostolic services;

c) *The tradition of the Eastern Churches* Finally, reference should be made to the monastic and eremitic tradition, the variety of forms of religious life in the Eastern Churches and their respective richness in liturgical rites and their age-old traditions. Monastic life in the East with its liturgical, ascetic and communal traditions so near to the experiences of the Eastern non-Catholic Churches, deserves to be strengthened and developed as an expression of the richness of the traditions of the Fathers and in order to promote a spiritual ecumenism with the monks and nuns of Churches in the East, which have preserved the rich patrimony of the first centuries.

CONTEMPLATIVE INSTITUTES

20. The Second Vatican Council has clearly stated the importance of institutes totally dedicated to the contemplative life: 'There are institutes which are entirely ordered towards contemplation, in such wise that their members give themselves over to God alone in solitude and silence, in constant prayer and willing penance. These will always have an honoured place in the mystical Body of Christ, in which 'all the members do not have the same function' (Rom 12:4), no matter how pressing may be the needs of the active ministry. For they offer to God an exceptional sacrifice of praise, they lend lustre to God's people with abundant fruits of holiness, they sway them by their example, and they enlarge the Church by their hidden apostolic fruitfulness. They are thus an ornament to the Church and a fount of heavenly graces' (PC 7: F1, p. 615).

In recent documents the Holy See has emphasised the importance of this way of life and has noted certain characteristics of the contemplative life, especially the following: liturgy and prayer; the obligation of asceticism and work; the importance of the cloister according to the diverse monastic traditions of East and West, and the necessity of a particular vocational discernment and an appropriate formation of their members according to the demands of a personal, communal and ecclesial commitment (Instruction on the Contemplative life and the Enclosure of Nuns, *Venite Seorsum*:: F1, pp 656-675; The Contemplative Dimension of the Religious Life, *La plenaria*, F2, pp 244-259; Instruction, *Potissimum Institutioni*). Their membership of 'the diocesan family' (MR, 18: F2, p. 222) should lead to their increased presence in all dioceses, especially in the younger Churches (AG, 18: F1, pp 834-835), and to their inclusion, in keeping with each one's charism, in the life of the local Churches. This should ensure that people would esteem them all the more and be more inclined to offer them concrete help when they need it. Their particular witness to the transcendence of God should be a stimulus for all the faithful. While remaining faithful to their proper spirit, monasteries are invited in turn to offer timely help to the people of our time through prayer and the spiritual life. especially through an appropriate participation in liturgical prayer (MR, 25: F2, p. 227.

BROTHERS

21. The religious life of brothers is today the clearest example of consecration in the variety of its charisms, as exemplified in its rich diversity of apostolic and social services on behalf of humanity. The Second Vatican Council has stated: 'lay religious life... is a state for the profession of the evangelical counsels which is complete in itself' (PC 10: F1, p. 616). Frequently, the character of the lay religious life for men is not clearly perceived, since many of the faithful think that the brothers should linked with the ordained priesthood, while in fact it represents consecration in its simplest form.

'Religious life began as very much a lay movement. It grew out of a desire of some Christian faithful to derive more abundant fruits from the grace of their baptism and by profession of the evangelical counsels to free themselves from those obstacles which might have drawn them away from the fervour of charity and the perfection of divine worship ...Thus the lay religious life in the Church as an expression of total consecration for the Kingdom, is an expression of the holiness of the Spouse of Christ and contributes effectively and in an original way to the fulfilment of the Church's mission of evangelisation and her many apostolic ministries. We cannot imagine religious life in the Church without the presence of this particular lay vocation, still open to so many Christians who in it can consecrate themselves to the following of Christ and the service of humanity' (John Paul II, 24 January 1986).

The members of lay religious institutes are a sign of the multiplicity of the Church's apostolic services, each with its own function in the pastoral mission of the Church. The decree *Perfectae Caritatis* has pointed out that the Second Vatican Council held lay religious life in "high esteem, for it is so useful to the Church in the exercise of its pastoral duty of educating the young, caring for the sick, and in its other ministries' (PC, 10: F1, p. 616). Called in virtue of their vocation to the evangelical service of humanity and to collaboration in the work of salvation, lay religious, prompted by their own charism, give themselves to all in the universal love of Christ, caring for the weak and sick, asserting their solidarity with the poor and marginalised and helping to establish true peace and justice in this world, in a universal brotherhood of communion, a fellowship which is inspired by the title they bear — 'brother'.

SECULAR INSTITUTES

22. 'While it is true that secular institutes are not religious institutes, at the same time they embody a true and full profession of the evangelical counsels in the world, recognised by the Church. This profession confers a consecration on people living in the world, men and women, laymen and clerics. Therefore they should make it their chief aim to give themselves to God totally in perfect charity. The institutes themselves ought to preserve their own special character — their secular character, that is to say — to the end that they may be able to carry on effectively and everywhere the apostolate in the world and, as it were, from the world, for which they were founded' (ibid 11: F1, pp. 616-612)

Secular institutes have their own characteristics in keeping with the charism of their founder, and assign different roles to the laity and the clergy. While the life of the clergy is characterised for the most part by a priestly spirituality and apostolate as a sign of their special, consecration, the life of the laity has the sanctification of the temporal order as its point of reference.

Such 'religious secularity', an experience of the consecrated life special to our century, is found in a mystical cross-current of two powerful forces in the Christian life, and draws its richness from each. The lay members of secular institutes are consecrated by the sacraments of Baptism and Confirmation, but they also assume the profession of the evangelical counsels as an obligation, along with a stable, recognised bond as a way of emphasising their consecration to God. They remain lay persons, committed to the secular values proper to the laity, but live a 'religious secularity' insofar as they live as consecrated persons in a secular world' (Paul VI, 20 September 1972). In this way the laity, while living their consecration in the world and participating in the Church's evangelising work, commit themselves to work in the temporal order, acting inside it, like yeast in dough, so that through their activities and witness the temporal order might be directed according to God's plan, and the world might be enlivened by the power of the Gospel.

SOCIETIES OF APOSTOLIC LIFE

23. Next to the institutes and other forms of consecrated life, but distinct from them, are the societies of apostolic life. They are mentioned here because of their external similarity to religious institutes and the general principles they both have in common. The Second Vatican Council made note of their proper character without, however, describing them (PC, 1: F1, p. 62). *The Code of Canon Law* (See CIC, 731) and *The Code of Canon Law for the Oriental Churches* (See CCEO, 572.) clarify the matter by describing the fundamental elements which characterise them and by giving them a new title from what was set down in the 1917 Code for the Latin Church. The basic features of the societies of the apostolic life are derived from this description.

Societies of apostolic life have a specific purpose in the Church's apostolic life: they were founded primarily for the work of the apostolate. Their legislation, including the life style of their members, was composed with this purpose in mind. The members of these societies of apostolic life live in community according to their own rule of life and endeavour to achieve the perfection of charity, observing their constitutions, which offer them the suitable means of achieving perfection. The first of these means is the apostolate, since all of the faithful are sanctified each day in the conditions, duties and circumstances of their lives. Added to the apostolate are the various counsels, proposed by the Lord to his disciples, as well as the common life.

Some societies of apostolic life in the Latin Church profess the three counsels of chastity, poverty and obedience through a bond defined in their constitutions. But in this case the practice of the evangelical counsels is essentially ordered to the apostolate, thus giving them a different emphasis from that of those who belong to the institutes of religious life, as described in chapter VI of Lumen Gentium and in canon 573 of *The Code of Canon Law.*

NEW FORMS OF EVANGELICAL LIFE

24. The Church today, as in other times in her history, is the scene of stirrings of spiritual and apostolic renewal, and is witnessing the rise of new forms of evangelical life. Coming to be by the power of the Spirit, these new forms are based on the practice of the counsels of chastity, poverty and obedience and have a specific style of spiritual life, individual and communal, which corresponds to the spiritual aspirations of people today and the needs of the Church and society. Some of these new expressions are true and proper forms of consecrated life and have received Church approval. Others are in the process of receiving such approval from bishops in one of the canonical forms of consecrated life, or as a totally new form. Canonical recognition of these new forms is reserved to the Apostolic See (See CIC, 605).

Some new communities are being formed today which have features in common with consecrated life, but in reality do not belong to the category, consecrated life, since they lack due canonical recognition or do not meet the requirements laid down by the Church. Some, for example, have married people as members. Many such experiments, sometimes marked by great enthusiasm, merit wise counsel and authoritative guidance so that they can find their proper place among the People of God.

Today there are also many individuals and groups of Christ's laity who have embraced the counsels of virginity or celibacy, and even voluntary poverty and obedience, without a public profession of the evangelical counsels. Although these are not institutes of religious life or comparable to them, they enrich the Church by the practice of an evangelical life according to the counsels, and they exhibit the vocation to holiness and to basic Gospel values which is open to all disciples of the Lord. They encourage others to achieve holiness in the world and are a specific instance of new charisms and services for the renewal of society. And they provide an encouragement to those in the religious life.

QUESTIONS: PART 1

1. How is the consecrated life perceived and evaluated today, particularly in reference to the public profession of the evangelical counsels of chastity, poverty and obedience?

2. What important aspects of the spiritual life should be present in the consecrated life?

3. Name the positive and negative factors involved in living and bearing witness to the communal dimension of consecrated life.

4. From the perspective of each institute's proper charism and the spirit of the founder, what urgent concerns of the consecrated life need attention, so as to bring about each institute's authentic witness to the Spirit in service to the Church in today's world?

5. What are the greatest difficulties today facing consecrated women and men in offering an authentic Gospel witness to their special consecration in the midst of the People of God?

6. What important possibilities and problems exist today in certain forms of consecrated life, particularly in monastic life, in communities totally dedicated to the contemplative life?

7. What important possibilities and problems exist in lay congregations today?

8. Consecrated life for women is affected today by the attention given to the woman question, woman's vocation and her role in the Church and in the world. What opportunities and problems are being revealed in this area?

9. How are secular institutes present today in the Church and in society with their proper values? What are the most important opportunities and difficulties facing members of secular institutes in offering their specific witness as consecrated lay people in the universal Church and in the local Church?

10. In what specific ways are societies of apostolic life present today in the Church and in society, and what characteristic problems do they have.

11. Are there new forms of consecrated life in your country? Describe their spiritual, communal and apostolic life. What values and problems exist in the area of ecclesial discernment? Are there other expressions of evangelical life which deserve special discernment and guidance

Religious Life in the Church and the World Today

RELIGIOUS LIFE APPROACHING THE YEAR 2000

25. In the last decade religious life has changed considerably because of changes in the Church and rapid changes in modern society.

It is generally agreed that as the year 2000 approaches religious life is facing a new phase in its evolution, having lived through a particularly significant period in the last hundred years. At the beginning of the century religious life underwent a spiritual reawakening, an expansion into new geographic areas and an increase in numbers: then in the next fifty years it developed and became more consolidated in its life, laws and work; the Second Vatican Council called the religious life to a profound renewal in its spiritual life and apostolate (See PC, 2-3). Today, after the period of conciliar renewal and adaptation of legislative texts and of structures, the religious life is experiencing a new phase in its history.

The celebration of the Ninth Ordinary General Assembly of the Synod of Bishops is a suitable occasion to undertake an objective assessment of the present situation, so that religious life might receive from the pastors of the Church, gathered together, the necessary help to maintain the vibrancy of its life and works, and to look confidently to the future.

Religious life is not everywhere in equally good shape. We need to ascertain its weak points and its strong points if our reflection is to be confident and objective. In this way, everyone would be helped to overcome what might be obstacles to living the religious life and would be helped to respond to new challenges.

FRUITS OF RENEWAL

26. An evaluation of religious life over the last ten years should be done in the light of the principles of renewal and adaptation contained in the decree *Perfectae Caritatis*, number 24, with which the Second Vatican Council encouraged a renewal of the life and rules of institutes. Though it is difficult to discover how faithfully these principles have been observed over all, it can be said that in the last ten years religious life has seen substantial advance in terms of activities, perseverance in prayer, study, communal dialogue and concrete commitments.

Generally speaking, the following positive results seem to have been achieved:

a) A clearer understanding of religious life's biblical and theological foundations, and *its relationship to Christ, the Holy Spirit and the Church*. This awareness prompted a renewal in the theology of the religious life, beginning with the biblical bases of consecration and of the evangelical counsels, and led to an effective renewal of religious life and a clearer perception of its values. Individuals are more aware of the need to have recourse to God's Word, to practice *lectio divina* and to seek silence so as to dedicate themselves to prayer and contemplation. These values find renewed application in initial and ongoing formation to the religious life.

b) A clearer *understanding of the liturgy and better celebration of it*, as part of the Church's over-all liturgical renewal, which has led to a better appreciation, by the majority of religious, of the celebration of the Eucharist in common and the Liturgy of the Hours as essential moments of community life.

c) A greater acceptance of *the meaning of community life*, with its Gospel demands and its forms of effective familial and spiritual interaction. This has meant that people are valued more than structures, attention is paid to the needs of individual members of communities, a sense of personal commitment and co-responsibility has been developed, as has a community life based on more mature, simple and genuine interpersonal relationships.

d) A greater awareness of the *charismatic aspect* of each institute's life and work, together with the study and rediscovery of each institute's foundational charism and origins, of its spirituality and mission, more in harmony with its original spirit and adapted to the needs of the Church.

e) A keener *ecclesial sense of the religious life*, which finds expression in more generous sharing in apostolic activity, thanks to the rediscovery of a sense of the Church in the lives of founders and the development of new relationships of communion and collaboration with priests and the laity.

f) The last decade has seen signs of the presence of God in history, in genuine models of sanctity and the apostolic life, and in the remarkable witness of charitable activities for those who are most in need. An additional extraordinary sign in our times is the *supreme witness*, especially in mission territories, of men and women religious *martyred* because if their dedication to Christ and to others.

NEW DIMENSIONS OF THE CONSECRATED LIFE

27. In tracing the path taken by the Church in the last ten years one is aware of new

tendencies in religious life which constitute the new developments, the *res novae*, of the present situation in the Church. Among these are certain elements of major importance:

a) With the development of a *theology of the local Church* and the awareness that the religious life belongs to the mystery of the universal Church which is made present in the local Church, new attitudes of participation and communion are developing among its members. Such attitudes are finding expression in a keener awareness of belonging to the diocesan family, a more visible presence in it, and a more active and concrete involvement in pastoral activity.

b) Over the last ten years *communication and collaboration among the various institutes of religious life and societies of apostolic life* have increased, thanks to the establishment of international, national, regional and diocesan bodies and a keener awareness of communion between institutes with different founding charisms. Such collaboration is also shown in the initiatives being taken in spiritual and pastoral programmes, including inter-congregational formation. Such formation must be authentic and must have positive results. That is to say, it must encourage fellowship between all who share the same ecclesial vocation to the religious life, each individual retaining the identity given by his or her own institute. To ensure this, such formation must conform to the directives published by the Holy See. (See *Potissimum Institutioni*, 2 February 1990).

c) Of importance is the *increase in the number of vocations in younger Churches and in Eastern Europe*, not only because existing charisms are thus spreading further afield, but also because abundant new charisms are appearing in some countries: indigenous institutes committed to service of the local Church.

d) A new *sensitivity towards the oppressed and marginalised*. More attention is being given to ethnic minorities and where new kinds of poverty exist in contemporary society this has led to the adoption of new forms of apostolic and missionary activity, in new areas of the apostolate. This is a concrete response to the demands of evangelical charity and justice, in keeping with particular charisms and out of a desire to make the Church present and active among the 'least' of men and women, with whom Christ himself is mystically identified.

NEGATIVE ASPECTS

28. A realistic assessment of the strengths and weaknesses in the religious life should take note of the problems which still remain, nor can they be ignored during the preparation for the Synod and when it takes place.

a) In certain institutes or in certain places there are signs, among individuals and groups, of *discontent* with changes in constitutions and departure from past practices. Many assert that balance has not been achieved between the different aspects of religious life, in a style of life authentically renewed in its spiritual values, especially in liturgy and prayer, asceticism, obedience, poverty, the common life, and apostolic commitment.

b) In some sectors of religious life there are symptoms of *individualism and secularism,* contrary to the meaning of consecration and the pursuit of perfection. A levelling of standards of deportment and a lessening of the content of spiritual and community life has resulted in a certain loss of identity in charism and activity, which has meant a less effective public witness of religious life in society.

c) Regretfully, there are some instances of tension with the hierarchy and *manifestations of dissent in both theory and practice* in relation to authority and the Magisterium of the Apostolic See and bishops, or in the celebration of the liturgy, all of which is contrary to the ecclesial nature of the religious life, the proper communion with the pastors of the Church and the submission owed to them.

d) Certain countries have a serious problem with regard to vocations. The continuing decrease in the number of religious available for apostolic work, which has led to the abandonment of certain apostolic activities, means that *some institutes are in danger of extinction.* This situation ought to be faced with realism and discernment because of the series of problems which arise on the personal and pastoral level. In the area of vocations, young men and women at times display a lack of enthusiasm for present forms of religious life, while seeking to return to more traditional ones, or to newer simpler forms of service to the local Church.

In the light of these real problems it is right that inquiry be made into their causes and that action be taken to remedy them.

THE QUESTIONABLE AND THE CHALLENGING IN MODERN SOCIETY

29. It might at first sight seem a contradiction in terms to speak of the positive and negative aspects of the religious life. However, this is how things are today. The reason for it, in part, is the emergence of new developments in society some of whose effects are positive, while others are questionable. The following are a few instances.

a) The cult of freedom, the assertion of human rights, and the increasing drive towards democracy today at all levels, have had their influence on the religious life. Where on the one hand these phenomena have highlighted the centrality of the human person, on the other they have also spawned individualism and have lowered esteem for authority and Church discipline.

b) Movements towards political and social emancipation, resulting in an awareness of economic inequality between the rich and the poor, and the existence of oppressive economic structures in certain capitalistic systems and totalitarian regimes, have moved more sensitive religious in certain areas to make a preferential commitment to the poor, based on an assessment of facts and the concrete social situation. Nevertheless, this has not always been done with due Gospel discernment; on the contrary, sometimes the situation itself and social action are taken as the only basis for understanding the nature of religious life and its apostolic service in the Church and in the world.

c) The emergence of new cultures and awareness that local Churches are rooted in people's own cultures have led to a search for forms of religious life which are more in tune with people's traditional values, coupled with a commitment to live with poorer people and in indigenous cultures and communities, frequently in marginalised communities, thus inserting the Gospel more deeply in such places, especially since vocations are especially flourishing in the younger Churches. Nevertheless, in some cases the abundance of new vocations in third world countries where there is great ecclesial vitality, combined with the scarcity of new vocations in the first world, has led some institutes to seek out native vocations at the cost of removing them from the environment suited to their way of life and apostolate, often causing problems in their formation.

d) The improvement in the status of women, one of the signs of the times, has had notable effects in the religious life of women, especially in certain countries. Thus, women religious are present in ways more in keeping with their dignity and mission, and endeavours are under way to put their special gifts to greater use in the life of the Church. However, in some cases a mistaken idea of feminism has laid claim to the right to participate in the life of the Church in ways which are not in keeping with the hierarchical structure willed by Christ.

e) The growing secularisation of life and structures, materialism and practical atheism which dominates in many countries, the misuse of the media, the weakening of the faith, the break-up of the family — all these have a negative effect on religious life. Religious often feel themselves immersed in a world which is at odds with their ideals. In such a situation they are expected to give a positive and Gospel-inspired response to the new legitimate expressions of the modern age, but at the same time, on a personal and social level, *they must resist the evil in the world, and not be overwhelmed by it*. They are called to bear witness to the gospel and the glorious cross of the Lord, the one means of transforming the world and its structures. Indeed, religious have today the crucial problem of confronting the impact of the modern age and the 'post-modern' culture on society, an impact which is deeply contrary to evangelical values. This must be done without losing the fervour of their consecration; on the contrary, religious must draw from it the capacity to react in fidelity to the Gospel and the prophetic dimension which is expressed in the call to conversion. Today's world needs evangelisers of God's love and heralds of transcendence and the supernatural, who bear decisive witness to the eschatological sense of life, culture and work, to the obligation to do good to others, offering to this world the spirit of the beatitudes and the charisms of the Holy Spirit, who leads history towards the Kingdom.

f) The general search for religion and transcendence in life, the desire for God, the need which they young have for silence and prayer and which is often expressed in a vague religious experience or leads to their being proselytised by the sects — all this challenges religious to offer a clear response to our world in a way of life which is spiritual, genuinely evangelical and ecclesial. The great spiritual traditions of religious life, especially those of the monastic and contemplative life, can make an invaluable contribution, in an appropriate pastoral program of Christian spirituality, to the spiritual renewal of society. The spiritual life of the laity, especially of those in certain movements and Church associations, is a stimulus to the renewal of the religious life.

g) The charisms of religious life are being called upon today — inspired by the spirit of the founder — to serve as the basis for new commitments and responses in Christian charity to the *new and older kinds of poverty* in our world. The necessary preferential love for the poor, as set forth in the Magisterium, is a constant call to religious to make renewed efforts in the field of charity and justice. The new poor call upon and challenge religious today. There are also many young people who are misled and deluded by modern culture, or who live the life of hopeless poverty which is typical of many third-world countries. These also need education, someone in their midst, guidance, dialogue and communion to bring about a new life-culture and hope for the future.

THE VARIETY OF GEOGRAPHIC AND CULTURAL SITUATIONS

30. The state of religious life varies from place to place. The experience of religious and their apostolic activity depend on how the Church fares in this or that place as well as on social and cultural conditions. Without intending to give an exhaustive description of the many varied geographic and cultural situations, one needs to look at certain problems and constants which await supplemental information to be supplied by the consultation in preparation for the Synod.

a) There are serious problems in some western countries. Especially noteworthy is the void created both by the scarcity of vocations and by departures from the religious life. Religious are changing to new ministries and new forms of presence where increasing socialisation has resulted in some apostolic activities being taken under State control, either totally or in part. Many institutes have consequently felt obliged to attempt a re-organisation of their activities, to seek the collaboration of the laity, to extend their apostolic activity in the pastoral and missionary field into new kinds of presence and various other areas in the apostolate. In this situation, thanks to international and national collaborative organisations formed by religious, there is an increased sharing of information as religious face problems together and search for solutions.

b) Especially noteworthy is the very promising revival of the religious life in some Eastern European countries which have emerged from totalitarian communism but have not yet achieved political, economic and social stability. In many of these countries there has been, for all practical purposes, an actual rebirth of religious life. Religious communities which have remained faithful for so long and have sometimes paid for their faithfulness with their lives have been getting vocations. These communities need theological updating and ecclesial renewal. In accord with the bishops, new modes of presence have to be sought which would combine the common life and apostolic commitment with a special mission for the renewal of society. In countries where the majority of the population belong to other Christian Churches, one expects the religious, bearing in mind the richness of Eastern monasticism, to make an appropriate contribution to ecumenical activity.

c) Religious life in the younger Churches (See AG, 18, 40) is of particular interest, though it differs from place to place. New institutes are coming into existence in the framework of native culture and, frequently, of the local Church. By all accounts these are most promising developments, which must be promoted and nurtured until they achieve maturity in their way of life and their activities, opening themselves towards the universal Church, which is in the nature of the religious life. A basic problem today is that of achieving the right balance between people's identity as religious and their own culture. Religious who live among people of different traditional religions also face the problem of inculturation. In other words, they need to be able to proclaim the Gospel, celebrate the liturgy and practise the spirituality deriving from their own ascetical traditions in a way that would promote inter-religious dialogue, without prejudice to their own Catholic identity.

d) Finally, in some countries there are many religious who still live under hostile political regimes. They are not free to live in community, to profess publicly that they are believers and religious, nor to engage in apostolic work on behalf of Church and society. These brothers and sisters should not be neglected in prayer and in familial help during the preparation for the Synod and its celebration.

CONTINUING IN THE PATH OF RENEWAL

31. One of the basic calls which the Church addresses to religious today is that to continuous spiritual renewal, with special emphasis on the following:

a) The fact that the renewal of religious life is still incomplete is a reminder to all that religious consecration, with its Gospel demands of love of Christ, imitation of his life and dedication to his kingdom, is a never-ending journey. It should involve a constant striving after the holiness to which religious are called. They are invited to give thanks for the gift which they have received, in an attitude of continuing conversion, in accordance with St Paul's exhortation: 'I urge you then, brothers and sisters, remembering the mercies of God, to offer your bodies as a living sacrifice, dedicated and acceptable to God; that is the kind of worship for you, as sensible people. Do not model your behaviour on the contemporary world, but let the renewing of your minds transform you, so that you may discern for yourselves what is the will of God — what is good and acceptable and mature' (Rom 12:1-2)

b) Consecration and the public profession of the vows of chastity, poverty and obedience, demand an *appropriate life-style,* authentic in its supernatural motivation, true in its ascetic demands, rich in diverse complementary aspects, and lived in communities where there is proper community life and holy rivalry. Witnessing publicly that one is a religious and acts as a religious involves wearing a religious habit, in accordance with the prescriptions of the Church and one's institute.

c) All are agreed about the originality of the Council's teaching, which has led to a better understanding of founders' charisms, and this should find expression in a spiritual commitment and an active presence. The spirit of the founders will thus be made more vibrant and active, as will the patrimony of each institute, for the good of the Church. One will thus avoid a theoretical and practical interpretation which is at variance with the genuine spirit of the charism.

d) The renewal of religious life is achieved through an *intensification of communion and ecclesial service,* in keeping with the charism proper to each institute and the new needs of the Church and the world. Communion with the Pope and bishops is the guarantee of authenticity, so that all can participate actively and responsibly in the many endeavours undertaken in the life of the universal Church and in local Churches.

e) In this ongoing process of renewal the *service rendered by authority* has its own part to play: chapters of individual institutes, superiors — who should be authentic animators of spiritual and apostolic renewal — and each community. And one must not overlook the *obligation on each member* to live out his or her vocation and consecration in God's sight. The same can be said for each member's personal and binding responsibility to promote the faithfulness of all members to the institute's charism. The essential criterion here is faithfulness to the Constitutions approved by the Church, which provide the reference point and norm for conformity with the charism of each institute.

SOME IMPORTANT PROBLEMS

32. In addition to the need for continuous renewal, there are various problems in religious life, among them the following:

a) The promotion of *vocations and formation*. If the future of communities depends on renewal and the appropriate formation of their members, the vitality of religious life today depends on the promotion of vocations, together with prayer to the Master of the vineyard in whose gift is every vocation, and initial and ongoing theological, moral and spiritual formation of candidates. In this regard, attention should be drawn to the instruction Poti*ssimum Institutioni*. This provides a practical summary of the doctrinal foundations of formation, it covers matters requiring special attention, pedagogical guidelines, deals with contemporary problems and the needs of successive stages of the formation process, including ongoing formation. This last is of particular importance today in the spiritual renewal of religious. Because candidates sometimes display a certain fragility, lacking roots and a solid tradition, in their formation it is important to insist on basic human values and a true supernatural motivation. Important too is the integration of the different elements of formation, emotional maturity, the progressive assimilation of evangelical, religious and charismatic behaviour, and effective identification with the history and life of the institute (See Potissi*mum Institutioni*)

b) *Unity of consecration and mission*. Religious life, especially in institutes dedicated to the apostolic life, nowadays seeks the necessary unified way of life, in which a balance is achieved, without tensions and illusions, between all the values in an existence dedicated to the apostolate. What is looked for is a harmony between all the essential elements: consecration and mission; particular charism and elements common to all religious life; personal responsibility, communion and obedience; membership of the universal Church and service to the local Church. The secret of this unity of life, for the fulfilment of God's will in one's vocation, is constant commitment to an organised spiritual life which combines liturgy and personal prayer, asceticism and the employment of whatever is required for one's life and apostolate, the common life and apostolic dedication, without prejudice to one or other of them. Such a unity of life calls for an intense theological life based on contemplation, with a firm commitment to the institute's ideal and constant exercise of real personal and communal discernment, achieved by traditional or new forms of asceticism and familial correction.

c) Inculturation. Another fundamental problem today is inculturation, which is the subject of discussion in the Church and is given added importance by the increasing number of indigenous religious in younger Churches. Religious and members of other institutes have always promoted people's authentic values, grafted onto the riches of Gospel revelation. One needs however to note the change which has taken place. There was a time when it was religious from the First World who transmitted essential values and a way of life. Nowadays, however, it is the new religious in the younger Churches who are endeavouring to incarnate and to transmit their own values. Dialogue and the exchange of gifts within the catholicity of the Church (See LG, 13) are needed so that, in communion and unity, genuine riches might be revealed in their splendour, making it possible for a variety of charisms to take root in different places and cultures, thus ushering in a new flowering of religious values and forms of religious life. The instruction of John Paul II in the encyclical Redemptoris Missio offers clear and sound teaching on this matter.

33. On the threshold of the third millennium the celebration of the Synod provides an occasion for all members of the Church, and especially for religious, to reconsider their own renewal in the light of current challenges and opportunities. Their dynamic communion with their founders calls them to maximum generosity in putting themselves at the service of Christ, in harmony with the common apostolic mission and with that 'element of real originality in the spiritual life of the Church along with fresh initiatives for action' (MR, F2, p. 217-218) which belong to each authentic charism. If these founders were alive today they would not fail to respond to the Church's appeal for a renewal of evangelical life, a deep spirituality and a generous involvement in the new evangelisation.

QUESTIONS: PART II

12. In your view, to what extent has the renewal of religious life according to Vatican II been realised, and what are its most notable results? What are the positive elements of the renewal? What are the negative aspects and their causes?

13. What means exist for promoting and achieving a decisive spiritual and apostolic renewal in the religious life, while maintaining the necessary 'unity between consecration and mission'? What challenges of society deserve an appropriate response?

14. The problem of vocations is becoming quite serious in some countries. What are the external and internal causes underlying the decrease in vocations and the lack of perseverance? What problems and solutions exist for the promotion of vocations?

15. What are the possibilities and problems existing today in the field of initial, ongoing and inter-congregational formation?

16. What aspects of the inculturation of the religious life deserve to be examined? What are its perennial values and possible cultural enrichments?

17. How are the problems treated which result from the drop in numbers in communities and the abandonment of ministries, especially those which have a valid social significance in education and health-care? How is the closing down of an institute dealt with or its difficulty in surviving?

The Role of Religious Life

1. THE CONSECRATED LIFE IN CHURCH COMMUNION

34. 'The ecclesiology of communion is the central and fundamental concept in the council documents' (Christifideles Laici, 19). The Extraordinary Synod of 1985, celebrated twenty years after the council, recalled what the Church had said about itself in the Second Vatican Council. The celebration of the next Synod ought to lead to a better understanding of the vocation and role of religious within the organic communion of the Church, where there are different yet complementary vocations, conditions in life, ministries, charisms and responsibilities. In this way, religious institutes and the societies of apostolic life, and all their members, will be able to give expression to their organic communion with the entire Church

and place their unique charismatic gifts at its service.

ECCLESIAL DIMENSION OF THE RELIGIOUS LIFE

35. The Second Vatican Council has highlighted the ecclesial meaning of religious life: that it belongs to the Church's mystery and mission. In the mystery of Church-communion, religious life 'is a special way of sharing in the sacramental nature of the People of God' (MR, 10: F2, p. 217). Taking their place in the mission of the Church religious put all the graces of their life, their Gospel witness and unique apostolic works at the service of the Gospel.

Lumen Gentium states: 'Being means to and instruments of love, the evangelical counsels unite those who practice them to the Church in a special way. It follows that the spiritual life of such Christians should be dedicated also to the welfare of the entire Church. To the extent of their capacities and in keeping with the particular kind of religious life to which they are individually called, whether it be one of prayer or of active labour as well, they have the duty of working for the implanting and strengthening of the kingdom of God in souls and for spreading it to the four corners of the earth. It is for this reason that the distinctive character of the various religious institutes is preserved and fostered by the Church' (LG 44: F1, p. 404)

The decree *Perfectae caritatis* has several times emphasised the duty of religious to participate in the life of the Church, in all its undertakings and in various areas of activity: biblical, liturgical, dogmatic, pastoral, ecumenical, missionary and social (PC, 2, c). Awareness of being a part of the Church-communion and of being at the service of the Church ought to characterise the vocation, formation and the entire life of all religious, in their different missions, contemplative and apostolic, as the decree itself states (See ibid. 7-11).

The ecclesial character of the religious life and the theological and practical implications of being part of the Church-communion have been fully treated in the document Mutuae *Relationes*. The teaching and the norms given there are still applicable today even if now, given the understanding of Church-communion and mission as well as the contents of the exhortation *Christifideles Laici*, there is a need to extend these 'mutual relations' to include the laity as well.

Religious, as well as others who live the consecrated life, develop and manifest a genuine ecclesial sense, not only their consciousness of *being with and in the Church*, but also in their consciousness of *being Church*, identifying themselves with it, in full communion with its doctrine, its life, its pastors, its faithful and its mission in the world (*Potissimum Institutioni*, 21-24). In this way they will be 'people who experience communion', witnesses and builders in God's plan of communion, which is at the summit of all human history. All this will be achieved through that same communion of life, prayer, and apostolate which renders them signs of familial communion in the midst of the People of God (See 'Religious and Human Advancement': F2, pp 260-284).

COMMUNION AND OBEDIENCE TO THE POPE AND BISHOPS

36. The ecclesial character of the religious life is expressed and realised through a special bond with the Petrine ministry, which ought to be concretely manifested in a relationship of loving communion and obedience to the Roman Pontiff, who

is the 'perpetual and visible source and foundation of the unity both of the bishops and the whole company of the faithful' (LG, 23: F1, p. 376). 'Institutes of religious life, in as much as they are dedicated in a special way to the service of God and of the entire Church, are subject to the supreme authority of this same Church in a special manner. Individual members are also bound to obey the Supreme Pontiff as their highest superior by reason of the sacred bond of obedience' (CIC, 590).

In virtue of this special bond: 'In order the better to provide for the good of institutes and the needs of the apostolate, the Supreme Pontiff, by reason of his primacy over the universal Church and considering the common good, can exempt institutes of religious life from the governance of local ordinaries and subject them either to himself alone or to another ecclesial authority' (CIC, 591; see LG, 45). This special relationship between religious and the Holy Father ought to be translated into a deep spiritual communion with his person, submission to his Magisterium, total and ready acceptance of his directives and a generous co-operation in his ministry as pastor of the universal Church, which he exercises through the competent departments of the Apostolic See.

A recent document from the Apostolic See has emphasised the importance of the universal dimension of the religious life in the ecclesiology of communion and has highlighted its basis in relation to the Petrine ministry: 'in the context of the Church understood as communion, consideration should also be given to the many institutes and societies which have the charisms of religious life and apostolic life, with which the Holy Spirit enriches the Mystical Body of Christ. Although these do not belong to the hierarchical structure of the Church, they belong to her life and holiness. Given their supra-diocesan character, rooted in the Petrine ministry, all these ecclesial realities are also elements at the service of communion among the various local Churches' (Congregation of the Doctrine of the Faith).

37. Religious and members of societies of apostolic life 'in fulfilling the duty towards the Church inherent in their particular form of life must show respect and obedience towards bishops in accordance with canon law, both because these exercise pastoral authority in their individual Churches, and because this is necessary for unity and harmony in the carrying out of apostolic work' (LG, 45: F1, p. 404). Such a relationship supposes, on the one hand, the just autonomy of institutes which these same Ordinaries ought to safeguard and protect (See CIC, 586), and, on the other, submission to the authority of the bishops, especially with regard to the tenets of the Faith (See ibid, 753), the care of souls, the public exercise of divine worship and the other works of the apostolate according to the prescriptions of law (See ibid, 678).

Bishops too have a role in promoting religious life: 'It is the duty of bishops, as authentic teachers and guides of perfection for all the members of the diocese, likewise to be the guardians of fidelity to the religious vocation in the spirit of each institute. In the exercise of this pastoral duty, the bishops shall take care to promote relations with religious superiors, to whom the religious are subject in a spirit of faith, in open communion of doctrine and practice with the Supreme Pontiff, the offices of the Holy See, and with the other bishops and local Ordinaries. Bishops, with their clergy, should be staunch advocates of the religious life, defenders of religious communities, promoters of vocations and firm guardians of the specific character of each religious family, both in the spiritual and in the apostolic field' (MR, 28: F2, p. 228)

STRUCTURES FOR COORDINATION

38. To foster communion among the institutes of religious life and societies of apostolic life and to establish opportune contacts and co-operation with episcopal conferences as well as with individual bishops, certain co-ordinating structures are very important.

Among these structures of co-ordination mention needs to be made in the first place of the conferences, unions or councils of superiors general which exist on the world, regional or national level. Their task is: to further the achievement of each institute's goal, while always safeguarding each one's autonomy; to foster each institute's nature and spirit: and to promote a more fruitful collaboration among all institutes for the good of the Church. Such conferences and councils are erected by the Apostolic See, which also approves their statutes (See PC, 23; CIC, 708-709).

In the relations between such conferences and councils, as well as with their respective episcopal conferences and individual bishops, much depends on a correct and exemplary sense of hierarchical communion, not only in the solution of common problems but also in the cooperation of all for the common good of the Church.

RELIGIOUS LIFE IN THE LOCAL CHURCH

39. The dependence of religious on the Roman Pontiff clearly manifests the universal dimension of the religious life. The submission to bishops which is required of them and their dedication to the service of local Churches give concrete expression to the testimony and apostolic service which they render in the midst of the People of God. 'The local Church is the historical space in which a vocation is exercised in concrete form and it fulfils its apostolic responsibility. It is here, within the ambit of a definite culture, that the Gospel is preached and received" (MR, 23: F2, pp.225-226). On the other hand, the presence of the charisms of the religious life in the local Church assists everyone — clergy and faithful — to open themselves to the universal and missionary dimension of the Church, and through the presence of the gifts of the Spirit, makes the local Churches an image of the universal Church.

From the very beginning of his pontificate Pope John Paul II described this relationship in speaking to superiors general: 'Wherever you are in the world, with your vocation for the universal Church, you are, because of your mission, in a given local Church. Therefore your vocation for the universal Church is realised in the structures of the local Church. Every effort must be made to ensure that religious life may develop in the individual local Churches, in order that it may contribute to their spiritual upbuilding, in order that it may constitute their particular strength. Unity with the universal Church, through the local Church, that is your way' (Discourse to Superiors General, 24 November 1978).

The decree Christus Dom*inus* describes a special relationship between religious and the local Church when it says that because of what they are religious priests belong to the diocesan presbyterate, as wise collaborators in the episcopal order. It further states that the other members of institutes of religious life, both men and women, belong to the diocesan family and make a noteworthy contribution to the hierarchy (See Christus Dom*inus*, 34: F1, p. 584)

40. To ensure an organic inclusion of religious in the local Church it is necessary to observe the recommendations in the decree Christus *Dominus,* the directives of the document *Mutuae Relationes* and the norms of canon law cited above. Among these recommendations the following should be kept in mind: the principle of obedience to the pastors of the Church, faithfulness by religious to the nature of their institute and submission to their own superiors, which the bishops themselves ought to recommend, the legitimate autonomy of institutes, co-ordination and collaboration with the clergy and the faithful of the diocese, and an appropriate participation of religious in presbyteral and pastoral councils (See MR, 52-59: F2, pp 238-241).

The harmonious presence of religious in the life and programmes of the local Church presupposes a mutual understanding which is fostered by a study of the theology of the local Church and an effective interest in its life, as well as an adequate knowledge of the theology and role of the religious life through an appreciation of its various charisms and apostolic services (See ibid, 29)

The document Mutuae Relationes states: 'Between the diocesan clergy and religious communities, efforts should be made to create new bonds of fraternity and co-operation. Great importance should therefore be attached to such ways and means, including simple and informal ones, as may serve to increase mutual trust, apostolic solidarity and 'fraternal harmony'. This will not only bring to mind the right idea of the local Church, but it will encourage each one joyfully to render or request assistance, to look for increased cooperation and to cherish the human and ecclesial community in whose life each one is inserted as the fatherland of one's vocation' (MR, 37: F2, p. 232)

Because of the pastoral needs which have led many institutes to accept parish ministry in dioceses, it is particularly urgent today to safeguard the necessary balance between the parochial ministry and each institute's life, particular charism, spirituality and discipline— this for the sake not only of the institutes themselves but of the entire diocese. But this is not enough. It would be a grave impoverishment of religious life, and of the local Church itself, to limit the contribution of institutes to that of the parochial ministry only, without encouraging and welcoming the richness of their spirituality and their proper charismatic service. In reference to religious priests Pope John Paul II has recently stated: 'Priests who belong to religious orders and congregations represent a spiritual enrichment for the entire diocesan presbyterate, to which they contribute specific charisms and special ministries, stimulating the local Church by their presence to be more fully open to the Church throughout the world' (*Pastores Dabo Vobis,* 31). Members of other institutes of consecrated life and of societies of apostolic life ought to offer their unique contribution to pastoral activity, in keeping with their proper charism and the needs of the local Church.

IN COMMUNION WITH THE LAY FAITHFUL

41. As previously stated, a renewed ecclesiology of communion has brought about a closer communion between religious and the laity. This was clearly seen during the celebration of the Synod on the laity and was explicitly mentioned on several occasions in the apostolic exhortation Christfideles Laici.

It should be remembered that the religious life, particularly in some of its forms, was always notably close to the people, especially through the pastoral ministry, and an orientation towards service of the people. What is new about the relationship with the laity today comes rather from a renewed experience of communion arising from a commonly shared baptismal dignity, the universal call to holiness, the rediscovery that everyone is called to a new evangelisation and from closer pastoral collaboration. The rediscovery of the vocation and mission of the laity in the Church, in turn, ought to lead to a more authentic living of the different yet complementary vocation of the religious life.

It can also be stated that the same theology of Church-communion and mission set forth in the exhortation *Christifideles Laici* can and ought to lead to a better understanding of the vocation to the religious life and its fulfilment in the Church and in the world. In fact, the lengthy description of the participation of all the baptised in the priestly, prophetic and kingly office is awaiting further development in reflection and specific experiences within the context of the religious life (See *ibid* 14) The assertion that all are called to holiness (See ibid, 16) serves as an incentive to religious to respond faithfully to their own vocation and to help all the baptised so that they can respond to their call. The secular character of the laity is, in turn, a reminder that 'all the members of the Church are participants in her secular dimension, but in different ways' (15). It also recalls 'the significance of the earthly and temporal realities in the salvific plan of God' (55).

In the light of the principle of the complementarity of vocations and charisms in the Church, the same exhortation states: 'Priests and religious ought to assist the laity in their formation... In turn, the laity themselves can and should help priests and religious in the course of their spiritual and pastoral journey' (61). It is right, therefore, that the members of institutes of religious life and of societies of apostolic life, by reason of this reciprocity, remain open to the just expectations of the laity in what concerns their way of their life, their witness and their service in the midst of the People of God.

On the basis of these principles, the diverse reciprocal relationship with the laity in the Church ought to be encouraged. Today many lay groups have been formed whose members are bound under different titles to the spirituality and apostolic work of various institutes and participate in the same spiritual family (third orders, associations, volunteers...). In this way the communion between the laity and religious in the Church is expressed; on the one hand, they are able to enrich their own lives with the spirituality proper to a religious family, and on the other, they contribute to the spread of the spirit of its charism in society. These same principles ought to lead to a better understanding of the laity's collaboration in apostolic and social works. Analogously speaking, the participation of religious in lay movements, as well as in spiritual and apostolic groups of the laity, ought to be seen in this same theological perspective, without detriment to the affiliation and discipline of these religious in relation to their proper institute (See *Potissimum Institutioni*, 92-93).

Religious Life in the Church's Mission

RELIGIOUS LIFE AND THE NEW EVANGELISATION

42. Nowadays the call to the new evangelisation is central to the mission of the

Church, involving everyone — clergy, religious and laity. In the coming years it will require the greatest effort and the best planning to achieve this. In this regard, religious institutes and societies of apostolic life ought to cooperate, each according to its unique charism and apostolic service.

One of the essential tasks of religious life at the present moment is to become fully involved in the new evangelisation. Those who are called to live the Gospel experience ought to take upon themselves the work of making the Gospel known in today's world.

Women and men religious, especially, who have given themselves totally to God for the sake of the Kingdom, ought to be the first to undertake the task of a new evangelisation, putting to work, in accordance with their profound communion with Christ, the best talents and energies deriving from their spiritual and apostolic charisms. It must not be forgotten that 'the apostolate of all religious consists first in their witness of a religious life which they are bound to foster by prayer and penance' (CIC, 673).

The members of secular institutes, according to their specific form of consecration in the midst of the world, are called upon to put their most genuine apostolic efforts at the service of Christ and his Kingdom.

Arising from the vitality of communion with Christ, the new evangelisation demands a witness which can lead to a renewal of charismatic fervour. It requires a profound renewal in proclamation and ministries, achieved in perfect ecclesial communion, in such a way as to make the new evangelisation really 'new'. The new evangelisation today also urges adoption of that 'boldness in initiatives" (MR, 12: F2, p. 218), characteristic of that authentic apostolic creativity which is among the charisms of the Spirit. It will be new in its methods also. In the first place, it calls for a commitment to live the Gospel which one preaches, and to incarnate it in one's personal life and in the life of one's community, in such wise that the proclamation of the Good News might be sustained by the very strength of a Gospel witness. The more that religious evangelise by means of the dynamic and irresistible energy of the light and warmth of the truth and charity of Christ, so much more effectively will their lives witness to the Gospel they profess.

43. One should remember, first of all, the call to the new evangelisation *ad gentes*, made by John Paul II in the encyclical *Redemptoris Missio* and addressed to all institutes of both contemplative and apostolic life, in virtue of their total dedication to the service of the Church, in keeping with their nature and mission (See *Redemptoris Missio*, 69-70). A still more pressing invitation was issued by the Holy Father to institutes of men and women whose special charism involves mission (See ibid, 65-66). The mission *ad gentes* is fundamental to proclaiming Christ, a work which has not yet been completely finished, not only in nations still awaiting the proclamation of the Gospel of salvation, but also in nations which have for centuries accepted the proclamation of Christ. A renewed enthusiasm to be present and at work among people is necessary in these nations so as to bring the Gospel to bear on people and places, according to particular situations and the needs of society.

There is no need to limit the new evangelisation to the initial proclamation of the Gospel or to a pastoral programme of Christian initiation. Everywhere there is a need to remake the Christian fabric of human society. In this work religious have an urgent task and serious responsibility. What is also needed today is a more thorough knowledge of catechetical teachings, and a proclamation of the truth of the Gospel in the midst of the greatest problems of human existence, that is, the relationship of all to God, the Creator and Redeemer, respect for life, the dignity of the person, and the universal distribution of goods. This should be done in such wise that the truth of the Gospel might throw light on today's serious moral problems. Furthermore, it is also necessary to promote the maturing of the Christian experience for individuals and groups through pastoral programmes of spirituality, rich in initiatives. The new evangelisation should develop the Christian vocation of all the People of God, should encourage response to the universal call to holiness and form authentic apostles of Christ for our world. The spiritual and apostolic legacy of institutes of religious life and of societies of apostolic life should be directed towards this particular service of the faithful as a contribution to the new evangelisation.

The promotion of the unity of all the baptised is the task of the new evangelisation, so that the witness of all Christ's disciples, united in accordance with his desire and priestly prayer, might prompt the return to the Father's house of all God's children scattered throughout the world. Religious have a special role in this ecumenical task, in dialogue with similar spiritual experiences of those in other Churches and Christian confessions, in a spiritual ecumenism of conversion, prayer, dialogue and mutual edification, always in keeping with their proper identity in the faith and their charism.

Depending on the diverse circumstances where the institutes of religious life and societies of apostolic life are called to work, such a task also includes dialogue with the followers of other religions, where the 'monastic' life, dedicated to asceticism and contemplation, is often found. The goal of the new evangelisation is the will of God, 'who desires all to be saved and to come to the knowledge of the truth' (I Tim 2:4). The proclamation of Christ in word and action to individuals and to all humanity is in line with his own sentiments and looks to the fulfilment of his prayer: 'that all may be one.., so that the world may believe' (Jn 17:21,23), The institutes of religious life and societies of apostolic life are called to give themselves generously to this task.

THE ROLE OF THE RELIGIOUS LIFE IN THE WORLD

44 The Second Vatican Council states. 'Let no one think that their consecrated way of life alienates religious from other people or makes them useless for human society. Though in some cases they have no direct relations with their contemporaries, still in a deeper way they have their fellow men and women present with them in the heart of Christ and cooperate with them spiritually, so that the building up of human society may always have its foundation in the Lord and have him as its goal: otherwise those who build it may have laboured in vain' (LG, 46: F1, 406). Considerable tasks face religious in today's world. The Church appeals to them to undertake these tasks in the spirit of the Gospel for the renewal of society. What is needed is an apostolic presence geared to evangelisation, the authentic expression of the Church's pastoral activity.

a) A specific *witness of God's love in the world*. There is a spiritual presence of religious, of contemplatives especially, whose prayer bears fruit in society. But, realistically, it must also be said that their presence is needed, as citizens of this world and pilgrims travelling towards the heavenly homeland (See Heb 13:14). With their charisms and services they seek to make effective *the Gospel of the beatitudes and the works of mercy.* Religious are present in our society today in a multiplicity of apostolic service to others, each institute with its own charism, a splendid expression of the charity of Christ. There is the work of religious for people's integral formation. There is education of children and young people; the care of the sick, the suffering, the elderly and those in want; help to people with special needs and to the marginalised. Some religious, in keeping with the spirit and regulations of their institute, are called to work for others in the professions (See 'Religious and Human Advancement': F2, p 265 ff).

b) *Care of young people.* Young people, the future of the Church and of humanity, offer much scope for initiatives by religious. In some First World countries young people live a life in which the search for high ideals encounters profound disillusionment with failed ideologies and surrender to short-lived substitutes from the world of entertainment and sports. They are often the unwitting victims of manipulation and exploitation, consumerism and facile pleasures leading to a dehumanised and degrading way of life. In other countries, especially in the Third World, young people face extreme poverty, unemployment, and with no future prospects because of lack of education and work. The love of Christ for young people, for their education and their total development is reflected in the special charisms sown by the Holy Spirit in the Church.

It has been mainly though not exclusively religious who have established Catholic schools. Many institutes, especially religious institutes, were founded for this purpose, at a time when the education of the young was threatened by hostile attitudes. Today there is still a need for this apostolate and for new and courageous educational ventures to be undertaken.

At the present time, when the example of the Holy Father, John Paul II, encourages everyone to take on the care of young people, those who have inherited a particular charism for education have a special responsibility. They are called upon to do their best to restart a dialogue with young people so as to form them after the heart of Christ, in an effective and attractive Gospel-based project.

c) *The preferential option for the poor.* This option has led many to make generous and dangerous choices. Religious life is certainly not inconsistent with an option for the Lord's poor. On the contrary, it has been a constant feature of the charisms of the apostolic life, often inspired by the words and actions of the Lord, who was sent 'to preach the Gospel to the poor' (Lk 4:18) and who invites people to practice the works of mercy to the 'least of these, my brothers and sisters', as if it were done to him (see Mt 25:40). In the last ten years the presence of communities among the poor and their involvement in places where misery and marginalisation are the norm have been the sign of a religious life which fully embraces not only poverty but the very life of the poor, their risks, their trials and their problems. Such an option, however, should be to the detriment neither of the essential elements of the religious life and of its charism, nor of the essential values of communion with God and with one's brothers and sisters. The option for the poor ought not to become the sole ideology, leading to internal divisions and causing dissent over doctrine and the norms of the pastors of the Church. Nor should it lead to choices incompatible with the life of faith and ecclesial communion (See *Libertatis Conscientia*)

d) *Presence in culture.* Over the centuries, religious institutes have considerably influenced the transmission and the formation of culture. This was true in the

Middle Ages, when Europe was being formed, when monasteries became places for the transmission of the cultural riches of the past and the formation of a new humanistic and Christian culture. This also happened whenever the light of the Gospel has shone for the first time on countries and cultures. Many religious have worked for the advancement of culture and have often defended indigenous cultures which they have studied and researched. Today what is particularly needed in the mission of the Church is work for the advancement of culture and the establishment of a dialogue between culture and faith capable of clarifying the great problems of society, which are fundamentally problems of culture and life. Granted the role of the laity, religious also have their proper task, especially those who through a special gift of the Spirit are called to promote dialogue between the Gospel and reason and human culture. They should endeavour to offer wise responses to the many problems and challenges of today's culture, in the area of philosophy, theology, scientific research and university studies. For this they should utilise the media and the Catholic universities and other institutions entrusted to their care.

e) *Meeting the needs of humanity according to God's plan.* At the same time, religious ought not to be unmindful of the Church's responsibility to safeguard the great values of nature and conscience, in accordance with the Gospel, in today's world. The cause of peace and justice, the defence of life, the fulfilment of the moral law engraved on the human conscience, the preservation of creation, all are values which ought to be defended and promoted, because they have their roots in the Gospels and in humanity. Religious, and some have been outstanding in this regard, ought to be particularly sensitive to these problems. Their communion and collaboration with the Magisterium of the Church in this area can be of great service in building a civilisation of love in communion with the laity, all the while respecting the laity's special contribution in the apostolate.

QUESTIONS: PART III

18. Describe relations between religious life and the Holy Father and his Magisterium.
19 Evaluate the communion between the consecrated life — that is, the institutes of religious life and the societies of apostolic life—and the bishops and their Magisterium. Give concrete examples.
20. How do the co-ordinating structures of the religious life function in your country at the level of international, regional or national conferences of major superiors? How do these structures relate to the Apostolic See and to the episcopal conference, respectively? How do they function in dioceses? How do they relate to the diocesan bishop.
21. Describe the presence and the participation of religious in the local Church. What are the main positive experiences and the main difficulties? How, in the concrete, is the universal dimension of religious life made a part of the exercise of each institute's charism and apostolic services in the local Church? Specifically, how is the presence of religious in the parochial ministry perceived and what problems does it pose?
22. How is the relationship between religious and the laity perceived and coordinated? Give examples of positive and negative experiences. What are the expectations of the laity with regard to the religious life and its presence and role

in the Church and in the world? In what ways is the multiform mutual relationship between those in the religious life and the laity encouraged?

23. If they are to participate more fully in the Church's mission what important tasks, what kinds of presence and what new strategies in the apostolate are needed by religious in view of the new evangelisation (in promoting better Church communion? in the mission ad gen*tes*, in ecumenism, in inter-religious dialogue, in culture and inculturation, etc.)?

24. What situations in today's society challenge religious to make new choices in fidelity to their life and their special charism? (in the works of an institute, in professional work done by individuals, in activities increasingly assumed by the State, in youth work, in the preferential option for the poor, in education, hospitals and charitable work, in the media, etc)

25. What other important aspects concerning religious life should be discussed during the Synod?

Conclusion

MARY, THE MODEL AND MOTHER OF THE RELIGIOUS LIFE

45. Under the influence of the Holy Spirit religious choose 'that kind of poor and virginal life which Christ the Lord chose for himself and which his Virgin Mother embraced also' (LG, 46: F1, p. 406), in union with St Joseph, himself an exceptional teacher both for those called to the contemplative life and for those called to the apostolate. Through the example of her virginal consecration and total dedication to the Lord, Mary adds a unique dimension to the religious life and makes visible a special profile of the Church.

The Virgin Mary, Mother of God, through her unconditional response to the divine call and her interior consecration by the Holy Spirit, is the model of vocation and total self-giving to God. Through the perfection with which she lived her virginity for the sake of the Kingdom, through her humility, evangelical poverty, and total obedience to God's plan, she is first among the Lord's disciples and an unparalleled example of the following of Christ the Lord. Through her total dedication to the mystery and mission of her son, she is a resplendent model of apostolic and ecclesial service. The charisms of the religious life shine forth in her life as in a mirror, making her the 'rule of conduct for all' (St. Ambrose, *De Virginibus*).

The Virgin Mary is often present at the origins of many expressions of the religious and apostolic life, as well as at the source of many calls to follow Christ. While numerous institutes bear the name of Mary in their title, all, guided by their founders, have spontaneously acknowledged the maternal presence of Mary as a source of communion in their midst and, implicitly or explicitly, have acknowledged some aspect of the life and mystery of Mary in their life-style and apostolate.

At this point in time religious are called upon to make a special effort at renewing their presence and role in the Church and in the world, with eyes fixed on Mary. As mother of the disciples of Jesus, Mary invites us to put into practice faithfully the words of her son (See Jn 2:5). Her maternal presence in the midst of the community, as at the beginning of the Church (see Acts 1:14), is the guarantee of faithfulness, renewal, and the communion of all in the Church. She ensures a more generous collaboration in the work of a new evangelisation, that is, in proclaiming salvation in Christ, the redeemer of humanity and centre of the cosmos and history.

A RENEWED PRESENCE OF CHRIST IN THE WORLD

46. Religious life in the Church, its charismatic variety and its apostolic richness, constitutes a special presence of the incarnate Word, crucified and risen. Through the influence of the Holy Spirit on the founders, he has wished to manifest in these multiple charisms various aspects of the Gospel, the power of its word and the richness of its mystery, so that the Mystical Body might show forth the multiform grace of Christ its head. The different experiences and forms of the religious life are charisms given by the one Spirit, fragments of a single Gospel, words of the unique Word which is the Word made flesh, different ways of making present in space and time the one mystery of the Lord. In our day also a particularly harmonious communion of those living the religious life in the Church can and should help to express better the fullness and richness of Christ, who is always present with his grace and power in our world.

Furthermore, in the basic unity arising from consecration and the extraordinary variety of charisms, 'the Church is not only well equipped for every good work and prepared for the work of her ministry unto the building-up of the Body of Christ, but also to appear adorned with the manifold gifts of her children, like a bride adorned for her spouse and to manifest in herself the multiform wisdom of God' (PC, 1: F1, p. 611). The variety of charisms of the religious life is also an indication of the beauty of the Church and the presence of the Spirit throughout her history.

Religious life in the Church calls attention to and is marked by the presence of many men and women who 'under the inspiration of the Holy Spirit became hermits or founded religious families' (ibid). Among the innumerable charismatic gifts of the Spirit are the Fathers and Mothers of the desert, hermits, consecrated virgins, the great fathers of Eastern and Western monasticism in the first centuries of the Church, the founders of canonical life and of the mendicant orders, the promoters of contemplative life and of the various reforms which have given renewed vigour through the centuries to the various forms of the religious life. Furthermore there are founders of new families of apostolic life, for both men and women, who have given a generous stimulus to new religious congregations and societies of apostolic life. Finally, there are those who have given new inspiration to a consecrated life in the world through secular institutes. The consecrated life serves as a summary of Church history and Christian spirituality through the ages and in its presence and charisms point to the communion of saints in glory.

47. Today's world has need of Christ and his saints as they are made luminously and effectively present in religious life through the splendour of its charisms, making visible for humanity in our times the countenance and grace of Christ. The Church wishes, in the splendour of the faithfulness to the divine plan shown by religious, to reveal Christ to the world and to be the universal sacrament of salvation. Through the multiple yet complementary expressions of her grace and God's gifts, she desires to make the light of Christ and his salvation shine forth for all of humanity. Furthermore, she wishes, in the communion of saints and in

the uninterrupted tradition of holiness to make the founders and their charisms present in our age. Thus in the communion of saints their sons and daughters, present in the pilgrim Church today, may work together in a new evangelisation putting to use the richness of all the gifts of the Spirit sown in the Church throughout her history.

On the threshold of the third millennium the celebration of the Synod on the religious life and its role in the Church and in the world calls together all those living the religious life so that with the fervour of saints renewed by the Spirit they might respond in a more intense Church communion to the grace they have received, that they might make Christ present and might make of themselves a living testimony in the Church for the renewal of society, for the unity and salvation of all peoples, and for the praise of God's glorious grace.

Statements

The [US] Leadership Conference of Women Religious

The national board of the U.S. Leadership Conference of Women Religious issued the following suggestions apropos the 1994 Synod of Bishops on Consecrated Life. Having welcomed the opportunity to contribute to the dialogue, they said that in their statement 'we articulate five themes that we strongly recommend shape the deliberations of the synod, as well as several hopes for the synod.'

We write as American women religious, leaders of congregations committed to active ministries in the United States and abroad. Our world-view has been shaped by the experience of post-Vatican II renewal, in which we invested enormous energy, creativity, scholarship as well as individual and congregational talent. Our understandings are further shaped by the ongoing struggle to meet new needs while respecting long-standing commitments, by the effort to transform institutional commitments into viable modes for the future and by the sheer pressure of maintaining congregational vitality without adequate financial resources. More recently our experience has been chastened by the phenomenon of steadily diminishing membership — a reality that has it own mysterious rationale in God's design.

Nevertheless, we emerge form a period of enormous change more confident than ever of the need for the witness of religious life in today's world. The pain of the dispossessed and marginalized in our world cries out for hope and healing. We look to the synod to challenge us to new authenticity and generosity in our way of life. In particular, we call on the synod to reflect with us on the charismatic identity of religious life, to clarify the functions of hierarchy and religious life for the life and holiness of the church, to affirm the intrinsic unity of consecration and mission, to recognize the unique perspective of women religious and to probe the implications of cultural diversity for religious life now and in the future.

CHARISMATIC IDENTITY: It is our hope that the question of how hierarchical and charismatic gifts of the church are related will be approached without preconceptions and with the benefit of fresh insights available today through new theological explorations, particularly those that reflect on the presence of the Holy Spirit in the ongoing life of the church. For this purpose the writings on religious life by U.S. women religious in our constitutions and other documents are important articulations of our self-understanding of charism, and they need to be read and studied by those who attend the synod.

An important distinction is set forth in the quotation from *Lumen Gentium*, Chapter 6, in the introductory section of the *lineamenta*: 'The state of life, then, which is constituted by the profession of evangelical counsels, while not entering into the hierarchical structure of the church, belongs undeniably to her life and holiness" (F1, p. 405).

These lines focus for us the important question of the relation between the hierarchical and charismatic gifts bestowed by the Spirit upon the church. Religious life, belonging not to the hierarchical structure but to the life and holiness of the church, is a charism, a gift of free grace for the building up of the body of Christ. Many church documents, e.g., *Lumen Gentium, Mutuae Relationes*, have set forth the understandings of religious life as a charism and of how members of religious institutes are related to those who hold ecclesial office. By now there is a body of official writing, including the approved constitutions of religious institutes, that generally includes concepts that have been repeated over time and reiterated particularly since Vatican Council II.

Through the period of renewal of religious life since Vatican Council II, we have been studying our founding charisms, developing our ministries in our desire to address the contemporary world and its needs, and reconsidering our forms of governance to facilitate our mission. We have given much thought to how the authority resident in us as religious institutes needs to function for ourselves and in relation to the church, to whose life and mission we belong. We have been actively engaged in ministerial service and have a truly vast experience in ministry that we brought to the task of renewal mandated after Vatican II.

Our experience, together with our studies of our histories and traditions, has led us into a deepened understanding of our charismatic role as gift within the church and into honoring the freedom of that gift in relation to the hierarchical church. Because much of our thought and reflection on these questions is new to the histories of women religious and is directed specifically to our character as actively ministerial congregations, we urge that what we have to say on the question of the relation between hierarchy and the charism of religious life be carefully considered.

HIERARCHY AND RELIGIOUS LIFE: The distinctions between religious life and hierarchy are often experienced by women religious as they are borne out in practice. Despite the acknowledgment that religious life is a charism distinct from the hierarchy and a grace with its own unique influence on the life and holiness of the church, we find often that we are perceived as a cadre of church professionals available for assignment to church ministries in dioceses and parishes. A kind of "parochialization" (absorption into parochial roles) has been the result.

While our members have made profound contributions to the growth of the church in our country through ministries of this kind, we find through reflection that our apostolic mission has a wider scope. Our histories reveal that our forebears were often those who stepped out in risk into new arenas of ministry that pushed the boundaries of our apostolic service in unexplored directions and that had positive influences on the life of the church as a whole.

We believe that the freedom for that kind of ministerial innovation and creativity must be preserved. It belongs to the very nature of our charismatic gift to the church. As *Mutuae Relationes* states:

"A certain apostolic diligence is urgently necessary in order to devise new, ingenious and courageous ecclesial experiments under the inspiration of the Holy Spirit, who is by his very nature creator. A responsiveness rich in creative initiative is eminently compatible with the charismatic nature of the religious life" (No. 4).

For active ministerial institutes, mission is the organizing principle of our lives. Within our religious congregations, authority exists to direct that mission which shapes the expression of every dimension of our reality. For carrying out the purposes of our congregations our leaders require a sphere of freedom within which to move and motivate our members.

The seeming tension that exists between the authority of the hierarchy and that of religious leaders in this respect is not of necessity conflictive. But it does require respectful mutuality in acknowledging the responsibility of bishops for the faith and unity of the church, and that of religious leaders to direct their own institutes (cf. *Pefectae Caritatis*, 14, 18; *Lumen Gentium*, 18).

We firmly believe that such mutuality and collaboration are possible. We have made mutuality and collaboration values to be achieved as have our bishops. We have been called to that mutuality and collaboration by *Mutuae Relationes*. We believe that they can be attained and that the work of the synod can be instrumental to that end by the clarification that it can bring to the respective functions of hierarchy and religious life for the life and holiness of the church.

CONSECRATION AND MISSION: Related to our sense of our charismatic identity is our consideration of the meaning of consecration, particularly as we reflect upon our active ministerial character. It is our perception that too often in formal documents consecration is set over against mission and that it is identified with the vows to the exclusion of the other dimensions of religious life.

On the other hand, the effort of much of our theological reflection in the past 20 years has been toward the integration of the elements of our active ministerial religious life. The life of the church to which we belong is a life in mission. By our vows we intensify our baptismal commitment to that life, and the intensity of our ministerial commitment is the witness that we bear to Jesus Christ. The freedom that the vows make possible is the milieu of mission to which we are consecrated by him who prayed: 'Consecrate them by means of truth — "Your word is truth." As you have sent me into the world, so I have sent them into the world; I consecrate myself for their sakes now, that they may be consecrated in truth' (Jn 17:17-19).

We find no diminishment of the understanding of consecration when its meaning is understood in the context of our sending in mission by Jesus. It is our sincere hope that the synod document will reflect the biblical import of consecration as mystery, grace, relationship and blessing. This is the basis for understanding active ministerial religious life, which has emerged in the last century but which has not yet been officially distinguished from the forms that preceded it.

WOMEN RELIGIOUS AS WOMEN: The issues that we have presented are all offered from our unique perspective and experience as *women* religious. Our identity as women is not an insignificant or secondary aspect of our reality as religious. We are embodied persons, and the special characteristics of our embodiment lend substance and style to our ways of perceiving, relating and responding to the world around us.

Our growing appreciation of our dignity as persons has given us a new freedom to act with creativity and initiative. It has resulted in a new sense of responsibility for preserving and developing the unique gifts of our charisms, and for responding to the needs of the human family in fidelity to those charisms. In keeping with our identity as women, we have developed styles of personal prayer that are appropriately feminine, and of liturgical and communal prayer that celebrate our lives. If the work of the synod is to be credible to women religious of the church, who are the largest number of those committed to religious life, the uniqueness of women's reality must be brought to bear upon the deliberations.

The climate of openness to women in our society today must be reflected in the agenda, processes and language through which the synod will be conducted. It will not be enough to engage in a series of consultations that include women if their contributions are then evaluated by persons who are unable fully to comprehend and assimilate not only the meaning of words but the fullness of experience that gives rise to them. We urge the synod to consider opening their discussions to the possibility of hearing firsthand the voices of women religious.

In many ways the synod, like other official church convocations, stands before the judgment of the church's women, and other women as well, in an age that finds the practice of exclusively male groups making decisions for women incomprehensible. We therefore believe that we speak for all women in the church when we ask to be included in the formal sessions of the synod in order to speak for ourselves and for the future of the religious life for women.

While we offer these recommendations from our stance within the United States, with its diversity of cultures, we know that we are reflecting aspirations of women religious throughout the world. As our members have labored literally in all countries of the world, and as we who are leaders have met in international groups of women religious, we have found more similarities in our experiences and our hopes for women in general and for women in the church than we have found differences.

We have learned over and over again the disappointment and disaffection of women religious worldwide when they are not able to bring their concerns into the forums of ecclesial decision-making. Our hope is that in this synod women will have a voice, that the church will honor its frequent assertions about the value placed upon the ministries of women religious by welcoming them to an arena where their identity and their future are being explored and possibly determined.

CULTURAL DIVERSITY: We call in the synod to probe the implications of adapting religious life to diverse cultures. Insertion into a local culture is essential to the credibility and viability of a religious congregation. As the *Lineamenta* notes: "The consecrated life is not found in the same state everywhere. In fact, experiences and apostolic activity depend on the situation of the church in a particular place as well as on social and cultural conditions" (No. 30).

Grasping that reality is one of the greatest challenges facing religious life today. One implication of insertion into multiple cultures is that religious congregations will vary widely. This reflects an infinitely varied God and enriches the life of the church with a diversity of spiritualities, liturgical expression, customs and ministries. It makes possible the enculturation of the good news among people of widely different backgrounds and customs, within our own country as well as across national boundaries.

In the face of such diversity, the challenge for the church is to celebrate the differences as gifts of the Spirit rather than to attempt to standardize the charismatic. In a world where people hunger for expressions of their unique identity, both religious and the church must build bridges between the local and the universal, finding ways to encourage this rich diversity.

The sower of Matthew's parable cast his seed on soil both fertile and arid. So religious life today is present in societies where its development is nurtured and in others were it is choked by the challenges of a hostile environment. Religious present the witness of their lives to societies that are pluralistic, apathetic, aggressively secular, agnostic, narrowly theocratic. Like the church, religious life must find a way to relate to each environment that is appropriate and that reveals the face of God in a manner that the culture recognizes.

Our ministry commitments today increasingly draw us into situations of collaboration with groups or agencies that do not share our faith tradition or even, in some instances, our ethical perspectives. Sensitive questions of cooperation will have to be dealt with if we are to respect others' consciences, avoid ethical compromise and give clear witness to the Gospel.

IN A SPIRIT OF HOPE: With a commitment to prepare for this synod by prayer and to participate fully in the preliminary consultations, we conclude these reflections in a spirit of hope:

That the synod will build on the learnings of women religious expressed in documents we have developed in the past 25 years.

That women religious will be included as full participants in the deliberations of the synod.

That the documents produced by the synod will be expressed inclusively in language that shows its intent to address both women and men religious.

That the synod will have a reconciling influence in bringing about mutual respect among proponents of diverse views of religious life.

That the synod will encourage a rich diversity in the expressions of religious life in a way that supports our efforts to live and to minister in a world that is increasingly pluralistic.

That, as a result of the reflection of the synod, we will be challenged to live our religious lives more authentically and generously.

That the synod will raise up and celebrate with the people of God the inestimable gift of religious life for the mission of the Gospel and our contemporary world.

(US) Conference of Major Superiors of Men

The following is a shortened version of a statement which was approved by the US Conference of Major Superiors of Men at a special hearing held on 6 August, 1993. It contains slight amendments made to an earlier draft which had been presented at a meeting on 26 March, 1993, copies of which were presented to various offices of the Roman curia. Expressing the hope that the Synod would prove to be 'a moment of grace' for religious and for the Church and adding that American religious 'welcome possibilities for greater mutual undersanding with bishops', the statement said that the *Lineamenta's* 'strong emphasis on "communio" and "consecration" should be complemented by other themes of great importance for understanding US religious.' It added: 'The renewal of religious life in the United States has been marked by the transformation of North American society, including economic, demographic and cultural shifts of great magnitude.' It also said: 'New forms of this radical discipleship are appearing in our time, and this fact, along with new insights into the meaning of our human and Christian existence, call us to openness, hope, and courageous response to the many challenges of the present day.' There followed a section entitled 'Historical and theological Perspectives' after which the statement continued:

SOCIAL AND CULTURAL CHANGE : In response to Vatican II's call to read the 'signs of the times,' we recognize the enormous changes in our culture and society since the council. There have been radical shifts in political, sexual, economic, social and religious relationships. For example, the recent emergence of democratic values in Eastern Europe has taught us the discipline that such values demand of people. The increased number of roles women perform in our society and church have challenged our traditional understandings of the roles of men and women. The growing gap between rich and poor and between the Northern and Southern hemispheres has brought us to question the sincerity of our option for the poor. So much social change has been the source of chaos and confusion, causing hardship for many, especially older, religious.

We do not see these instances of confusion as moral failures, but simply the reality of living in a pluriform culture that impacts the church and religious life. These shifts have radically affected our self-understanding as religious and as a church. Thus our anthropology and ecclesiology have developed even since Vatican II.

We must ask what it means to be human today and how that is expressed authentically in religious life and its structures. What kind of spirituality develops as a result? How do religious relate to and function in the larger ecclesial community? These questions and their answers are different than they were 30 years ago.

NORTH AMERICAN CONTEXT OF RELIGIOUS LIFE: Our experience of religious life has been influenced by the dynamic and diverse context of North American culture on the brink of the 21st century. Facets of this culture are having a profound influence upon our experience. Among these considerations are the following:

Pluralism: North American culture manifests pluralism on practically every level of its existence, particularly but not exclusively in urban settings: a confluence of diverse races, ethnic groupings, economic and social levels and religious identities — Catholic, Protestant, Jewish, Muslim and a growing number of Asian Religions. An enormous wave of immigration, particularly from Asia, Latin America and Eastern Europe accentuates this diversity.

This same diversity and the new immigration are dramatically changing the face of the North American church, with a huge growth in membership among Hispanic and Asian groups.

Religiosity: Religious practice and identification are significantly higher in the United States than among any other Western country. While acknowledging that some of this religious practice represents sentimentality and individualism, nonetheless the strong religious cast to American society cannot be ignored.

Globalization: More than ever in its history, the fate of the United States is entwined with global realities. The impact of a global economy, the reality of world-wide electronic communication, the legacy of political and military dominance, and recently accelerated immigration have contributed to the impact of globalization on US. consciousness.

A democratic political heritage: Individual freedom and the right of participation and representation in social and political structures are powerful cultural assumptions in North America. Our appreciation for democratic processes is very different from that of people of some other cultures.

Transformation of traditional institutions and structures: Practically all fundamental institutions of North American Society have undergone profound transformation since World War II and the time of the Second Vatican Council — e.g., the nuclear family (with changing family employment patterns, single mother families, divorce rates), education and political life. The church has not escaped the critical scrutiny that has been applied to all institutional life.

NEW SOURCES OF ENERGY: Our North American cultural reality has both life-giving and destructive potential and, as it should, has had a profound impact on the experience of religious and monastic life. Within this cultural context, there exist new sources of energy which may become elements for the revitalisation of traditional forms of religious life. Among them we may cite the following:

1. We see a surge of lay involvement in the church and growing signs of collaboration between laity and religious. This new partnership, having roots in the traditions of non-clerical membership in religious communities, has led to the appearance of lay associations sponsored by religious communities, teams of lay and religious missionaries, and collaboration among lay and religious in the staffing and direction of corporate ministries once held exclusively by religious.

Many human services now performed by laity have developed under the inspiration of religious institutes. Many laity seek to discover authentic spirituality in dialogue with religious life traditions.

2. The perspectives brought to theology and religious life by women have also had
a profound impact on religious life in the United States. Exploration of new forms
of authority and structures for community life, a renewed understanding of our
images for God and church, a new consciousness of the sins of sexism and
exclusion — all of these have been the positive results of authentic Christian
feminism.

3. While the youth of contemporary American culture are often characterised as
self-absorbed and psychically wounded, there is powerful contrary evidence of
profound idealism and authentic religious hungers among young people. The
rapid growth of lay volunteer groups, the increasing numbers of young lay men
and women who are studying theology and the number of young people involved
in service activities conform this.

These stirrings of life within our contemporary culture have resulted in the
appearance of many new forms of religious living. Lay associations existing
either in conjunction with traditional forms of religious life or independently,
communities of married couples, ecumenical associations dedicated to Gospel
living, feminist communities and those exploring spiritualities of Native American or Asian religions are some of the signs of emerging new life.

As religious living in this culture we are also aware of the enormous challenges
and problems facing traditional forms of religious life. A great many religious
communities are experiencing a critical lack of qualified new members, and some
face the real prospect of not surviving. Rapid change has left many individual
religious under-employed and bitter about change that they do not understand or
agree with.

Some religious congregations have been unable to create authentic Gospel
communities and have settled for superficial forms of communal life that do not
give authentic witness to Gospel values. The comfortable style of living of most
religious is often indistinguishable from a middle-class lifestyle and offers small
corporate witness to poverty. The way we exercise authority and deal with each
other can sometimes be as oppressive or abusive as the exercise of political power
within secular society.

We recognize the need, therefore, for honest reflection on our lives and the
need for repentance and continued renewal. We want to do this not as a rejection
of our past experience nor in reaction to the complexity and limitations of our
cultural context, but in a spirit of hope and confidence. We trust that God is present
in our times and in our culture as much as God's Spirit has been active in the past.
While we embrace our world as the Gospel compels us to, we also recognize that
we and our world are in need of ongoing redemption. Yet if religious life is to be
born anew in the United States, it must be capable of responding to the signs of
the times as they are experienced within this culture and this moment in history.

CONCLUSION The profound transformations that have swept through the
church since the Second Vatican Council have changed the face of religious life
in the United States. For many religious, these changes have involved a sense of
loss and grief as well as liberation and new possibilities. These changes may be
calculated in historical and sociological terms. But from the perspective of faith,

we must also perceive the presence of God's purifying Spirit at work within them.

The loss and uncertainty that follow in the wake of any powerful changes and even the threat to the survival of some religious communities bring us face to face with the core reality of our faith, the paschal mystery. The way of discipleship that gives shape and meaning to every form of authentic religious life compels us to understand our contemporary experience in the light of the mystery of Jesus' cross and resurrection. We may experience loss and death, but we also experience the resurgence of new life. If we believe in the abiding presence of the risen Christ in the church, then we trust that we are moving from death to new and abundant life with the crucified and risen One. We live, therefore, in hope.

For the sake of reflection and discussion, we propose the following questions in the light of what has gone before:

> 1. Does this statement reflect your vision and understanding of religious life? 2. Is it clear in your experience of renewal that radical discipleship of the Lord Jesus is exemplary for and in solidarity with the Christian life of all the baptized? 3. How is generous Gospel living in community a real and life-giving phenomenon among you — and how isn't it? 4. Why do people join your institute? Why do they stay? What is life-giving for your new members? 5. How can you characterise what your institute (monastery, congregation, province) has learned from the past 30 years of renewal of religious life? 6. Are you expressing communal prayer in open, spontaneous dialogue over the Gospel as well as in structured ways through the Liturgy of the Hours? How is that impacting upon you own common life, mission and vocations? 7. How does your expression of hospitality — the sharing of life and fellowship with those outside your institute — enable your mission to the local church? 8. Are you critically and positively involved in fostering the promotion of apostolic engagement by laity, by women in ministry and by youth? 9. What is your experience of working with the local church? Do you experience a fundamental respect for your institute's charism? Do you have opportunities to dialogue about your charism and its relation to the local church with diocesan ordinaries? 10 What do you want the Synod of Bishops 1994 to say to you?

Major Superiors of German Women Religious

What follows is a shortened version of the statement, which was issued in July, 1993, specially translated by Geza Thiessen and John de Paor. The references to numbers and to questions are to the Lineamenta, q.v. After an expression of welcome for the synod and of satisfaction that it has stimulated a good deal of discussion among religious, the statement goes on:

GENERAL REFLECTIONS The language used in the *Lineamenta* makes access to its contents difficult. It is a language which is foreign to today's experience. Terms such as 'life consecrated to God', 'consecration', 'bridal' (no.7) are no longer easily understood in our society. Besides that, its use of language shows that the document very often relies on ideal concepts and pays little attention to historical and cultural developments, (e.g.,among others, in its statements on the image of women). The juridical language suggests that the aim is to organize religious life (theologically and legally), rather than involve people together in a common search. Its wide range and the many cross-references to earlier Church documents make it difficult to understand what the text really wants to say.

Statements which contain at heart a positive challenge and could set some process going are often so wrapped up in qualifying clauses that hardly anything remains of their power to renew. Thus, the *Lineamenta* appears rather as admonishments to caution than as offering encouragement, and is somewhat less future oriented than many of the statements of Vatican II or the conclusions of the Wurzburg Synod of 1974.

Also, the basic tendency of the *Lineamenta* is deductive. It starts from definitions, it puts before us the most important statements of the Church's teaching office on the religious life since Vatican II and thus gives us to understand what religious are and what their mission is. In this way there is too little consideration of the fact that religious life since Vatican II has undergone an enormous inner and outer radical change, which, in a great openness to the guidance of the Holy Spirit, and after much searching, demands open questions and vision. Today there is considerable uncertainty about what religious life is and it must be lived with questions unanswered.

In the following we wish address some of the questions. The choice of questions was made at a session of the Assembly of the German Religious Superiors.

QUESTION 6: OPPORTUNITIES AND PROBLEMS OF THE CONSECRATED LIFE Opportunities: With greater flexibility (of small groups), it is possible to give spontaneous help more easily where there are pressing social needs. It is possible more easily to have contacts with important alternative groups in society (e.g. Amnesty International) and their areas of human concern, as well as with other human and Christian groups which are not included, addressed or affected by present structures. There are possibilities of having others take part in one's community life (eg the 'Cloister for a time' project, among others).

Both contemplative and active communities are more particularly called by their spiritual ideal to live and show forth the 'primacy of being over having'; this can be a direct and redeeming sign for our time and our society. They can make the 'sisterly' dimension of the Church a living experience because they are not very much perceived as hierarchical institutions. They can show, by their model structures in the midst of the current tensions within the Church, that hierarchy and laity need not confront each other as ruler and ruled, but are bound together in one shared mission and form one community of life and faith, which, when lived in God-centred loving unity, is a sacramental event for the well-being of the world.

Problems: Ever-increasing ageing; few entrants; many departures. Isolation and the feeling of loneliness, work overload, generation conflicts, lack of internal communication, tensions between community goals and individual charisms, little scope for the individual, functional competence is more important than the personal/spiritual. Lack of vocational identity and danger of self-secularization. The constraint of having to abandon one important work after another — though this is, in part, experienced as a 'salutary constraint', because many works are no longer opportune or are taken over by other institutes. In communities some can be further advanced along the path of renewal than others. 'Obedience', 'chastity/virginity', 'poverty' are concepts which are used widely in a negative sense. In fact, there is an ever widening world which is untouched by religion and where celibacy along with many other 'churchy' things are no longer understood. Those who enter are also influenced by this. Sometimes there is a practise of enclosure which appears as 'encapsulation', and not simply as self-definition and identity. Distress, perplexity and anger at many of the ways that Church authorities have of dealing with religious communities (this conflict was felt very strongly in the Carmelite nuns affair).

In the text of the *Lineamenta* there is a tension between action and comtemplation for which a theological re-working at the Synod of Bishops is a matter of urgency; this tension is at the root of each and every renewal in the Church. On the one hand the unity of contemplation and action is emphasized (11.e, 32.b), and on the other what is shared in common by 'communities of the apostolic life' and 'institutes of a life consecrated to God' is limited to 'external similarities' (23). This separation is disastrous for both sides: the apostolate is understood as being oreinted towards function (23) and the eminently 'apostolic' dimension of contemplation recedes into the background.

Should not the Bishops invite qualified theologians, from the religious orders or from outside them, to clarify this basic theological question?

QUESTION 7 : POSSIBILITIES AND PROBLEMS OF LAY CONGREGATIONS
Much of what has been said in reply to question 6 applies here also. The cooperation of clerical and lay vocations bears witness to the variety of gifts. There is a problem in deciding what are today's greatest needs: the founders applied themselves mostly to the pressing social problems of their day! What service should we engage in, concretely, in response to God's will? How can we live in greater solidarity with the really poor? The major work of each institute must indeed be analysed.

QUESTION 8: WOMEN'S COMMUNITIES AND WOMEN'S HOPES. Nowadays the role and self-understanding of women are undergoing a radical change and this carries with it many consequences. On the one hand there is uncertainty, retention of the old views, one-sidedness, unreal identity. On the other hand there is experimentation, new breakthroughs, creativity, new joys in relationship, an increase in influence and responsibility for sharing in the formation of Church, society and the political spheres. Against the background of such conflicts, communities of women are faced with the question of what it means today to be a woman in religion, and what form it should take for the future. In this context, inculturation must be seen as an urgent task both in our culture and in our Church.

With regard to 'motherhood according to the spirit' (19a) the comments of the German communities of women vary in their emphases. While many see in it a great value, a specially entrusted mission and a basic element in the life of women religious, others point out that, in view of the changed self-understanding of women, they do not recognise themselves in this 'spiritual motherhood', but that they would wish to be 'sisters among the people' and that their efforts must above try to reach the goal of becoming sisters.

It is important that the efforts of today's religious women to find their mission in society and the Church be not hastily judged, rather, it should be taken seriously and tackled as the responsibility of all. Not dismissal, but dialogue in mutual, active interest, and with a view to the common mission of the Church is what is necessary. The professional potential of sisters, as also the pastoral, is still too little utilised. There is a whole range of offices which could quite well be undertaken by women. The gifts of women for setting up relationships and community (this also in the spiritual sphere), could be made to bear fruit if they were taken more into account or integrated into today's search to live out *communio*. Here, sisters could make a major contribution, for example in retreat teams, in teams for the formation of priestly and other religious vocations, and in the general area of pastoral work, especially where an over-emphasis on functional operation does not yet allow for togetherness in the Spirit.

Within communities of sisters possibilities of formation are, occasionally, refused as undesirable, although proper theological studies and training for their vocation, as well as continuing formation would be desirable. There is still, here and there, a dependance on male religious orders and superiors which is dificult to understand. Time and again communities of women and brothers are assigned chaplains who have no zest left in them and no strength to journey with the sisters/brothers on a new path into the future. On the other hand, there are happy examples of priests who bring with them their own charism, and share this in teamwork with that of the community; they are thus a sign of Church which is alive.

QUESTION 10: COMMUNITIES OF THE APOSTOLIC LIFE What happens when life has so changed that the original objectives of the founder no longer really come to grips with the concerns of our day? While the insistance on the 'charism of the founder' is in principle understandable, it sometimes leads to rigidity and can make renewal impossible. More important than concrete objectives is indeed the question: how do we live out the original ideal? and how do we take part in today's new evangelisation? Not all the concepts employed, such as 'consecration, vows, promises', etc. are clear.

QUESTION 11: NEW FORMS OF THE CONSECRATED LIFE The existence of new communities, of which there are very many in our country, is a sign that God has not ceased to call people, especially the young. These are to be seen as a gift of the Holy Spirit to the Church, and they live in close spiritual relatonship with the religious orders. In their frequently courageous initiatives, they are a fruitful challenge to the religious orders to ask themselves: from where do these new spiritual groups receive their impulse? what is their witness? and what does this signify for us?

On the basis of lived *communio* the experience is well known: when new forms, or better, new communities of the consecrated life find no room in the Church, when they are harshly judged and their charism not wanted nor taken up, this means that at times the Spirit is given no room to work.

QUESTION 12: RENEWAL SINCE THE SECOND VATICAN COUNCIL Positive aspects: Better collaboration between the religious orders. Since the Council the constitutions have been revised in the light of Vatican II and the new Canon Law. Better and more meaningful concelebration of the eucharistic liturgy and the Liturgy of the Hours. A deepening of life through the Word of God. *Lectio Divina* has taken a firm hold in the daily life of many religious. Better appreciation of the individual religious, of their capacities and gifts. Improved human relations inside the communities and with the laity. Return to the sources: the founding charism and one's own spirituality. Better initial and on-going formation of members. Adaptation to the present day. Some congregations have made the option for the poor': to the marginalised, eg in the hospice movement, ministry to drug users, prostitutes, etc.

Negative aspects: Considerable confusion among religious. An identity crisis. After Vatican II many experiments were made which were not all successful and even had negative results. Many religious have left. Tensions with authority at the level of Church and of order/congregation. A crisis of values (*Werte*). We have not learned how to use properly the great gift of freedom.

As regards the basic meaning of Vatican II the whole Church is faced with a turning point. This is seen, among other things, in the fact that the interpretation of the Council is once more in debate. A new generation is now assuming authority in the Church which did not consciously live through the Council and so must first work through the Council period and the documents. There are thus in our orders/congregations different generations who, each with its own attitude to Vatican II, must meet together and ask themselves: what is our stand on the Council? how do we understand it? how has the Holy Spirit marked our particular community in the conciliar and post-conciliar renewal periods? and what new shape has it taken?

QUESTION 13: RENEWAL PATHS The orders and congregations are at decisive turning points in their renewal. Many structures, as also the laws and duties which go with them (this includes the laws of the State), the strength of familiar traditions and the uncertainty about the 'whether' and 'how' of survival can obscure the vision of hope which God has made part of the founding charisms. There is need for a new faith vision. This is already beginning to appear in outline. Many religious communities have had very painful experiences and feel, therefore, that on their own they cannot advance into a new future. Any particular charism of a given community cannot be brought to life on its own. All efforts to achieve this seem to be fruitless. Then the realization grows that this new coming to life of one's own charism can only happen in a concerned dialogue with, and a believing acceptance of, all the charisms with which God has endowed our times. Concretely this means that there must be an end to emotional defences against other new or old communities or movements, judging one another as progressive or conservative, with mistrust or competition-linked reservations. All such must give way to a readiness to dialogue about the works of the Spirit, drawing its orientation and criteria from the discernment of spirits.

Religious orders and spiritual movements must move together, on the one hand, to uncover their deeper affinity of vocation and to allow renewal to happen through and with each other, and on the other hand, to discuss the question of the continuation of their institutions and, where necessary, to find common solutions.

Contemplative and apostolic orders have thus opened up to each other. Both must seek to live the tension: action-contemplation. This tension, which finds its origin and pattern in the 'thou' of God, is at the centre of the life of religious orders and congregations and there is always the danger, even in our time, that one will be separated from the other. It is striking that precisely the new spiritual movements and communities seek for ways, once more, to bring both of these into a balanced tension. This may be a call to the orders: to seek to live again, and perhaps in a new way in each particular form of religious life, this tensionful unity of action and contemplation.

What is needed is a creative openness to the Holy Spirit when encountering new situations. This awareness of charisms has a central importance for the renewal of institutes' lives. It means to discover one's own charism, those of one's own community, of the other communities and movements, of the local Church, of the universal Church, to read therein God's directions, to obey the Holy Spirit and to translate forthwith into action this impulse of the Spirit.

Of special importance is the dialogue between religious orders and congregations, as also with religious communities of other Churches, Protestant (Lutheran), Anglican, etc. Experience has shown that a religious order has only limited power to renew itself. Each particular charism needs contact with the other charisms bestowed on the Church in order to be made viable. *Communio* is essential.

QUESTION 14: VOCATIONS Today there are many possibilities for forms of Christian life and vocation in the Church. Changing values in our society, pluralism, high standards of living, lack of future prospects for young people, young people asking fewer questions about God's plan in their lives, poverty of faith, and parents being opposed to their sons or daughters taking up vocations in the Church.

Religious have little contact with young people, they are not sufficiently present in society (this partly because of declining numbers). Pressures for results and overwork is not witness. There often seems to be a lack of energy in the institutes for radical renewal, which, if realized in concrete living, could be a prophetic answer in the Spirit of the Gospels to the dramatic developments in the Church and in the world. Consequently, religious life has little power to attract. In a society which is reluctant to make commitments, communities have failed to live, among themselves and for the outside world, a convincing concept of commitment (allied to freedom).

Life without a partner, without a sexual life, is seen as more and more difficult. Many structures and ways of communicating are seen as old-fashioned and contrary to the views and values of a modern society where performance is emphasised.

The diocesan clergy hardly ever present religious institutes in an attractive manner as a real possibility for life according to the Gospels; indeed when individual people show interest they are actively dissuaded. If at all, the priesthood is almost the only possibility which is portrayed positively.

The Church on the whole — and this includes the institutes — is experienced as an institution which is authoritarian, which creates guilt-feelings and which does not have attractive structures for solving conflicts. Often one has the chance to meet people on a more personal level than is offered by fixed, rigid structures. However, even this does not necessarily attract new members. It seems important, generally, to promote a sense of the value of vocation for a Christian life and to live it; from this should come spiritual/Church vocations. Pastoral ministry which is only on the level of action and is detached from the inner life of the community is fruitless.

Young people can see whether the members of a community are unified, whether tensions are resolved in the spirit of Jesus, or whether hidden 'embolisms' quench the Spirit in the body of Christ. They sense clearly whether religious are really God-loving people, whether they are happy in their vocation, or whether work, disordered relationships, hardened structures, cold-heartedness etc. drive love (thus Jesus himself) away.

In addition, one finds among young people a great openness to a life built on the word of God. For this we need people who have the courage to be on fire with God's word and who live it in everyday life.

QUESTION 19: COMMUNION WITH THE BISHOPS AND THE MAGISTERIUM Is it not the orders and congregations who, in a time of crisis of authority, have the chance to live '*communio*-authority', i.e. to live the example of a communal type of authority?

Office and charism are given to one another. They must be held together in tension. Today, especially, it is important that the Synod document does not emphasize subordination solely (see *Lineamenta* 2, 4, 15, 18, 27, 28, 39) as the determining factor in the relationship between ecclesial authority and the orders. It is yet more important that the great value of obedience which grows out of freedom and love, and the blessing of a hierarchy which is led by the Spirit, are properly articulated. It would be desirable that the Synod should build bridges for religious, i.e. give encouragement and awaken joy for a life of union with the superiors and with one another, as Christ lived it in example (cf. John 17).

There is an urgent need in our Church for dialogue between people of all vocations and offices, those who live out the urgent call of the Spirit.

QUESTION 22: RELATIONS BETWEEN RELIGIOUS AND LAITY There are already attempts at closer cooperation, but there is still too little of this and of togetherness. Lay people are not only partners in work, but also 'partners in vocation'. The common foundation of baptism and confession of Christ must be yet more emphasized. *Communio* must be lived with all those who are called. There are more and more lay people who live their calling consciously and with conviction. Such people are a helpful challenge to our religious life. Are we also ready to share our spiritual gifts with them, to approach conflicts in the spirit of love, and to dispense with power structures, for example, in employer/employee relationships, etc.?

QUESTION 23: NEW EVANGELISATION This is the kernel of renewal for every community and the central task of religious life today in union with all other vocations. It must take place in a positive relationship to the world (see *Gaudium et Spes*) and demands keen awareness of the signs of the times. It cannot mean always following the 'golden mean', it demands daring and following new paths. It should not succumb to a tendency to make the Gospels 'liveable' by watering them down. It is not confined to proclamation of the Good News. It also takes place through involvement in movements which work for peace, social justice, human rights, care of creation, in open communities which make it possible for people to live, pray, and believe with others. As yet, religious institutes often do not find themselves gripped by enthusiasm for this new evangelisation.

CONCLUSION In all these questions we are addressing a reality which we must face, if we want to obey the Spirit. Is there not at present a totally new form of religious life emerging, a form, which is not just the sum of 'back to the sources' and 'openness to the signs of the times' but a form, which cannot (yet?) be defined, a form which, nevertheless, already displays a great sacramental force, because it lives deeply rooted in the mystery of *communio*?
The Synod wants 'to understand the Lord's plan in its fullness'. In the light of all that has been said, should the Synod not then become a forum for mutual sharing of reports in worship and celebration.
    At any rate, we ask those responsible for the Synod to include enough male (especially brothers) and female religious in their consultations in order to develop and concretely enter upon shared perspectives on the future of the communities, and indeed, of the whole Church.

Conference of German Religious Superiors (VDO)
Conference of Religious Superiors of the German Orders and Congregations of Brothers (VOB)

The following statement was issued by the two conferences after their joint AGM in June, 1993. It was specially translated for this book by Geza Thiessen and John de Paor. Having welcomed the decision to hold a Synod, the statement added that this was a difficult time for religious and for the Church as a whole, and hoped that the Synod's approach would be marked by encouragement. It went on:

GENERAL REMARKS We feel somewhat about the text of the Lineamenta because it is written in a language, which is *quite inaccesible and in many places almost unintelligible* nowadays for the religious themselves and especially for young people who might be interested in religious life. We also know from bishops that they consider the language of the *Lineamenta* as too difficult and out of date. With regard to the formulation of the results of the Synod, a style of *language which invites assent* would be preferable to that of the *Lineamenta* which is more exhortatory.

In German many terms present still greater difficulty. It is not helpful, for example, to speak of 'consecrated' (gottgeweihtem) life, because to be 'consecrated' is not really special to religious, it is true of every life, above all it is true of the life of every baptized Christian. In general, there is need, in the *Lineamenta*, for clarification of important basic words in contemporary faith discourse.

In many cases we did not find the questions raised in the *Lineamenta* very helpful. We feel that the questions expect very definite answers, already assumed in the text, instead of helping to elucidate the different experiences and valuations of the bishops and religious.

We can understand that the juridical questions of religious life, especially after the introduction of the new canon law, are regarded as very important by Church superiors. As for ourselves, we hope that the Synod will not be concerned primarily with canonical arrangements between the orders and the hierarchy, between the order and individual members, but that it will speak about the particular charism of an order and the prophetic character of the orders as well as the sisterly/brotherly togetherness in community. To us, the *Lineamenta* bears too much the stamp of canonical formulations.

We are aware of the difficulties in which the world finds itself, especially in this time of radical change. We think, however, that in the *Lineamenta* world and society are described in pessimistic vein. Catchwords like 'secularism', 'individualism', 'feminism' are used in one-sided warnings against the 'world'. We would be grateful if the Synod were not to look at 'secularism', the current emphasis on the person and the individual, or the position of woman in the Church and the world primarily in a negative way. Could not one see these developments rather as an encouraging opportunity to face the signs of the times and the imperatives for the Church and the world?

We welcome the attempt to expand and strengthen the structures for dialogue between bishops, bishops' conferences and religious communities (cf. Preface to the *Lineamenta*). At the same time we would like to ask the bishops to effect a real *communal dialogue* during the Synod and when preparing documents. Different parts of the *Lineamenta* (eg nos.3, 25, 47) give the impression of a 'talking about' rather than a 'talking with' the religious communities.

In this connection *the presence of members of religious orders and congregations* at the Synod seems to us indispensible. As male relgious, we find it especially important, and take it for granted, that this active participation at the Synod will be open to representatives of female orders and communities. Only where a real collegial togetherness of Pope, bishops and religious is possible, in these questions and at this Synod, will it be seen as a credible model of dialogue and as an encouragement for young people to venture into religious life in community.

Thus, we would like to express our wish to the Synod that the participants' discussions and, afterwards, the statement of the Pope, will not be stamped by that world-view which deters young people from entering religious life. Let the Pope and the Synod rather encourage sister-brotherliness in the orders and in the Church as well as an approach to the world, which wVatican II helped us to rediscover ill awaken hope in people.

RELIGIOUS AND THE CHURCH Vatican II helped us to rediscover the ecclesiological model of *communio* and of the 'pilgrim people of God'. Through this a changed view of community and a different form of leadership has developed in many communities.

Along with the German bishops we have the impression that, contrary to the emphasis on communion, participation and thus mutual enrichment, the *Lineamenta* portrays, above all, the perspective of subordination under leadership, as, for example, the office of St. Peter. This seems to us an insufficient expression of sister-brotherliness and partnership. Indeed, it does not at all correspond to the feelings of religious today. And so we would be happy if the Synod were to exhibit less of the subordination aspects and more of the mutuality of charisms, which also includes the office of leadership. It is our belief that, precisely here, the Church has the duty to act and can attain to model status in a world which is all too often very hierarchically structured.

The intention of this is not at all the abolition of authority and obedience, but an understanding of these which is in accordance with the Gospels. Because of positive experiences we would like to ask the delegates at the Synod to consider this aspect in their discussions and statements.

The charism of religious life and of spiritual communities is a gift for the vitality and variety of the Church. Thus, both office and charism are addressed and invited to be open to to the impulses of the Holy Spirit in our time.

We ask the bishops to prevent the possible impression that charism can and is allowed to unfold only where the office regulates and guides it. Rather we hope that the Synod may present this cooperation of charisms in such a manner that the enriching element of the charism of religious life is emphasized.

In the *Lineamenta* there are no considerations of dual membership of religious in a spiritual movement and their own community, or even in two different orders. Cooperation and membership of religious in spiritual movements is, of course, possible and can be fruitful. However, because tensions can arise thereby, a word of clarification from the Synod will be very important. We assume that if such a case arises, the Church will never approve of structures of double obedience, but that it will act in such a way that the cooperation between orders and spiritual communities will enrich each one's own situation and their unity.

RELIGIOUS ORDERS AND SOCIETY In the relationship between the orders and society two aspects are particularly close to our hearts. Orders have functions in and for the Church as well as outwards to society. Therefore, it would be important to look at the situation from both points of view.

Thus, for example, on the one hand, a discriminating view of the situation of orders in the individual regions is necessary in order to do justice to the actual cooperation between the orders as they concretely appear, especially the apostolic communities, their tasks and aims, and the cultural context of the respective society (see in this context *Lineamenta* nos 29c, 30 and question 16).

On the other hand, the concrete situation of orders in the West European communities especially cannot be considered apart from the critical view and attitude to the Church which obtains in the respective societies (cf. *Lineamenta* no.14).

The secularized and atheistic world which we have in Germany, especially since reunification, presents a huge task for all Christians. Here too, new areas of work arise for the orders and religious communities, for which we expect encouragement. One aspect of this is solidarity with all people which we as orders wish to manifest. Another is the dialogue with those who think differently, with those who are estranged from the Church, as well as lively ecumenical relations with other denominations.

ORDERS AND THEIR SELF-UNDERSTANDING We welcome the fact that in the *Lineamenta* there is a clear awareness of the charismatic variety in religious life. However, it seems to us that the meaning and interpretation of the individual charism of the orders require some further reflections (eg.*Lineamenta* nos 5, 12e, 16 and 17).

We therefore ask the bishops: To leave sufficient space theologically and practically for the particular charisms of the communities (see Guidelines for Formation in the Religious Orders, *Potissimum institutioni* no.17). To encourage the orders to interpret their founding charism in the contemporary context, because it cannot be retained and guaranteed without reference to history, but needs to be interpreted in changing conditions. To encourage, then, an analysis of the socio-cultural and ecclesial environment of each of the world religions. And to create the conditions in which the institutes are able to make their own charism fruitful in the local and in the universal Church (see PO, 9, LG, 12, AA, 3).

In this context the *Lineamenta* gives us the impression that this Synod could lay down that renewal should be brought to a conclusion and that this renewal can be achieved only with reference to the founding charism of the orders. We are grateful for the founding charism which brought each of our communities into existence. It is important, certainly, to regain the noble-hearted courage of our beginnings. Nevertheless, other times may require changed forms, which does not mean to discard old ideals but it is to adapt to new demands. We hope that the Church will not provide us in this instance with restrictions but with encouragement and accompaniment.

In no 32b of the *Lineamenta* the required 'unity of life', especially in the apostolic institutes, is addressed. This unity has been and is being made difficult through the continuous 'monastisation' of the active orders, in which the structure of monastic and contemplative life has been made the norm for other communities. Because of this, many institutes and individual members of orders have experienced and still experience considerable tensions.

It seems important to us that the Synod should take this problem of monastic colonising into consideration and that, in what it teaches and in practice, it should support the orders concerned in their search for new ways (*Lineamenta* no.12e, question 6, and PC, 8).

We feel, furthermore, that the *Lineamenta* shows little awareness of what apostolic orders really are in today's Church. Some apostolic orders, for example, would hardly see themselves as 'clerical institutes' (cf. CIC can 588) because in their ranks they have lay as well as clerical members. It seems incompatible with the dignity of lay religious as equal members of one and the same institute that they are excluded in principle from leadership positions in their orders because of canonical regulations. Here we hope that the Synod will clarify the self-understanding of the apostolic communities especially.

In the self-understanding of clerical religious the vocation to priesthood is superimposed on the vocation to religious life. We ask the Synod to promote the self-understanding of the vocation to religious life.

When the *Lineamenta* talks about the evangelical counsels it over-emphasize the vow of chastity. In general, it keeps very much to the well known definitions. In this way, possible mistakes in using modern language can be avoided. Modern religious, however, search for a way to understand the evangelical counsels, in our day, as an answer of holistic love, and thereby express the process-like nature of such a life model. Here we ask the Synod for clarifications but also for the courage to name, beyond the three vows, new signs in accordance with the Gospels, which are important for religious life today; for example, pacifism in a time without peace, justice for a world which is full of injustice and oppression, or sharing in a world of hunger and poverty.

The question thus arises as to what we in religious life want to signal to the world. This should not primarily be the habit or the enclosure (cf. *Lineamenta* no. 31b). Rather, the orders desire to be known to the world by their style of community life, by the manner in which they live the common faith and hope, and by their concern for people.

In the *Lineamenta* the prophetic mission of the orders in society is mentioned only once (no 29e, see 'Religious Life and Human Advancement', Introduction nos 4a, 24, 33b; 'Guidelines for Formation' no 25). A look at the history of religious life shows that the prophetic dimension has been characteristic of this life right from the beginning and that it has had its effect outside and within the Church. The prophetic character of religious life within the Church, which can sometimes demand critical protest inspired by the Gospels, often seems to us to be undervalued. Prophetic service, therefore, requires alertness to new needs and the courage to tread unknown paths. We hope that the Synod will speak more decisively about this prophetic dimension of religious life inside and outside the Church. Besides the encouragement to the orders themselves, the local Churches can thereby receive the impulse for a new appreciation of the prophetic character of religious life.

Religious communities in our local Churches have often endeavoured to set a higher value on the person than on structures. Experience shows that, as a result, the life and work of religious has been very much enriched. The *Lineamenta* also counts this among the 'Fruits of Renewal' (no 26c). This encourages us to hope that the Synod will make this point even more strongly and will encourage the communities to follow this path further. In addition, conclusions will flow from this for a comprehensive understanding of religious life in the Church. Here, also, it is true that community members need to be more highly valued than structures of a theological and canonical nature. We therefore ask the bishops to pay special attention to this point, whether in discussing religious life or in taking practical decisions.

TOWARDS THE SYNOD OF BISHOPS We see the Synod as a great opportunity for the Church to put new life into the different charisms and offices and to make them fruitful for each another.

The particular theme of the Synod should be an occasion for conferring as members of a family, bishops and religious, women and men, and for giving encouragement to religious life and life in spiritual communities. Here we request that when choosing the male and female participants in the Synod account is taken of the number and variety of the different orders, communities and secular institutes.

The *Instrumentum Laboris* should contain questions, rather than present a systematic outline.

In agreement with the German bishops we ask that the following questions be addressed:

What are the important theological emphases for the self-understanding of religious orders and spiritual communities in today's Church?

What meaning do the signs of the times have here?

How can the founding charism and the demands of our times in their tension/unity relationship be lived in such a way that the orders find a path to the spiritual centre of their life and work?

Where and how do new beginnings become manifest in orders and spiritual communities?

How can the cooperation between dioceses and orders be strenghtened, so that, for the well-being of the local and universal Church, the dioceses and orders are each strengthened in their own task? Where are the difficulties in this area?

How can the orders and spiritual communities live with the overload of work which, at times, they face, as well as the problem of old age, and how should they deal with the death of institutes (cf. *Lineamenta*, question 17)?

What does the universal Church expect from the orders and spiritual communities?

Union of European Conferences of Major Religious Superiors

The following statement was 'proposed' to European national conferences of major religious superiors after the meeting of the Union in Prague, September, 1993. This English text was written at the meeting.

INTRODUCTION As members of religious institutes in a continent which has produced half of the world's religious, we hope that the Synod will offer words of encouragement to religious living a life consecrated to Jesus Christ for the Church and the world. The renewal process, started by Vatican II, must continue. For the religious in Europe, this implies both discernment and inculturation, communion and freedom, creativity and fidelity.

RECOMMENDATIONS: 1. The theological meaning of consecration will have to be deepened. This is also true of mission. Consecration and mission are essentially linked. Both need to be inculturated in a world which, nothwithstanding its ambiguities, is primarily the good creation of a loving God. We hope for the recognition of the charismatic and prophetic character of religious life.

2. Community life, with its great variety of concrete forms, belongs to the essence of religious life. The theology of community life needs to be developed according to the different charisms. Apostolic community life is not to be identified with monastic life. Religious who are called to be alone in mission need to be prepared for this and be supported by a warm and healing community.

3. (i) Women religious expect a real and full recognition of their place in the Church by the People of God and in particular by its male members, be they laity, priests or bishops. The majority of religious sisters belong to Apostolic institutes. They should be regarded as partners in ministry.

(ii). A theological training of high quality has to be provided, not only for candidates (future sisters and brothers) but also in on-going formation.

(iii). When religious, male and female, are working in the service of the Church, they should receive a fair remuneration and this should be part of their contract.

(iv). More religious, women and men, should be appointed as vicars for the religious life.

4. The vocation of religious brothers is a unique vocation in the Church; too often brothers are forgotten in official documents and in vocation programmes, even by religious themselves.

5. A closer co-operation with the laity, or even their association with religious institutes, is seen as a positive sign of the times. This requires more formation and education on the part of religious institutes and of the laity.

6. We challenge ourselves to cooperate more on an inter-congregational level. This would provide opportunities for a higher level of training (on-going formation), and a more efficient discernment of apostolic commitments.

7. (i) Religious are called to link faith and justice, faith and culture. In the Europe

of today, this means a creative presence, according to each charism, in the marginal world of the materially and spiritually poor and in the world of the young. Their presence among Christians of other Churches, on the margins of the Church, among the faithful of other religions, and among agnostics, leads to dialogue. Religious will respond to the needs of migrants, refugees etc. Living close to these people, they are called to find a new language, to bring the Good News to everybody.

(ii) Religious are called to witness to Jesus Christ, dying and rising; to promote reconciliation in the world and in the Church; to liberate people from the superficial dimension of life.

(iii) Religious, through their international or inter-regional networks, are called to challenge others to open their minds and hearts to the European and intercontinental dimensions of evangelisation.

8. (i) While we acknowledge the deficiencies within our institutes, we think that the decline of vocations in Europe should also be considered as a socio-cultural phenomenon and as a challenge for us in a new culture.

(ii). The problem of the shortage of secular priests cannot be solved by calling upon religious priests.

9. Religious are at the heart of the Church. They are ill at ease when, on account of their activities or because of what they say, they are considered to be a rival group.

10. While in several countries *Mutuae Relationes* has had some effect, in many others it needs to be implemented and taken further. Care should be taken that courses in religious life form part of the programme in seminaries.

11. The language of the *Instrumentum Laboris* and of subsequent documents should reflect the spiritual dynamism, the concern for renewal and for inculturation, of the religious institutes. Religious are not asking for a new definition of religious life, but a life-giving word of hope for the future.

Religious themselves are the principal agents of their own renewal. They must trust more in the power of the Spirit of Jesus living in them.

Sisters of Notre Dame de Namur, England and Wales

I, We, the Sisters of Notre Dame de Namur in [England and wales], would like the Synod on 'The Consecrated Life and its role in the Church and in the World', to address the future of religious life:

>1 With an appreciative consciousness of the *present*, recognising the value to the Church and the world which religious are, as they witness to Christ in their various ways, and diverse situations.

>2 By underpinning its reflections with scripture, theology and spirituality, rather than concentrating largely on canon law and Roman documents.

>3 With an awareness that the theology of religious/consecrated life which is emerging is one of relatedness *to* rather than separation *from* the world.

4 With a consciousness of the love and loyalty with which consecrated women have served the Church, from New Testament times to the present day. Pope Paul VI expressed the following sentiments regarding apostolic religious; 'Their apostolate is often marked by an originality and a genius that compels admiration' (as quoted in the Introduction to the *Lineamenta*).

It is our hope that the Synod will allow women religious the freedom to express that originality as they talk in faith alongside the poor and oppressed.

5 In a spirit of communion and collegiality which presupposes flexibility, trust, honesty and mutual collaboration. This requires dialogue between bishops and a representative group of women and men with lived experience of religious life, remembering that:

a) Men cannot speak from the reality of religious life as lived and experienced by women.

b) Women form the majority of members in consecrated life.

c) We need the complementarity of female and male in any dialogue concerning consecrated life.

Many religious are experiencing a 'Calvary' situation at the present time, and would welcome a statement written from an experiential standpoint, rather than one emerging from a theoretical base — one which offers more Gospel-based freedom to walk with 'resurrection' hope into the heart of the world situations of the future.

6 In a spirit of discernment rather than debate and with respect, openness and prophetic vision — a vision which allows women to be present *and* active at the Synod itself.

We ask that the Synod would aim to be an exploration of consecrated life rather than an arena for the emergence of a static definition. We sense in the theoretical and even doctrinal nature of the *Lineamenta* a move towards a 'reinstitutionalizing' of religious life.

We prefer the use of the term *vita apostolica* to that of 'essential elements of consecrated life' (p 17 *Lineamenta*). This term came strongly to the fore in the eleventh century, and indicated a close following of Christ, in poverty, in prayer and mission of good works. But traditions of culture and expectations of society greatly restricted the ways in which female consecrated persons could operate. Only in this second half of the twentieth century have conditions evolved socially which make it possible for consecrated women to explore the *vita apostolica* freely and fully. Previous attempts to do so by people like Mary Ward, St Julie Billiart, our own foundress and others have been hampered when the Church, often using Canon Law, has tried to bring women back to a more enclosed and monastic life. Men religious (Franciscans, Dominicans, Jesuits and others) have not been so encumbered.

7 With a working conviction that Male *plus* Female equals Human. In ancient Roman law, a woman *belonged* to her father and was *given* in marriage to her husband. This element of pagan masculine ownership of women influenced the thinking of Church and Society long after the demise

of the Roman empire.

We hope that this Synod of the Twentieth Century will operate in such a way that women religious will feel affirmed and empowered as they respond freely and fully to the signs of their times.

II As consecrated religious approaching the twenty first century, we would, therefore, like the Synod to address the tension between the concept of religious life as static and the dynamism of our present reality as consecrated apostolic persons in a secular world. We seek to be present as 'leaven' in today's rapidly changing society and not set apart in an inflexible mould which witnesses little to the people among whom we work. Included in the above statement is:

a) A request for the re-appraisal of laws and regulations which deny the freedom of women and give the impression that women have a second class role to play in apostolic life.

b) A request for an informed recognition and acceptance of vowed community life as lived today. The geographical, historical and static bondings which were synonymous with former images of religious life may not be so apparent, yet community living derives its strength from a radical living of Gospel values, coupled with and enhanced by a deep collaborative relationship with the People of God, especially the poor.

We hope that, in this way, a balance can be struck, between institutionalisation and freedom to witness.

c) A request for affirmation of our endeavours in exploring new forms of membership and association, new types and lengths of commitment, the possibility of more open community, with inter-congregational and/or ecumenical dimensions.

The 'harvest' is great and today's young people need to be introduced to labouring for the Kingdom in ways which will tap their generosity for longer or shorter periods and through structures which speak the 'Good News' to them.

d) A request for a development of a theology of consecrated life, based on the Gospels, the needs of today's world and the spiritualities of individual congregations. We hope that women religious will have an opportunity to subscribe to the formulation of this.

e) A request for a holistic approach to the consecrated life, understanding it to be part of the life of the universal Church.

This presupposes collaboration with other laity and with clerics of the Church in their apostolic, as distinct from, their sacramental role.

Finally, we would like to record our appreciation for the opportunity given, yet again, to re-think our commitment to Christ through his Church in the world of today and of the years ahead.

ENGLISH AND WELSH RELIGIOUS

What follows is portion of a collation of the responses of eight groups of religious to questions put by the England and Wales CMRS. The full text is in Religious Life Review, July-August, 1993, pp 240-144.

HOW SHOULD THE SYNOD ADDRESS THE FUTURE OF RELIGIOUS LIFE?
With a clear expression of the apostolic religious vocation, i.e. a theology of the apostolic religious life, based on lived experience. (The model of religious life in the *Lineamenta* is much closer to the monastic religious life than to the apostolic.). With the insight and vision of religious life expressed in recent writings — the document specifically mentioned was Religious and Human Advancement. (Text in *Vatican II: More Postconciliar Documents*, Austin Flannery, OP, Editor, pp. 260-284, Dominican Publications, Dublin). With an openness to new forms of religious life. Within the context of fidelity, on the part of the whole Church, to Vatican II in respect of subsidiarity, collegiality, ecumenism, collaboration etc. Within the context of the vocation of every baptised person, to marriage, to religious life or to the single life. With an understanding of the intrinsic rather than the utilitarian value of religious life. With an emphasis on values rather than on structures, the 'spirit' rather than the law. With an implicit recognition of what is negotiable and what is non-negotiable in our lives. With reference to the 'prophetic' and the 'relational' aspects of religious life. With a new understanding of how to live out the vows in today's world. With an openness to the world of today and its needs — the world writes the agenda for apostolic religious. With respect for the international dimension of religious life and its place in other cultures, not just the West European. With recognition of the relationship of religious with religious of other world religions. With an openness to the place of women in the Church, the contribution of women religious and their full participation in the Synod. With a sympathetic understanding of the problems religious face today (ageing communities, lack of vocations, the weight of their institutions). With acceptance of religious, trust in their intuition, with hope and with encouragement. In a non-directive manner. In a language appropriate for people of today. With acceptance of the idea that the Synod is the start of a process of reflection, not the end of one. Consequently, the Synod should not produce any definitive statement. The Synod members should write the document themselves. A further meeting of men and women representatives of religious orders with the bishops could take place before a susbstantive document is written.

WHAT IS YOUR VISION OF RELIGIOUS LIFE IN THE FUTURE? The end of institutional religious life and its refounding in contemporary culture; fewer religious; new authority structures; new concepts of community; mixed communities of sisters, brothers, priests and laity, married and single, collaborating in ministry; small communities; loving, stable relationships in community; community life adapted to different cultures; community life witnessing to counter-cultural values; a religious life which helps women and men become fully mature; emphasis on the 'incarnational' dimension, living the life of the time and the place; religious much more 'in the midst of people'; communities at the 'cutting edge' of society; possibility of short-term commitments/temporary vocations to the religious life; the main emphasis on spirituality, on the contemplative dimension of prayer, on a life centred on the Eucharist and on faith-sharing; some religious adopting an eremitical way of life; closer collaboration between all congregations, creating a national net-work to help empower people at all levels; well thought out formation programmes adapted to each person and aiming to make him/her both free and responsible; serious on-going formation.

Irish Contemplatives

The following statement was drawn after several meetings of representatives of all the contemplative communities of women and men religioius in Ireland.

1. We would like to convey to our Bishops an intent to be all that the Church wants us to be viz. to be a powerhouse of prayer within the Church, to offer God a choice sacrifice of prayer on its behalf and by the example of our lives to draw others to him.

2. We would thank the Church for affirming us in our vocation and affording us the protection of enclosure in order that we may live out our lives in silence and solitude. The first section of *Venite Seorsum* gives an inspiring exposition of the contemplative life. The second section regarding the norms is out of date and if this is revised or another document drawn up we feel that contemplative men and women should be allowed to contribute and collaborate in writing it. Why should there be one form of enclosure for men and another form of enclosure for women?

3. We would welcome a strong clear statement from the Synod reaffirming the value of the consecrated contemplative Life — simple and Christocentric. Could Bishops follow through their beliefs about our life by promoting a greater understanding of it among the priests, religious and laity of their diocese and encourage vocations to it. We would hope that our bishops, priests, religious, laity would share more frequently in our prayer and liturgies and that enclosure would not be seen as a barrier to that sharing.

4. We would make a strong request that consecrated women be well represented at the Synod. They are far more numerous than men and they find it offensive to be excluded from something so vital in their lives. Avoiding any aggressive tone, we would ask for more recognition for women religious.

5. We ask that elitist language in our regard should be avoided.

6. We ask that St. Thérèse be declared a Doctor of the Church.

Superiors General
on Religious Life Today

The Union of Superiors General is holding a special international meeting in Rome in November, 1993, in preparation for the 1994 Synod. In preparation for the 1993 meeting the Union solicited the views of superiors general, worldwide. In an article in an Italian journal, *Testimoni*, 30 Jan., 1993, entitled *Vita Religiosa Maschile: Autoritratto con Chiaroscuri* (Male Religious Life: Self-portrait with Light and Shade) Luigi Cuccini summarised some of the results of the enquiry, as they had been presented by Fabio Ciardi, OMI. He points out that while it was not a scientifically-conducted survey, but a simple canvassing of views, at the same time it does indicate 'how men religious — and in this case, the major superiors especially — view the religious life and its prospects.'

Of the replies received by 7 October, 1992, 51 were from general curias, 22 from national conferences of religious, 15 from individual provinces, two were written by theologians. They showed a remarkable convergence of viewpoint. What follows is a shortened version of Cuccini's article, in our own translation:

In the first place, there is a more profound and more theological understanding of the meaning of the religious life and its essentials. Theological reflection has made considerable progress and has re-discovered religious life in its evangelical, Christological, ecclesiological and pneumaticalogical dimensions. There has been a fruitful return to the Gospel and a clearer appreciation of consecration. The vows are seen in positive light as consecration and readiness to give oneself, more than as renunciation.

A new spiritual sensibility has placed more emphasis on the contemplative dimension of the religious life and on the primacy of 'being' over 'doing'.

Spirituality, its biblical and theological roots restored, pays more attention to synthesis (unity of life). The need for 'a more incarnated spirituality' is especially underlined, one allied to duty and service, capable of discovering God and the will of God in concrete problems of each day and in the signs of the times.

Also important is the renewal which has taken place in people's prayer life. The renewal of the liturgy and the rediscovery of the word of God have opened new prospects for prayer, which has become more community oriented and less formal. Obsolete devotions have been jettisoned in favour of new, simpler and more authentic forms, more suitable to sharing. In a word, what is emphasised is 'the effort to set aside empty formalism in favour of a more authentic life-style, simpler, more evangelical, lived in interior liberty.'

THE FOUNDER, THE COMMUNITY: All are agreed that the founders of institutes have been the object of intense study, as have institutes' stories, their charisms and their spiritualities. It is one of the positive signs which is noted in almost all the replies.

Community, its biblical and theological foundations and its centrality in religious life re-discovered, is another of the essential elements noted — community understood as brotherly and sisterly life, characterised first and foremost not by observance but by lived gospel values.

In this context, what is much emphasised is the new 'sense of the person' which has developed as a response to the anonymity and, as it were, the treating of people in the mass, which happened in the past. Account is taken of personal charisms and talents; there is a more lively awareness of the 'human aspects' of living in community.

Words like liberty, maturity and personal responsibility, co-responsibility in decision-making, subsidiarity and sharing — such things have significantly changed community life and obedience. Authority has come to be understood as animation and guidance, in a spirit of service and not of power. There is less *dependence* on superiors, the atmosphere in community is more mature, the general climate is more familiar and simple, more serene. Common life is more authentic.

CENTRALITY OF MISSION: Attention is drawn to the importance of having outgrown a monastic conception of apostolic religious life which had been prevalent, in favour of a way of being and acting which is more responsive the charism as it has been taken into renewed constitutions.

At a deeper level, much importance is attached to the 'rediscovery of the centrality of mission in the religious project.' Several institutes have endeavoured to redefine their identity in terms of mission. Communities are understood as 'communities in mission' and religious as 'agents of evangelization', 'witnesses to the presence of God in the world', 'at the service of others'. With a central objective between all: 'the integration of consecration, community and mission.'

The rediscovery and the re-reading of the theme of mission has led to 'a more natural, less institutional relationship with the world'. There is greater freedom in the exercise of the apostolate, greater ability to immerse oneself in the world and in its problems.

Heeding the signs of the times is another important acquisition. There is a more vivid awareness of the new problems of modern society, of justice and peace. In short, 'greater attention to humanity and humanity's story.'

There is much insistence on the prophetic nature of religious life and not a few religious have paid for this with their lives. But behind all this, there is acceptance of the indissoluble link which exists between evangelization and commitment to justice, with a very firm acceptance of the preferential option for the poor. 'Everywhere one encounters', the responses tell us, 'the desire for greater closeness to and solidarity with people, for authentic communion with people and their problems.'

RELIGIOUS LIFE AND THE CHURCH: Everywhere one finds 'a greater understanding of the ecclesial meaning of religious life.' Religious feel that they are 'an integral part of the Church.' Hence 'the wish to establish authentic relationships and for communion with bishops, priests and laity, in an organized ecclesial communion, with greater attention to what is specific in the local Church of which one is part.' In this context the call to a close relationship with the laity is increasingly in evidence. From which there follows an increasing 'commitment to de-clericalization', the readiness of the community to welcome individuals and groups, the sharing of experience and research.

NEGATIVE ASPECTS AND PROBLEMS: One could go on to enumerate gains; in recent years religious life has known improvements that will be measurable only after a lapse of years.

But such progress has also encountered problems. It has known unfulfilled expectations, negative repercussions, paths which, in certain respects, put one in mind of decadence. On this point, notes Father Ciardi, the replies voiced 'harsh' judgements. Perhaps because of a sense of frustration experienced by superiors who find their service difficult, the path littered with obstacles and impediments? Or perhaps because the situation is such as to merit a severe judgement, without obfuscation? .

We shall endeavour to describe the data objectively, after which we will attempt an assessment. One mistake to be avoided is that of moralising. Further, on the positive side, it is important to differentiate between what has been achieved at the level of people's mind-set and of the new structuring of religious life, on the one hand, and the behaviour of individuals on the other. Thus, on the negative and problematical side, the behaviour of individuals is one thing — it can be more, or less, in conformity with the gospel and the spirit of religious life — but it is a different matter if one is talking about is the totality of objective situations and factors which could produce negative consequences. We shall, above all, endeavour to single out this last kind of factors. But let us first see what has emerged from the enquiry.

GAP BETWEEN THEORY AND PRACTICE: The first problem which is noted is the gap between the principles which are accepted and the life which is lived. There is a splendid theology of the religious life, but what is needed is to put into practice. The new insights are not always translated into life. Reformed normative texts have not been adequately interiorised. 'The principles of the evangelical, ecclesiological and charismatic renewal have not been fully assimilated.'

One consequence is a persistent and creeping 'crisis of identity'. The Council and recent synods, it is noted in particular, have given us a clear theology of the priesthood and of the laity, while it is not yet quite so clear what is the nature of religious life. If everybody is called to holiness and take part in mission, what is the point of the religious life?

The crisis of identity among the brothers is symbolic in this respect. But neither do we have an adequate theology of the priest-religious — how is the diocesan priesthood related to the priesthood of the religious? What relationship exists between the presbyterate, the lay life and religious life? There is an urgent need to clarify the 'ecclesiological status of religious life and of the organic communion which links together the various vocations.'

More concretely: the renewal is retarded and experiences many difficulties. 'People do not properly know how to give effect in their lives to the renewal prescribed in the renewed constitutions.'

It has to be acknowledged that the process of change has been inadequately guided. 'The *aggiornamento* has, as it were, fallen from on high and has not yet been absorbed into people's actual lives.' Resistance to change is mentioned very frequently. Religious attempt to return to their origins, but not always with a clear understanding of their charism. Some institutes acknowledge 'an insufficient sense of identity', 'ideological confusion', 'erosion of a sense of belonging.'

After the early years of enthusiasm for *aggiornamento*, one institute said, we have entered an era of disenchantment. 'Religious life is no longer what it was but has not yet become what it ought to be. Many blue-prints for a renewed religious life have been forthcoming, but they have not yet been brought to completion.' We are in a time of 'evolution and uncertainty.' One has the feeling of a transition as yet incomplete, or badly managed.

A DECLINE IN SPIRITUALITY?: It is when one goes from the general to the particular that 'the analysis becomes especially harsh'. Here are some observations: 'Religious life has been affected and frequently overwhelmed by the contemporary currents of individualism, moral relativism and pursuit of self-fulfilment.' One encounters at times 'a materialistic culture, consumerism as a life-style, secularism, bourgeois and worldly values, pragmatism, the exaltation of privacy [the Italian text uses the English word] as a fundamental and inalienable right, mediocrity, etc.' Each of the above terms was used by more than on institute, but what strikes one is the convergence, which suggests that one has here something widely experienced. At the level of spirituality the same points are made: superficiality in the spiritual life and in prayer, lack of faith, diminution of moral concern, relativism, a weak experience of God, crisis of spiritual identity, abandonment of ascesis and of the pursuit of holiness. 'By and large there is an end to legalistic spirituality, repetitive, devotional, but frequently nothing has replaced it, leaving nothing but a void', one institute reported. Another: 'It has been more a revolution for us than a renewal.'

The fundamental problem, people assert , is 'how to relate to the world, to modernity'. 'What is the identity of the religious in the modern and post-modern world? How does one live for God in this new society?'

Sometimes bewilderment comes across, scant perception of the drama of our epoch, the divorce between gospel and culture. We do not recognise ourselves in the world of today. There is fear of what is new.

As well as those who try to bring about social change, even to the extent of joining political organisations, there are those who take refuge in some new form of flight from the world: *fuga mundi*, become crusaders, or resort to restorationism, after a simplified model of social or personal life.

COMMUNITY LINKS: Notwithstanding the important advances in community, there are complaints about immaturity, the difficulty of living together and of collaboration, complaints about disunity, lack of commitment to the common life, apathy and disinterest, rivalry and criticism. In a word: 'the quality of community life leaves much to be desired.' Widely voiced is a complaint about 'individualism, subjectivism and independence.' Too many fall back into private life or turn in on themselves or their own problems. From a dependence and a certain way of conceiving obedience and life in common one has gone to a too unilateral insistence on the person, on privacy, personal charisms and individual apostolate, to the detriment of the community apostolate. The result, according to one institute, is 'the loss of a sense of belonging and of communion, self-marginalization and flight to extra-community membership.'

It is not always easy to bridge the generation gap. The Spanish Conference of Religious put it this way: 'the youngest lack solid principles, the old condemn the present and the middle-aged have lost the impulse towards renewal.'

In such a situation the exercise of authority is difficult. There is less respect, a slide towards democratic models, lack of clarity as to the function of a the local superior, lack of leadership. How does one renew and re-found religious life in such a situation? asks one institute, how balance the relationship between the personal and the community dimension?

VOCATION AND FORMATION: A widely experienced problem is the lack of effective personnel, the ageing of personnel and the lack of vocations, a sign, it is noted, that 'we are not attractive to young people.'

Hence the questions about the future and how to respond to new needs. And if that were not enough, there is the problem of the formation to be given to new generations, which appears to be weak. 'There are not in the higher reaches of formation people sufficiently well formed.' 'There is a shortage of masters and fathers in renewed religious life.' Failures in perseverance, people leaving, vocational instability, these are seen as connected to formation. 'It would appear that formation makes only a superficial impression. 'Dilettantism and experimenting.' in formation should be discarded.

More than one institute complained of candidates who have "difficulty with radical and definite choices, who fight shy of serious intellectual life.'

The picture can be very worrying. People speak of discouragement, lack of joy, lack of peace and hope for the future, of tiredness and pessimism, of resignation, of frustration. There are some who say that the present relative tranquillity in institutes could be 'a question of something latent', connected with tiredess and advancing yeas. This means that 'the unresolved problems could arise tomorrow in more acute form, with violence. We should be ready and on the watch.'

THE DECLINE OF MISSION: Some general remarks about the decline of mission: It has been said that religious, still seeking their identity in this moment of transition, run the risk that their life would be nothing more than the performance of a pastoral task, not something freely given, something brimming with spiritual energy. 'A great deal of apostolic work is done', a large institute says, re-echoing the sentiments of others also, 'but because there is no evangelical depth, it is unconvincing, not very effective, nor does grace shine through.'

A cause of worry is the increasing commitment of religious to parishes. There is the risk of their being identified with the diocesan clergy and losing their own identity, thus further increasing the clericalization of religious life. It is judged that there are insufficient religious in milieu which are in need of their presence. On the one hand, the commitments of traditional institutions block new initiatives. On the other hand, there is a lack of available personnel and of courage. An excess of mobility is followed by an excess of stability, with loss of gospel freedom and of the missionary spirit.

AN EVALUATION: It would be a mistake to draw general conclusions from this very negative portrayal. One needs to balance it with the first part of the report and, further, to bear in mind that what one has is replies to questions about problematic and negative aspects. However, it remains true that all of this has been described as happening and, not infrequently, in pessimistic tones. What is one to say?

First of all, one might say what those interviewed themselves emphasised, and that is that religious are called to conversion. Religious have to question themselves not only at the level of institutions and activities, but with regard to the quality of evangelical life to which they are vowed and which must evoke a concrete response in their lives.

All other discourse presupposes this: a life consistent with the vows, faithfulness to prayer, spiritual commitment, detachment, love of God and of others in his name, self-sacrifice in generous dedication to the cause of the Gospel.

The responses to the enquiry, given by major superiors for the most part, seem to *shout* a renewed appeal for humility and for the courage to embark on an honest examination of conscience which would convert everyone to a renewed and daily decision to be Christian in all the depth and extent of that term.

Today, as never before, religious life is judged by the quality of its evangelical life. This is the first thing made evident: our institutes need — and in the concrete lives of all its members, at that — a decided re-commitment to the evangelical life.

CAUSES AND CURES: If conversion is the first need (see Mk 1:15), other, more general, factors ought not be ignored, for they affect people's ability to live it to its full significance, especially in community life.

It is true, for example, that the positive elements listed in the first part have become part of the patrimony of religious life, but to what extent have they been effectively accepted and by whom?

The reality seems to be as follows: progress there has been, but the advance of the renewal of mind-set has been very unequal, inconclusive and patchy. Individuals have been profoundly renewed, others have remained what they always have been, still others have reached the half-way stage or, simply, have lost their way. Thus, the fabric of community is divided or, more accurately, unravelled. It is really difficult to achieve a situation where a superior is able to lead a community in accordance with a project on which all agree. Usually, all a superior can do is respect people's consciences and accept the *status quo* whenever a project is strongly opposed.

There is a lack of consensus for a community advance where the community is not content with the minimum necessary but is capable of taking decisions that matter, even at the level of spiritual commitment and evangelical cohesion, which is always the most difficult and costly area. It is obvious that there would be different rhythms as people acquire a new mind-set and a new consensus is built and that, therefore, there would be a period of anomie. But it must be said that this has lasted longer than, perhaps, was foreseen and who knows if, or when, we will come out of it.

OVERCOMING APATHY AND LACK OF INTEREST: On the debit side in this situation is the open and unacceptable lack of interest which male religious have about the problems of religious life, which is their vocation. Basically, it is for this reason that only a small minority of them — very often those who did it because of the needs of the ministry — have taken on the new mind-set which is the product of the reflection of recent years.

The consequence is a Babel of languages — where is the community in which the word obedience means the same for everyone? And, with the confusion of language, paralysis and everyone left to his own devices.

It is true that we do not as yet have an exhaustive theology of religious life and, thus, a new synthesis. But what is needed now, above all, is an effort by all to take on board the perfectly valid gains which have already been achieved. Just think of how difficult it is, a difficulty not yet resolved, to organise on-going formation for all!

In such a situation of fragmentation and anomie it is with difficulty that — in spite of the good will of individuals — a lamentable detachment of practice from theory has been avoided. The least that can be said is that, in order to arrive at a situation which people can live with, evangelical radicalism, which is the substance of religious life, is left to the generosity of individuals.

A remedy, certainly, is that male religious would abandon the stance of lack of interest in their vocation which is characteristic of them. But one would also need to study the composition of communities in which such consensus is possible, for it is indispensable for a truly communitarian advance. It may be sufficient, in this regard, to think about the problem of where to place the young religious.

MANAGING THE CHANGE: There is another points, just as relevant. In recent years we have discussed at length and have discovered aspects of religious life previously unknown — the enquiry provides ample confirmation of this — but it has all remained too much in the abstract, taken up only by individual consciences. How often have religious attended important conferences on formation in important aspects of religious life and charism, with implications for a profoundly new community organisation but have then returned home, where nothing changed. The individuals are left on their own, responsibility laid upon them for the renewal of religious life, which ought to have been a community responsibility. We did not know how to take charge of the change and set it in motion, nor did we want to; we lacked the courage of consistency at the level of the consequences of actual reform, a reform which ought to involve the community and the institute.

Thus there developed a mechanism which exposed us to a real risk of a vacuum. At the beginning there was enthusiasm, but later, when nothing changed, discouragement set in, even if not always and everywhere, with the result that people wanted to hear no more about reflection, or study, or renewal.

How different it could have been if every time people returned home they were yet further convinced of the inadequacy of the *status quo* and of the old order of things, without the possibility of a rebirth.

Major superiors have systematically run the risk — a sore point this in recent years — of being absorbed in ordinary administration (administering the old order of things) while what was needed was to implement the change. General chapters made decisions binding on provinces, while provincials found they could do no more than pass the matter on to local communities, those same fragmented communities, lacking consensus, unable on their own to solve their own problems.

It has to be said: there was too much of an expectation that the renewal would fall from heaven, dispensing us from the tensions and the divisions which every new birth brings with it.

The Future of Religious Life in the United States

What follows is a summary, by Father Sean Fagan, SM, secretary general of the Marist Fathers, Rome, of a lengthy document published in *Origins, 24* September, 1992 and described as an 'Executive Summary of a Study on the Future of Religious Orders in the United States'. The document begins by pointing out that the average age of members of many congregations in the US is 67, that numbers have decreased over the past thirty years by approximately 45% for brothers and sisters and 27% for religious priests. The study, which was conducted by Sister Miriam Ukeritis, St Joseph of Carondelet and Father David Nygren, CM, reflects the opinions of more than 10,000 religious priests, sisters and brothers (reflecting 126,000 in 816 groups). The overall response was 76%.

On the theoretical perspective of the study, the authors explain that they examined 'the implications of transformation for: (1) religious life as a social institution: broad-based beliefs, attitudes and behaviours common across all religious orders; (2) an individual congregation; (3) individual religious.' They went on:

HOW TRANSFORMATION TAKES PLACE: Transformation usually begins with a crisis that shows that the current shared understandings no longer suffice. The experience of crisis must be strong enough to 'unfreeze' present understandings by challenging their validity. After this takes place, various individuals and groups develop understandings that lead to new types of action and to changes in the structure.

There is likely to be considerable conflict between the traditional and the new. Leaders can have a strong impact on the outcome of this conflict. If they support only one perspective they decrease the creativity potential of others. They may increase the possibility of divisions. They can enable the groups to interact creatively. Emotions enter into the transformational experience. It can be paralysing and disorienting; it can seem a sequence of deaths and rebirths. Members can experience ambiguity and confusion, leading to additional tension.

It seems that religious life, congregations and individual religious are in the midst of a transformational process, and that the new understandings of religious life held by significant members have not yet been fully developed. The greatest environmental change affecting the process was the new understanding of Church proclaimed by Vatican II, and the call to religious to analyse and revise their basic principles and practice.

The next sections of the document describe the levels of change: across congregations, in individual congregations and as it affects individual members. It goes on to describe the various research units which helped the authors to assemble the data and the national survey which they carried out. The document continues:

ROLE CLARITY: The study placed good deal of emphasis on the question of how clearly individual religious perceived their role, that is, their 'purpose and function within the current structure of the church', which perception the study terms 'role clarity' contrasting high 'role clarity' and low 'role clarity'. 55% of sisters, 65% of brothers, 68% of priests had a high 'role clarity'. 30% of women religious admitted having a low 'role clarity'. 77% of contemplatives, 64% of monastic religious and 59% of apostolic and mendicant religious reported high 'role clarity' as did 52% of younger religious and 71% of older religious. 'This finding parallels research in many professions which points to greater role clarity among those who have a greater tenure in their profession.'

The more highly educated were less clear about their role clarity as religious, but this could vary with differing fields of study. Religious in 'disciplines such as business, education and health professions indicated they were less clear about their role as religious in the church when compared to religious whose training is in the more theoretical disciplines such as theology, humanities and the social sciences. The role demands of the health care providers or educators may present pressures that replace or compete with, rather than complement, the current role of religious in the church.'

Ambiguity regarding role can in general lead to anxiety, reduced ability to meet role requirements, decreased ministerial satisfaction lower trust and self-confidence, increased sense of futility and greater propensity to leave a religious order. The fact that a high proportion of religious do not see their roles clearly may lead to a further diminution of the number of religious. The current reduction in the number of women entering religious life—they used to out number men by three to one, now the numbers are equal—is perhaps not unconnected with the low 'role clarity' experienced by many religious women. Hence its importance.

Commitment, External Authority: Asked to what extent they agreed or disagreed that life-long commitment should be the norm for religious life, the sentiment most commonly expressed among all groups fell half-way between 'strongly agree' and 'strongly disagree'. All tended to believe that reliance on external authority would not favourably influence the future of religious life. There was a general rejection of the tendency to seek influence regarding thought or behaviour from outside sources such as the church or group authority.

Systemic change, Hierarchy: All, sisters, brothers, priests, experienced little connection between their work for systemic change (justice, peace, against discrimination in society) and their personal and spiritual fulfilment. Any positive relationship between hierarchy and religious, as well as the influence of church hierarchy and magisterial authority, were not typically rated highly by religious.

Inclusion of homosexuals, members of minorities, laity, the poor: Religious differed greatly as to whether declared homosexuals would be admitted to their communities, religious priests, for example, being the most open (43%) on the matter, brothers next (35%) and sisters third (16%). A high proportion of contemplatives and of older religious felt that homosexuals would not be admitted to their communities. 36% felt that members of minority groups would not feel at ease in their communities

For 65% the admission of lay associates 'as members' of their congregations would not destroy their own sense of membership, as against 16% who said that it would. 'The inclusion of lay associates, including women and married people, appears to have widespread acceptance among religious.'

Religious are agreed that the expansion of the role of the laity, feminist theology, ordination of women and inclusion of married persons in religious communities would have little effect on the future of religious life.

Although work with the poor is a stated ideal with most congregations and is espoused by the church, in practice there is little personal commitment to it. 'The greatest commitment to work with the poor ... would be found in a young apostolic sister. This group currently shows the smallest tendency to increase in size.

Anomie: loss of conviction about the vows, lack of clarity about the role of religious, very negative reaction to authority, lack of corporate mission and ministry and disillusionment with leadership 'pose significant threats to the future of religious life.'

Involvement and influence: For the study 'involvement' is both the desire to take part in one's congregation's activities and actually taking part in them. 'Influence' is wanting to have an impact on decisions and on the future of one's congregation and actually having such an impact. The study reported: 'A consistent pattern did emerge: The perceived or desired level of influence in one 's congregation is consistently lower than an individual' s experience or desire to be involved in the group . ' [In other words, religious reported that however great their involvement in their congregations and however much they want to be involved, they never achieve or even want a like measure of influence in their congregation.] The study commented: 'This raises serious questions about ownership (of ideals, objectives, norms) and group commitment' to ideal and stated goals.

Clarity about policies; Vatican 11. Members in general 'do not experience an overwhelming sense of clarity concerning their congregation's policies and procedures.' There is only moderate agreement that the congregations have accomplished what Vatican II called for.

Commitment to institutions. Overall, 93% are willing to work in a sponsored institution of their congregation and live there; this presents an opportunity to leaders to direct efforts towards a corporate mission. 'The focus on individual ministries that has evolved over the past several years may now be shifting or open to reconsideration by members.'

Spirituality: The survey endeavoured to ascertain whether spirituality implied enhanced conviction of the value of religious life, deeper belief in Christ and/or appreciation of the value of prayer since first profession. It also endeavoured to discover if common prayer, annual retreat, confession, devotion to Mary were seen as sources of personal spiritual fulfilment. All reported a high level of conviction that this was so, with sisters and contemplatives even more convinced; this sense appears to deepen with age.

Staying Power and Vows: All religious reported a moderately high to very high level of commitment to their congregations, with the older members even more highly committed. All religious report a strong determination to remain in their congregation and they rated their fidelity to their vows as ranging between 3.7 and 4.1 (on 5-point scale). Religious women saw chastity as most meaningful and least difficult, while men saw it as most difficult and least meaningful . Religious women found obedience more difficult than did religious men.

Action for the Poor: A high proportion of religious priests and sisters found that working for the poor and the sick 'made a somewhat valuable contribution to their spiritual and personal fulfilment'.

In General: 'The results would indicate that ... religious in general are moving toward a much more permeable system of membership, commitment, autonomy and inclusion. While on the one hand this reinforces innovation that includes diversity and broadened assumptions about religious life, the research also indicates that religious do not see how clearly they are influenced by cultural assimilation. Similarly, for many their own credibility may be threatened in the eyes of those they serve and the society in which they function because of the discrepancies between their espoused values and their practice. By their own admission, religious see indifference and a lack of passion to be a major threat to themselves as persons.'

Leadership is one of the critical forces that will assist in the clarification of the role identity of religious in the US. Especially among women, there is a fair degree of satisfaction with leadership.

Community life continues to engage membership and they feel committed deeply to congregational life, willing to be more involved than they currently are. It is clear that spirituality and a vital relationship with God is really important for many religious. Structured prayer, however varied the forms, continues to be valued. Individuals feel genuinely called to God to religious life and see an intensified spirituality as desirable. They are personally committed strongly to the community, derive satisfaction from belonging and most intend to remain in religious life.

The data suggests that if religious experience difficulty it is in the realm of impact and fidelity to vows. There are profound shifts in the interpretation of the vows and the willingness to live them. More fluid interpretations of poverty, obedience and chastity are widely observed.

Major problem throughout: lack of role clarity and the cast cultural shifts in American life, with significant influence on religious life.

LEADERSHIP : Leadership is recognised as a critical factor in the transformation of religious orders. It is urgent to select and train leaders who not only can manage the complexity of religious life that will intensify in the next 10 years, but who also can focus the attention of their communities on a vision that will unite individual efforts inspired by the mission of their founder/foundries. The most striking weakness is the inability to formulate a strategy to achieve a purpose or mission. There is increasing and widespread use of consensual processes and team leadership, but these often lead to mediocre management, representing the least common denominator.

Four categories of leadership emerged from the replies given by religious at leadership workshops concerning their vision for the future of their congregations the people they serve and religious life in general:

Value-based leaders expressed a sense of direction for the congregation or themselves in terms of the conceptual and cultural aspects of religious life. Able to give expression to their values, but unable to identify strategies to actualise them.

Visionary leaders expressed a sense of direction in terms of the structure and organisation of religious life. 'The articulation of a strategy to accomplish their vision marks the difference between visionary and value-based leaders.'

Conflicted leaders were unable to address change and often expressed frustration, anger, sadness and even despair; they blame others.

Incognizant leaders were unconscious or unaware of major issues facing their orders, fail to address any of the concerns facing their orders or the church; do not realise their role in enabling the action of God.

There is often a gulf between the responsibilities of office and the abilities some leaders bring to it.

The national survey measured members' perception of their leaders in terms of spiritual intensity; and as (i) 'transformational leaders', who provide vision and a sense of mission while instilling pride and gaining respect and trust, and (ii) ' transactional leaders', who orient subordinates towards achieving goals, monitoring performance and rewarding accomplishments; they take corrective action when necessary.

Data shows that while spiritual intensity was the most frequently observed behaviour of all outstanding leaders, charisma or individual consideration of members was the most significant predictor of satisfaction with an individual leader or leadership team.

The survey studied differences between outstanding leaders and typical leaders. The former try to find new ways to achieve goals and to make things better for the people their order serves. they take initiatives to deal with anticipated problems (five times more than other leaders). Outstanding leaders are more likely to use their power to influence group decisions or behaviour; to build consensus and team spirit by soliciting the views of others; to attempt to see issues from different perspectives; and to draw on divine assistance in their leadership roles. They begin new projects, act assertively, provide more opinions, particularly negative ones, to subordinates, develop the leadership capacity of others.

VIEWS OF VISIONING GROUPS: The survey included especially the views of persons who could provide specifically clear opinions about the future of religious life; future oriented individuals but rooted in their order's charism(92 took part, after requests to 550 orders). Aim was to learn about their personality characteristics and beliefs, and develop strategies and agendas to implement their predicted vision of religious life.

It was discovered that even with these, affiliation (to accustomed group) is generally stronger than vision. The national survey revealed a particularly high need for affiliation among members of religious orders. This tension needs to be considered.

Revitalised religious life, rooted in Jesus Christ and gospel values, will manifest that spirit in the world by challenging systems that oppress others, living in a style of visible simplicity and renewing congregations' fidelity to their founding purpose. Visionary groups see authority as power that is shared among communities of equals. They would like to see greater inclusiveness, sharing in the world's suffering. The dominant language of religious life has shifted from theological constructs to social and psychological paradigms. Many members no longer use sacramental or transcendental frames of reference to describe their experience of God. Multi-culturalism as normative is desirable, but confronting the personal and systemic racism that marks our society and religious orders could be the single greatest challenge in the area of membership.

Congregations ought to provide opportunities for structural expressions of emerging forms of religious life. To do this they will have to discern the contemporary expression of their founder's charism, redefine or establish boundaries for membership and behaviour, confront the discrepancies between espoused and lived values.

Individuals will shift from an internal to global focus. They will learn to cope with moving from values related to stability and security to those related to change and process that lead to a more clearly focused mission.

Facing a culture which has supported privatism and individualism religious will need to re-examine non negotiables. Relinquishing many previously held tenets, they will respond to the call of serving absolute human need in the spirit of their founder.

New members must demonstrate the maturity to live a life of sacrifice, possess or acquire the skills for leadership positions in global and church communities, and be able to sustain intimate relationship in the context of a celibate commitment.

VIEWS OF CARING PEOPLE: Special study of religious identified as 'uniquely caring, unusually helpful, thoughtful, understanding. ' In contrast to typical religious, these feel closer to and more trusting of God, who is seen as the source of healing and care. On projective measures they score higher in trust and lower in mistrust than others, and tend to portray authority as benevolent. They are less self-controlling and more spontaneously inclined to generosity. They say they find the experience of contemplative prayer very valuable, and show a greater inter-personal involvement in caring experiences. They experience more joy in caring and zest for living. Typical religious see caring as a response to a need in themselves such as caring out of duty or repayment, or in response to special needs like illness, rejection or trauma of others.

For caring religious, helping is not simply a transaction between two people, but there is a third force in the relationship; a benevolent authority, or God. Meeting a person in need, they create a three-way relationship in which Jesus and the gospel values are deeply involved.

Caring religious see themselves as partners with or assistants to the real source of helping. They do not feel ultimately responsible. For this reason and also because the helping in itself is joyous, caring religious do not as readily 'burn out'.

To the extent that responding to absolute human need is embraced anew as the ultimate mission of religious congregations, the formation and development of this motive for religious life is clearly essential.

Perhaps the future of religious life will be defined increasingly by those attributes or actions on behalf of others that mediate the presence of God. Caring religious live an operative Christology which is simultaneously imminent and transcendent.

This part of the study shows that the focus of individual formation must be increasingly spiritual. Those who learn to be authentically caring are inclined spontaneously to generosity, trusting and aware that God acts in and through them. This level of freedom requires viewing God as a benevolent authority in whose name one acts as mediator.

VIEWS OF INDIVIDUALS: Individuals identified as particularly knowledge-able about religious life and its future, and about leadership qualities were interviewed. The following points were made.

The mission of Jesus will be the central focus, and the spirituality of congregations will be rooted in their charism. Driven by pressing social and ecclesial needs, charity and justice will be the focus of mission and ministry, and most apostolic community life will be in proximity to the poor.

While maintaining a clear church identity, the structures of religious life will be based on mission rather than canons, and the unique charism of religious life will remain largely distinct from hierarchical functions. An inclusive atmosphere will be marked by multi-culturalism, a clear inclusion of women and the feminine, and a genuine respect for diversity.

Most striking discrepancy: Only a moderate commitment to participate in an activity which has become increasingly an espoused mission for many orders and quite explicitly by the church: work for and with the poor.

Religious community life will be marked increasingly by intentionality in terms of shared values, purpose and resources. Some congregations with similar charisms will merge; the number of apostolic groups will decrease, with smaller numbers of members. Monastic orders will increase in numbers because of greater clarity of focus. Congregations that are vital to the church will have an explicit focus, and their effectiveness will be enhanced by the members' commitment to the collective mission. Commitment to works of mercy is critical.

Most religious were motivated at the outset by their impulse to generosity and are sustained by their special relationship with God. By serving those with an absolute human need, religious will dedicate themselves to a high-cost, high-commitment life in communities that can be witness to Jesus Christ and the gospel.

CONCLUSIONS: SHAPING THE FUTURE: Dramatic changes must occur if religious life is to continue to be a vital force in world and church. Fidelity to the spirit of the founder and responsiveness to critical and unmet human needs are basic to their ongoing mission in confronting the current gap between the gospel and the surrounding culture.

1. Individualism and Vocation: There have been cultural shifts in US society, towards democratisation of all authority, individualism and cultural assimilation. 'Religious have spent at least 20 years focused largely on the internal reorganisation of congregational life. This structural perspective combined with a heightened awareness left many weary of bureaucratisation of vocation at a time when individualism was escalating in society and religious life as well. For many, the dynamics of change itself presented an additional burden.... the impulse to generosity among some religious is being eclipsed by self-preoccupation, psychological decompensation, stark individualism and a lessening of the willingness to sacrifice.'

'For others, the reaction is the opposite. In these congregations we observe individuals who, regardless of age, know the distinctiveness of their vocation as religious. Their profile includes a radical dependence on God ... and a capacity to enter the life of another for the sake of the other and not to meet their personal ... needs. They also possess a deep desire for oneness with God and with others. They are deeply committed to their congregation where, by objective standards, the costs of their work and membership are very high.'

Recent literature stresses preferential option for the poor as normative for religious life, but many feel no commitment to this. Many individuals have drifted to the periphery of their congregation; for many of these a call by the congregation to participate in its vocation and mission would be welcomed.

2. Leadership: Need for outstanding leaders. Several factors inhibit the exercise of effective leadership: 'the nature of authority is widely contested, consensual decision-making processes have little form, membership is generally unwilling to relinquish authority to those given responsibility and the concept of personal "call" often eclipses any willingness to work on behalf of the congregational ends. Furthermore, those elected to leadership are in some instances those least likely to succeed because they are elected to fill the need of a group that lacks ambition or the will to move forward. Effective leaders on the other hand are rooted in an awareness that they act with and on behalf of God. They treat members as though they are equally responsible for the life of the congregation, yet do not compromise the clarity of their role as leader. Effective leaders understand how to position the congregation strategically to be responsive to human needs, and they generally are granted authority by their members.'

3. Authority: Authority in religious life, as in the church itself, is perhaps the most pressing question for religious to resolve. Authority should provide protection, direction and order for the sake of the group, but in US culture it has undergone deconstruction. Ambiguity about consensus, subsidiarity, discernment and leadership, coupled with individualism, limited understanding of obedience, and separation of spiritual life from the life of the Christian community, have all contributed to the crisis.

The abuses of authority in the past are still alive in memory. Religious in US are clear in their lowered respect for the magisterial authority of the church and of the US hierarchy in general.

4. *Work and Corporate Identity:* In .the '60s and '70s institutions staffed or sponsored by religious suffered dramatic decline, and this removed a focus of corporate identity. Lack of clarity regarding an order's mission offers little to attract the commitment or passion of potential new members.

The orders that are refounding [the text has ' rebounding ', which I take, perhaps wrongly, to be a misprint. Ed.] or stabilising most are several monasteries who have carefully reinstated monastic practices and a sense of clarity regarding their life and work. Men's orders who retained the classic traditions of monasticism have not had to rely as much on compensation from parochial work.

'A related dynamic for religious involves becoming identified solely with one's work. This results for developmental reasons, from a lack of corporate identity, from the absence of community and spiritual support.... many individual religious and groups have relinquished the power of corporate witness for a variety of individual commitments in effective but unconnected ministerial positions.'

5. *Affiliative Decline and Role Clarity:* The authors of the study say that its most compelling finding is that 'a significant percentage of religious no longer understand their role and function in the church.... [which] can result in lowered self-confidence, a sense of futility, greater propensity to leave religious life, and significant anxiety. The younger religious experience the least clarity, and among them, women religious experience less clarity than their male counterparts.'

'Whatever clarity exists among men seems to emerge from the definitiveness of orders for priests and the incumbent role requirements as well as the clarity of the lay vocation for brothers. Women religious are divided upon the concept of consecrated life as distinct from or equal to their female lay counterparts. For both women and men religious, Vatican II substantially reinforced the role of laity in the church, but did not clarify for religious the unique contribution of their vocation.'

What holds many to their commitment to religious life is a sense of affiliation that is stronger than their sense of purpose or mission. Communal bonding continues in spite of 30 years of membership decline. Congregations will continue to decline if affiliative motives are stronger than a concern for the mission and the extension of the charism.

6. *Racism and Multi-culturalism:* 96% of American religious are white, despite the radical increases in US population of other groups. Not easy to attract members from these groups. Members of these groups find that the current

concerns of religious (authority, discipline, pious practices) are not theirs. Their structure of faith, ecclesiology, female and male relationships, understandings of the vows, relationship to the church, each present a very different dynamic as a function of culture.

7. *Materialism and the Gospel:* Religious of the future will derive their mission and their life in common from a firm relationship with the person of Jesus, will focus on the gap that exists between the surrounding culture and the gospel community, and they will be recognised by their simplicity of life, their visible presence among the most abandoned and by their joy in serving God.

Many religious at present are unaware of the degree of their assimilation into the mainstream culture and how invisible they have become to those who would most call out to them. To remain distinctive in the world, this trend needs to be reversed.

8. *Charism and Parochial Assimilation:* Vatican II has not provided a vibrant declaration on the clear role of religious in the church. Historically the orders arose to serve emerging or unmet human needs, independent of and yet complementary to the hieratic order of the church But given the shortage of diocesan clergy, religious find that parochial and diocesan work takes precedence over their involvement in the life of the order. This can easily lead to a compromise of the prophetic role of religious.

SUMMARY: The change process is deeply affected by the individual and communal choices made along the way. The critical component in the effort to change is to imagine a desirable future for a congregation and reinforce that movement by consistency in choices based on values and the traditions of the order.

The will of God must be considered, but no formula can create will where little exists. The purpose of the survey is to provide information that will help religious understand the choices before them and to orient them towards their possible futures.

The conviction of the authors is that there are many reasons to be hopeful about the future of religious life, although renewal efforts will continue to be threatened by significant cultural, personal and collective resistance